Blood in the Hills

BOOKS BY CHARLES W. SASSER

NONFICTION:

The Walking Dead (w/ Craig Roberts)

One Shot, One Kill (w/ Craig Roberts)

Homicide!

Shoot to Kill

Always a Warrior

In Cold Blood: Oklahoma's Most Notorious Murders

Last American Heroes (w/ Michael Sasser)

Smoke Jumpers

First SEAL (w/ Roy Boehm)

At Large

Fire Cops (w/ Michael Sasser)

Doc: Platoon Medic (w/ Daniel E. Evans)

Arctic Homestead (w/ Norma Cobb)

Taking Fire (w/ Ron Alexander)

Raider

Encyclopedia of Navy SEALs

Magic Steps to Writing Success

Hill 488 (w/ Ray Hildreth)

Crosshairs on the Kill Zone (w/ Craig Roberts)

Going Bonkers: The Wacky World of Cultural Madness

Patton's Panthers

The Shoebox: Letters for the Seasons

God in the Foxhole

Devoted to Fishing: Devotionals for Fishermen

None Left Behind

Predator (w/ Matt Martin)

The Sniper Anthology

Back in the Fight (w/ Joe Kapacziewski)

Two Fronts, One War

The Night Fighter (w/ Navy Captain William Hamilton)

Blood in the Hills (w/ Bob Maras)

FICTION:

No Gentle Streets

The 100th Kill

Operation No Man's Land (as Mike Martell)

Liberty City

Detachment Delta: Punitive Strike

Detachment Delta: Operation Iron Weed

Detachment Delta: Operation Deep Steel

Detachment Delta: Operation Aces Wild

Detachment Delta: Operation Cold Dawn

Dark Planet

OSS Commando: Final Option

OSS Commando: Hitler's A-Bomb

No Longer Lost

War Chaser

The Return

A Thousand Years of Darkness

Sanctuary

The Foreworld Saga: Bloodaxe

Shadow Mountain

Six: Blood Brothers

Six: End Game

BLOOD IN THE HILLS

The Story of Khe Sanh,
the Most Savage Fight of the Vietnam War

ROBERT MARAS

AND

CHARLES W. SASSER

Guilford, Connecticut

An imprint of The Rowman & Littlefield Publishing Group, Inc.
4501 Forbes Blvd., Ste. 200
Lanham, MD 20706
www.rowman.com

Distributed by NATIONAL BOOK NETWORK

British Library Cataloguing in Publication Information available

Library of Congress Cataloging-in-Publication Data available

ISBN 978-1-4930-4996-7 (paperback)
ISBN 978-1-4930-1976-2 (e-book)

∞™ The paper used in this publication meets the minimum requirements of American
National Standard for Information Sciences—Permanence of Paper for Printed Library
Materials, ANSI/NISO Z39.48-1992.

To all my Marine Corps brothers who died on those Khe Sanh Hills in 1967.

I will never forget you, brothers.

—Bob Maras

And to every Vietnam veteran who fought through his own hills.

—Charles W. Sasser

CONTENTS

Authors' Note

Time has passed since the "Hill Fights" of Khe Sanh fought in South Vietnam during April and May 1967. And time, as in this personal narrative of Marine PFC Bob Maras, has a tendency to erode memory in some areas and selectively enhance it in others. People may see the same action from different perspectives. Where errors or conflict in recollection occur, the authors accept full responsibility and ask to be forgiven.

Actual names are used throughout except in those instances where names could not be recalled or where public identification serves no useful purpose. Some dialogue and scenes have by necessity been re-created using the raw material of one Marine's memory. We have attempted to match personalities with the activities and action while maintaining factual content. The recounting of some events and time sequences may not correspond precisely with the memories of all individuals involved.

The authors apologize to anyone who may have been omitted, neglected, or slighted in the preparation of this book. While some interpretational mistakes are bound to have occurred, we are confident that the content of this book is true to the reality, spirit, and incredible courage of the brave US Marines who fought and died during the Hill Fights in the Republic of South Vietnam during that terrifying spring of 1967.

I (Bob Maras) wish to thank my father, George, for instilling in me common sense. It helped me to stay alive.

I should also like to thank Mike and Sharon Lewis of Farmington, New Mexico, who provided me the peace of their vacation home for three weeks in November 2015 to help put together this book.

Most of all, I thank my co-author, Charles W. Sasser, for making me talk about my nightmares. You and Dr. Hoffmann were right; it did help.

The authors are indebted to the following authors and works for helping to provide a historical perspective to this narrative: *The Hill Fights: The First Battle of Khe Sanh*, by Edward F. Murphy; *Last Stand at Khe Sanh*, by Gregg Jones; *The Battle of Khe Sanh*, by Captain Moyers S. Shore II; *War Without Heroes*, by David Douglas Duncan; *The Vietnam War Almanac*, by Colonel Harry G. Summers Jr.; and *NAM: The Vietnam Experience 1965–75*, by Tim Page and John Pimlott.

PREFACE

IN WASHINGTON D.C., "THE WALL" OF THE VIETNAM VETERANS Memorial, etched with the names of that war's KIAs and MIAs, is designed with a black mirrored surface that looks back at you as you look into it. Symbolically, the effect is intended to signify reuniting the past with the present. Peering back from its depths in 2002 was an older Bob Maras so unlike the nineteen-year-old youth I was when I took my senior trip to Vietnam right out of high school in 1966 and was thrust almost immediately into what Marine Lieutenant General Victor Krulak, Commander of Fleet Marine Force-Pacific, called the "bloodiest and toughest fight we had in Vietnam."

Also reflecting out of the dark depths of The Wall beyond the 58,191 names engraved into it were the now-older images of former Marine Sergeant Ed Crawford and Private Tony Leyba, old comrades from what military history now calls the "Hill Fights." For a long time the three of us stood there shoulder to shoulder, silently peering into the dark past, trying hard to see *through* The Wall, as though seeking something vital each of us had left in Vietnam thirty-five years ago.

The names on The Wall. They represented what we lost there. James Hill, Jaggers, Roldan, Todd, Doc Heath, and the others. All there for future generations to look back on, even one hundred years from now, and wonder, as we in the present generation look back on Civil War memorials.

Around three million visitors are drawn each year to the national Vietnam Veterans Memorial in Constitution Gardens adjacent to Washington D.C.'s National Mall. Like Crawford, Leyba, and me, the vets who come here have gotten older, but none of us outlive the memories of what happened in a violent land far away. Those memories come back fresh every day.

Construction of the memorial was completed in 1983. It consists of two 246-foot gabbro walls filled with names. The highest point is ten feet tall, the lowest points at either end are each eight inches in height. The design is meant to express "a wound that is closed and healing." One wall points toward the Washington Monument, the other toward the Lincoln Memorial.

A short distance away, larger-than-life bronzes of three soldiers in full combat kit prepare to defend. Visitors pause before them. They demonstrate America's diversity in war. One soldier is European American, one African American, and the third Hispanic American. In the Marines, there is only one color, and that color is *Marine Green*.

Loved ones of the dead and missing bring sentimental items to leave before the wall. According to legend, the custom began when a Vietnam vet tossed the Purple Heart his brother received posthumously into the wet concrete of the memorial's foundation. Since then, items as large as a Harley-Davidson motorcycle with *HERO* on its license plate down to a simple plain brown teddy bear have been presented to The Wall.

Names of men killed in action are denoted by a diamond. Crosses next to the names mark some 1,200 soldiers, sailors, airmen, and Marines who are still missing in action. Tentatively, I reached trembling fingers toward a name with a cross next to it: *Robert J. Todd*. Tony and I recalled vividly the day Todd disappeared.

The Wall and its names have generated a unique ritual called "rubbing." Relatives, friends, and loved ones come to The Wall with a sheet of paper, which they place over the selected name and rub with wax crayon or graphite pencil to make a memento.

Sergeant Crawford, Tony, and I were etching our eighteenth name from the stone when we heard sniffling and weeping. Startled, we turned to discover a small crowd gathered behind us to watch.

"Did you know so many guys who died in the war?" someone asked.

Tony turned away to hide the tears in his eyes. Sergeant Crawford's face resembled stone. I lowered my head.

"They were all from our battalion at Khe Sanh," I said.

CHAPTER ONE

Combat Landing

MARINES CLAIMED THEY COULD ALREADY SMELL THE COOKING FIRES, rot, and human shit of Vietnam from aboard the USS *Ogden* off the coast as BLT (Battalion Landing Team) 2nd Battalion, 3rd Marine Division, prepared to combat land on Red Beach, located four miles from Phu Bai. Wherever the hell *that* was. Not that it mattered. Common grunts in the By-God Crotch were like mushrooms—kept in the dark and fed bullshit. We were life support systems for our rifles, nothing more. Why clutter our minds with unnecessary details? Some general moved a pin on a tactical map and we moved with it. It was that simple.

"Your sergeant spots a gook over there," an instructor at ITR (Infantry Training Regiment) said, pointing indefinitely into our future, "and tells you to shoot him, then, by God, you shoot him. That's all you need to know."

Today, 22 April 1967, was what BLT 2/3 had trained to do over the past months. Everything was assholes and elbows aboard LPD (Landing Port, Dock) *Ogden* and her sister ship, LPD *Monticello*. USS *Princeton* was the third ship in the little flotilla. She was an LPH (landing port, helicopter), an aircraft carrier for choppers. LPDs and LPHs were to Marines what troop ships were to the fighting men of World War II—a method of transporting us and our gear to the war front.

About a mile off *Ogden*'s bow stretched a thin green line of earth against the horizon of the South China Sea. The war front. That was where our pin was being moved. Looked peaceful enough from here, but a rumor spread among the troops that a regiment of NVA, the North

Vietnamese Army, waited ashore to kick sand in our faces when we landed.

"Marines, get your shit together and saddle up!"

Golf Company's 3rd Platoon Leader, Lieutenant Andrew "Mac" McFarlane, seemed to be everywhere at once on the open deck as coxswains drove amphibious tractors (AMTRACs) from the ship's wells into the sea and the battalion distributed among the three ships prepared to board them for the landing. AMTRACs served as both landing craft and floating armored personnel carriers. Bobbing on the gentle sea still tethered to their mother ships, they reminded me of giant alligator turtles on farm ponds back in my home state of Oklahoma.

Lieutenant Mac cajoled, slapped Marines on the back, moved easily and confidently among us like the true motivational leader he was. At about thirty-five, he referred to himself as "the oldest second lieutenant in the entire US Crotch." A tall, lanky officer with a thin face and a sharp nose, he was a former enlisted man, a sergeant, who fought in Korea at the Frozen Chosin. He pulled double duty in Golf Company as 3rd Platoon Leader as well as commander of the Weapons Platoon.

Tony Leyba, my assistant gunner (AG) on the M-60 7.62 machine gun, and I were assigned to Weapons. The Weapons Platoon, with less than half the manpower of a regular rifle platoon, was a Golf Company asset. That meant we could be piecemealed out to any of the company's three platoons as needed. For control purposes, Mac and Company Gunnery Sergeant Bill Janzen were in charge of us.

"Maras," Lieutenant Mac said to me, "you and Leyba with the machine gun will be on the first boat to land. We may need your gun."

"Sir, yes, Sir."

In my mind, I pictured WWII Iwo Jima or Saipan with thousands of pissed-off little yellow men waiting ashore for a chance to waste our asses. I silently vowed to make John Wayne proud.

"Gentlemen! Suck up your balls," Lieutenant Mac shouted above the turmoil. "They need some *men* to kick gook ass. The Second Battalion is going to *war!*"

A month ago, the entire 2/3, some 1,300 Marines, clambered aboard the three boats following "Vietnam Training" at Camp Schwab, Okinawa. Since then we had sailed up and down the Vietnamese coast eager for the opportunity to prove ourselves. We considered it cool, *real* cool, that 2/3 was a Battalion Landing Team, which, according to our leaders, meant we were specially selected. We were genuine warriors who policed the war zone, made everything bad good, and went ashore like the cavalry in an Old West movie to rescue the good guys just in the nick of time when they got in trouble.

I was nineteen years old. A few of the other Marines were even younger. Not many though, since you had to be at least eighteen to be sent to Vietnam. So far, before reality set in, everything was a great adventure. We were an impatient lot, champing at the bit: *Hurry up and let us loose in the war. It's going to be over by Christmas when we get there and the enemy sees what we can do.*

We were a mixed lot. White and brown and black and from states, cities, towns, and rural areas all over the United States. From metropolises like Detroit and Los Angeles and my hometown, Tulsa, to dusty crossroads in Arizona or shacks in the hills of Kentucky and Tennessee where guys wore no shoes all summer. We had one thing in common and that made us brothers—the US Marine Corps and its uncomplicated warrior creed of *Semper Fidelis.* "Always faithful."

From the halls of Montezuma
To the shores of Tripoli,
We fight our country's battles
In the air, on land, and sea. . . .

You dug that kind of stuff when you were nineteen and had never been shot at.

Nothing happened aboard ship unless the PA system first announced it: *PREPARE TO DISEMBARK. . . . GOLF COMPANY TO RED THREE. . . . PREPARE TO LOAD AMTRACS.*

Decks on all three boats came alive with gray-green utility uniforms. They echoed with the clanking of rifles and E-tools and K-bar combat knives, vibrated with the shouting of sergeants and the stomping of boots as men scrambled over the sides of the boats and loaded onto

AMTRACs. We were on our way to make the world safe for democracy. Like Marines had done in the Battle of Belleau Wood in France during World War I, on Tarawa a generation later in World War II, and at Inchon in Korea.

The loaded tractors set out across the water for Red Beach like newly hatched baby turtles leaving their mamas. Hunkered inside the steel AMTRACs, all we saw were other Marines around us and perhaps a patch of blue sky directly above through an open hatch. Tony and I were wearing helmets and packs and were laden with ammo and grenades, me toting the M-60 machine gun, Tony with his M-16 rifle, both of us packing .45 sidearms. We occupied a place next to the ramp so that when it lowered we would be among the first out.

The evening before the battalion loaded up a month ago and set sail from Okinawa, the battalion commander, Colonel Earl Delong, assembled everyone in the base theater at Camp Schwab for a pep talk. "Pappy" Delong was an old salt. At least he was *old* compared to most of his Marines. He had been well seasoned in the Marine Corps.

"Remember your training," he advised. "That's critical. Everybody in this battalion is a good shot, so make your bullets count. We have the experience in this outfit. Some of your NCOs fought in World War II or Korea. Listen to them. They'll guide you through. Most of all except for mission and duty, look out for one another. That's the Marine Corps way. Make your battalion proud!"

Semper Fi!

Tony and I were privates, down near the bottom of the military pecking order. We had been together looking out for each other from boot camp on through ITR and BITS (Battalion Infantry Training School) where we drilled on unit crew-served weapons, everything from the M-60 machine gun and 3.5 rocket launcher to flamethrowers, 60mm mortars and the Browning Automatic Rifle (BAR). If a Marine company had the weapon, Tony and I could fire it. I suspected we were about to have an opportunity to prove our mettle.

"Maras?" Tony whispered next to me as the AMTRACs charged toward Vietnam. "Are you nervous, man?"

We knew each other too well to lie. But bluster and braggadocio in the face of pending danger was not the same as a lie. "I ain't paid to be nervous, Tony. It's out of my pay grade."

Tony sighed. "I think my pay grade stops at cleaning the pissers in the head."

He reminded me of the actor-comedian Buddy Hackett, but now a very anxious Buddy Hackett with cramps as we drew near Red Beach. He wasn't fat like Buddy. No combat Marine was *fat*. But he was a solid block of a guy with dark bristle on top of a round head covered by his helmet.

The closer we drew to shore, the quieter we became. Marines gave our weapons a last check, tightened our helmet straps, tapped each other on the shoulder or helmet for good luck. I gripped the machine gun tightly between my knees and waited, expecting at any moment a bombardment from shore, like at Iwo Jima. That was the way it happened in John Wayne movies.

Quiet like this couldn't be good; it was giving me time to think. I glanced at Tony. His head was lowered and I figured he must be thinking of Peggy. Or praying, like the good Catholic boy he was. I thought of Linda, my high school sweetheart. I married her on boot camp leave. A lot of boots before shipping out to Vietnam got married when they went home. Marriage formed a bond, an assurance of an anchor to bring us back, someone waiting for us.

"Maras?" Tony lifted his head. "Maras, if I don't make it, will you . . .?" He took a deep breath. "Will you tell Peggy what happened?"

I tried to josh him out of it. Buddies did that for buddies. A mood was something you didn't want to carry into combat. "Come on, Tony, don't get your skivvies in a knot. We're both coming back, okay? Peggy is counting on you to fart for her."

"You're cold, Maras. *Cold.*" But he half-grinned, sheepishly.

I chuckled, feeling the release of tension. Most of the time, you could count on Tony for a funny story or comment. One of his funniest was when his girlfriend Peggy had her heart set on becoming high school prom queen. She was afraid her chief rival, one of the most popular and self-centered girls in the senior class, would move in over her. Tony couldn't let that happen.

At the school dance where the voting and selection occurred, Tony whisked Peggy's competitor onto the dance floor to whirl with Elvis. In the middle of a light-footed but complicated series of rock 'n' roll steps, Tony passed wind in a gale that reverberated throughout the gym and rattled colored lanterns hanging from the ceiling. The dance went embarrassingly silent.

Pretending alarm and disgust, Tony grabbed his partner and shook her. "You *pig!*" he scolded. "Farting like that and you wanna be Prom Queen?!"

Peggy won the crown.

"Coldest thing I've ever done to anybody," Tony confessed to me as we heard breakers crashing against Vietnamese sand, his good Catholic boy persona crushed. "But I couldn't let my girlfriend lose."

I slapped his helmet. We both laughed and relaxed.

Lieutenant Mac's standing up in the AMTRAC immediately got our attention. "One minute!" he announced.

That brought back the tension.

Half of BLT 2/3 consisted of raw greenhorns like Tony and me. The "old" 2nd Battalion had got fucked up bad in a deadly ambush northwest of Da Nang that left the outfit's command sergeant major dead along with a bunch of other NCOs, men, and most of the brass. The battalion returned—what was left of it—from Vietnam to Okinawa to refit and seed in replacements. Golf Company, into which fate inserted Tony and me, had lost 26 dead and 46 wounded out of a company of 110 men.

A Marine lance corporal who had survived the ambush balked at the prospect of having to go back to Vietnam. He had barely made it back the first time. Returning to give the gooks another shot at him was beyond his ability to cope. When the battalion was preparing to load onto the boats, the disturbed Marine took off for the showers and repeatedly bashed his head against a tile wall until he cracked open his skull. Medics carried him out on a stretcher. He giggled hysterically through the blood and gore on his face.

"Don't go back there!" he ranted. "Don't go! You're all dead if you do! God, don't go!"

Chapter Two

The Graveyard

THE BATTALION WAS RAMPED UP, EVERY GRUNT'S SENSES HYPER-AWARE. "Red Beach" in gyrene lingo was a generic term indicating a possible hot landing with enemy opposition. The 9th Marine Regiment had done the first Vietnam Red Beach when it stormed ashore at Da Nang two years ago in March 1965 to kick this ragtag war into high gear. In all the old World War II movies, like *Sands of Iwo Jima* and *The Fighting Seabees*, a dramatic score with crescendos of drums and bugles accompanied land-ings. There was nothing like that now as our AMTRACs charged toward the sand. Just the rattle of weapons, some muted cursing, a few muttered prayers, nervous knees knocking together.

PFC Gene Kilgore occupied a space in the track on the other side of Tony. He slapped the black plastic stock of his new Mattie Mattel M-16 rifle. "This piece of shit had better work," he muttered.

Up until Okinawa, we had trained with trusty M-14s that replaced WWII-era M-1s. They were heavy-caliber, heavy-weight semi-automatic rifles, and they were dependable. On Okinawa, however, officers collected our M-14s and issued black metal-and-plastic M-16s that resembled children's toy guns. They were touted as lightweight weapons capable of fully automatic fire fed by 20- or 30-round magazines. Whereas the -14 fired enemy-stopping 7.62mm rounds, the new -16 loaded 5.56mm, a slight advance over the .222 rifles Sunday shooters used back home for plinking rabbits or squirrels. In selecting it as Vietnam's rifle, the Penta-gon apparently preferred its higher bullet velocity and magazine capacity.

It had problems from the beginning. On the range at Camp Schwab, M-16s jammed every few rounds when the battalion took them out for a test run. *Bang! Bang! Jam. Bang! Jam. Bang! Jam.* Marines exchanged startled looks.

"They're sending us to war with *these pieces of shit.*"

"So, I see this gook coming right at me," Tony hypothesized. "I got him dead in my sights. Sight picture, sight picture. . . . Squeeze the trigger. Oh, *fuck!*"

"*I'll* shoot him," I offered. The reliable ol' Pig, the M-60 machine gun, *always* functioned.

Same thing happened with the Mattie Mattels when we test-fired them off the *Ogden*'s fantail on the sea cruise to Vietnam. Seldom could you burn through a magazine without their malfunctioning. Failures were initially chalked up to our not cleaning the weapons properly. That didn't fly. Even though we were issued only enough cleaning equipment and rods for every fourth or fifth man, a finicky New York Fifth Avenue socialite could have sipped coffee from the barrels. Marines always kept our weapons that clean.

The unreliable status of the M-16 added to the tension as the amphib tractors rolled up on tan-white sand backed by lush tropical vegetation and low jungle hills in the distance. The AMTRACs dropped their "drawers" and excreted the battalion onto Vietnam soil. For perhaps the majority of Marines in 2/3, due to the previous ambush casualties, this was our first time on hostile shores.

We charged off the armored boats like 1,300 John Wayne impersonators prepared to combat evil and save the world. It was 22 April 1967 and Operation Beacon Star, later called Operation Bo Diddley, was under way. Our debut turned out to be rather anticlimactic and inglorious. Nobody shot at us. Nobody said a cross or unkind word. Fact was, nobody said anything to us because nobody was there. Just a gull that flushed and winged off down the beach screeching his indignation.

Marines had arrived ready to do battle with the hordes—and it was like we were on a day's outing at Miami or Waikiki Beach. Confused, even a bit disappointed, we looked at each other, looked up and down the deserted beach. Somebody laughed out of nervous relief. It proved contagious and more sniggers rippled through the invaders.

A private named Burnham figured it out. "Gooks heard the mighty 2/3 was coming and they split. They're probably back in Hanoi by now."

Tony Leyba threw back his head and called out at the top of his lungs, "*Good morning, Vietnam!*"

Platoon leaders and sergeants snapped us back into line. Golf Company's Gunny Sergeant Janzen, thirty-six years old and still feisty and hard-core, roared, "Cut the grabass. You guys are sounding like a gaggle of geese. Shape up or my boot will be up your asses and you'll have more to worry about than gooks."

The way I understood our mission at my lowly pay grade was that Viet Cong guerrillas supported by Hanoi and the NVA had established a presence in the ratty little villages in the Phu Bai area of I Corps. Communists moved into a village, generally the more remote ones, and took it over through a combination of stick and carrot. Go along with the program and the village elders were rewarded by not being assassinated; resist and they found themselves hung in the village square as a warning to potential opposition. Communists had been using this tried and true method since Vladimir Lenin—and along the way had slaughtered several million recalcitrants. Building communism was a brutal and bloody business.

BLT 2/3's role in Operation Beacon Star was to create a presence by patrolling VC-infested villages to search for and seize arms, combat rations, and other war matériel and, finally, to root out VC and kill them.

The battalion quickly formed for a road march in force along a cart trail that threaded up and off Red Beach. Echo Company took point, followed by Hotel and Foxtrot. Golf brought up the rear. Grass hooches with either tin or palm leaf roofs caught the notice of naïve young Marines who soon came to realize that much of the Third World existed in squalor and poverty. Naked, dirty-faced kids played in the mud along with chickens, ducks, pigs, water buffalo, and, presumably, various parasites. Snaggle-toothed *mamasans* with babies on their hips and baskets balanced on their heads stared as the battalion tramped by. From the rice fields, *papasans* in black "pajamas" paused in the tepid water with their trouser cuffs rolled up to the knees and straw cone hats pulled low to shade their eyes from sunlight.

Kids stood by the side of the trail hawking cans of warm Coca-Cola. "Joe? Joe, you buy Coca?"

"They had Cokes ready for us," Tony observed. "How did they know we were coming? I thought we were a secret operation."

"Nothing's secret in this country," said Gunny Janzen, who happened to be passing by checking on his men.

Shortly, we approached a Buddhist cemetery that looked to be about a thousand years old. Ancient trees shrouded in gray moss stood sentinel over little cupolas, shrines, and tombstones crusted in lichen. A lizard watched us from the top of the stone wall that surrounded the graveyard.

I expected the battalion to march on by. To my surprise, Echo and the Command Element turned in through the cemetery gate and proceeded to set up a battalion Command Post under a clump of gloomy trees from which to oversee and control the Area of Operations (AO). Darkness crept through the grave markers as the battalion established a perimeter and put out Observation/Listening (OP/LP) Posts.

I surmised the site had been selected because of the protection afforded by the high rock wall. Still, it had to be the spookiest place in Vietnam, an assumption that proved premature the longer I remained in-country. There were a lot of spooky places in Vietnam.

Things got even spookier as the sky turned purple and full night slithered in. Tony figured Dracula with slanted Asian eyes would probably rise out of the grave next to which he and I set up our 50-50 watch—one of us sleeping and the other keeping an eye peeled for the enemy, ghosts, or Dracula, whichever arrived first.

Foxfire glowed from a decaying pile of fallen trees nearby. Tony kept a wary eye on it.

"It's like eyes shining in the dark," he ventured. "I have a feeling Vietnam is glaring at us, telling us it doesn't want us here."

Chapter Three

Khe Sanh

At first I was embarrassed busting into the little Vietnamese villages ransacking through people's belongings without so much as a by your leave. Poor gooks in their grass hooches seemed so ignorant they probably didn't even realize the world was round or that the sun didn't rise out of the ocean as it seemed to. You could smell a village from a mile downwind.

The kids were cute little critters, the younger ones naked, the older standing aside in their faded black cotton pants as they silently watched big, round-eyed foreigners wearing helmets and armed with exotic weapons invade and go from hut to hut, poking knives into barrels of grain, up-ending baskets, nosing around and taking no guff from the elders.

Women in their woven-grass cone hats and baggy black pajamas were tiny things, and cute too. At least *some* of them were attractive when they were young. They aged fast working the rice paddies, became *mamasans* with their faces wrinkled and crusted in the hot tropical sun like cardboard left out in the weather. The withered crones they became glared silent resentment as we barged into their homes.

The men with their wispy little beards all looked like Ho Chi Minh. I could have sworn one of them *was* Uncle Ho. He stepped aside and watched with a pained expression on his face as Bill Rainey, Tony, and I barged into his hooch and tossed it for contraband. A fat, crudely rolled cigarette burned down to his fingers; he grimaced and dropped it at his feet on the dirt floor. Instead of stomping it out, he squatted and carefully salvaged what few grains of tobacco remained.

I stood over him. Poor bastard. I handed him a pack of cigarettes. *Lucky Strikes.* Little packs of six came with our C-rations. I didn't smoke, so I mostly traded mine for C-rat fruit cocktails or white cake. I figured I always got the better of the deal.

Uncle Ho seemed so grateful for a few butts that Rainey forked over a C-rat chocolate bar to a passing maiden to see just how grateful *she* might be. She snatched it out of his hand and kept going without looking at him.

"Damn!" he huffed. "The bitch probably doesn't even speak English."

It occurred to me that all these poor dirt farmers wanted out of life was to be left alone to grow their rice, bed their women on their woven sleeping mats, raise their children, and watch the sun rise and set. Instead, the commies came through promising a "workers' paradise," and anyone who refused it was shot and hung in the center of the village as a warning.

Then here *we* came chasing the commies, tossing people's houses, ogling their women, and further disrupting their lives. Poor fuckers were losers no matter what.

"Third Herd's" platoon leader, Lieutenant McFarlane, had fought in Korea and didn't trust *any* gooks. He warned we shouldn't turn our backs on them. Even the sweetest-looking little granny or a four-year-old kid might drop a hot Chicom grenade down our skivvies.

"Search and destroy" in Operation Beacon Star, at least for BLT 2/3, seemed to be mostly "search" with the companies sent out separately. After a hard day's work in the sun, we returned to the cemetery to set out OP/LPs and wait for the hordes to attack. Tony hunkered next to *our* tomb and shivered, still half-convinced that Dracula roamed the graves at night and would suck our blood.

"You won't doze off or nothing when you're on watch, right, Maras?"

"We could build you a crucifix or find some garlic to ward him off," I teased.

Nights after-action, such as it was, our squad and platoon leaders briefed us about hard-core VC and perhaps even NVA in the area. Already beginning to feel like old salts, our reaction was *Bring 'em on!* We were fresh, young, loaded with all this battle equipment, and raring to go. As Kilgore put it, "All dressed up and nobody to take us to the party."

Golf Company was on a trudge between villages, all strung out up and down a muddy road, when a sniper with a grudge and an old 50-caliber rifle took a pot shot at the lead elements, which included Tony and me. The machine gun always traveled near the front of a column. That 50-cal boomed like a cannon from out of a clump of mangrove on the other side of a rice paddy. I hit the dirt. I would have crawled *under* it if possible. This was my first experience getting shot at—or at least it *felt* like I had been shot at.

"I can't get any lower, me buttons are in the way," I quipped to ease the tension. That was the tagline from a cartoon in Bill Mauldin's classic World War II book *Up Front*, which seemed apropos for the occasion.

"I'm taking off all my buttons tonight," Tony responded.

Only that one shot and the sniper *di di'd* out of the AO. What we figured was the commie VC made some old guy shoot at us, or else they would gut his wife or first-born. Probably he didn't actually want to hit anyone because then things got serious and we would have to kill somebody.

Next day, a couple of guys in Hotel Company triggered a booby trap in one of the villes. Typical set-up with a trip wire attached to a live grenade slid into a discarded C-rat can. Stumbling into the wire jerked the grenade free, released the spoon and—*Boom!* The injured Marines were medevac'd out to the sick bay on *Princeton* waiting off the coast. Rumor had it that one of them may have died. Rumors also circulated that some other guys in Echo or Foxtrot were killed in an ambush.

Rumors always made the rounds in a big outfit in which contact between men outside their own units was limited. Nights in the cemetery, each company held its own sector inside the rock wall perimeter and communicated with each other primarily through the CP—the Command Post.

"If we had an FM/AM radio," Tony commented, "we could listen to Saigon Sally and find out what's really going on."

We had sometimes tuned in to Sally while aboard the *Ogden*. Sally played good rock 'n' roll, interspersed with patter such as, "*Marines of the 3rd Division, be aware that the Peoples' Republic of Vietnam does not want you here. Colonel Earl Delong, this message is for you: Your men will all die as they died before. . . .*"

That girl did her research.

"What we should do," I proposed, "is kick ass, take names, get this over with, and go home."

"You tell 'em, *Private* Maras. I'm sure they'll listen to you."

Supported by Golf Company, Hotel returned to the booby trapped village that had wounded our guys. Golf maneuvered to the back side of the settlement to sit on our duffs as the anvil while Hotel moved in as a hammer from the other side to drive any resident rats out to us. Lieutenant Mac placed Tony and me behind a rock pile in the center of the ambush line where our machine gun could cover the entire breadth of the village. So far, residents seemed unaware of our presence.

We watched as some gook emerged yawning from his hut, totally unaware of our presence. *Gook.* A strange word. Marines in previous wars had had their own terms to designate the enemy: In WWII, it was *Japs* for the Japanese and *Krauts* for Germans. In Korea, the enemy was known as *chinks.* For us, we learned *gook* in boot camp. It became part of the way young Marines in combat thought and spoke. It dehumanized the Vietnamese and made it easier for us to kill them. In return, the Vietnamese called us *round eyes* or whatever for the same reason.

The villager walked off a few paces from his hut and took a leak on Vietnam.

"That's how I feel," Tony approved. "Piss on Vietnam."

"*Good morning, Vietnam,*" I whispered back.

So far in this strange war, I had been shot at once. Well, *maybe* I had been shot at; that wasn't confirmed since the dude with the ancient 50-cal hadn't hit anyone and boogied out immediately afterwards. Neither Tony nor I had yet fired a round in anger. The Pig, we joked, was still a virgin. As were we. That could all end in a baptism of fire within the next few minutes.

I gave an involuntary start at the sudden crack of a rifle shot from Hotel's side of the hamlet. This was a fair-sized town laid out along a small creek on one side, with rice paddies on the other side, and backed by a low range of hills. On Golf's end lay the Buddhist cemetery. On Hotel's end, an old stone Catholic Church marked the edge of habitation.

As Hotel had spread out in combat formation and entered the ville, the rifle shot had snapped from one of the huts beyond the church. Hotel's Weapons Platoon led by Sergeant Ed Crawford found itself directly in the line of fire and went immediately to ground. Sergeant Crawford, a combat veteran of Korea, instinctively noted the source of the assault.

Ed was in his forties, which made him *old* in the eyes of nineteen-year-olds like me. He might even have been a *grampa*. Naturally soft-spoken with a laid-back disposition, he was a big man thick of shoulder and thin of hair with wise brown eyes and a rock jaw like that on any classic Marine recruiting poster. He had been previously wounded in combat a total of three times in Korea. After Korea, he went off active duty but remained in the Marine Corps Reserves, became a police officer in Upper Darby, Pennsylvania, married, and started raising three kids.

When the Marine Corps requested veterans return for active duty in Vietnam, Ed took a two-year leave of absence from the police department and shipped off to his third war. To the grunts of 2/3, Ed would always be *Big* Ed Crawford. I was fortunate enough to be one of the newbies Ed befriended and took under his wing during "Vietnam training" on Okinawa.

Marine rules of engagement (ROE) prohibited employing automatic weapons or explosives on buildings in a populated area unless we received intense fire from them. More shots rang out from the sniper's hooch as Hotel blew forward through the village. That did it for Ed. He was old school from a previous no-holds-barred war. Two or three rifle shots in his mind constituted "intense fire." He snatched a 3.5 launcher from his rocket man—and the hut went up in a ball of flame.

Hotel Company's commander, Captain Ray Madonna, was furious. "Crawford, what in the hell do you think you're doing? You're not supposed to do that."

"Cap, that cocksucker was trying to kill my boys. As far as I'm concerned, automatic fire was coming from that hooch. Show me the order *in writing* where I'm not supposed to blow him up and I'll adhere to it."

Echoes from the explosion were still rebounding through the village when all hell broke loose from around the old Catholic Church, which a hive of VC was apparently using as a sanctuary. From where Golf waited as anvil, it sounded like a real fight brewing. For us newbies, it would be our first real battle. We were eager to get in on it.

Then, something unexpected happened. PRC-77 radios began chattering all over the AO. I heard some of it since heavy weapons teams with machine guns and rocket launchers were required to stay close under the personal control of platoon leaders.

"Halt what you're doing!" blasted from the radio. It was the old man's voice—Colonel Pappy Delong himself. *"Return to the CP area. We're moving out ASAP."*

Astonished Golf and Hotel commanders jumped on their radios in protest, neglecting call signs and radio protocol in their intensity to transmit their circumstances. *"We're under fire. We have an enemy element trapped inside a church—"*

"Negative! Negative! Break contact immediately. Roger that?"

What kind of war was this? Right in the middle of an action and we're being pulled out.

Gooks at the church must have thought they were hot shit, standing off a battalion of Marines and driving it off. I glanced back at the village as a plume of smoke from Crawford's burning hut rose into the air and our two companies assembled out of small arms range to road-march on the double back to where we came from. We could only assume something really big had come down to draw us away from a fight we could have won.

Suddenly, all the old military drill about "stand around and wait" no longer applied. Before Jack Spratt could eat no fat, flocks of helicopters—CH-46 Sea Knights and smaller Sikorsky UH-34s—jerked us up and out of the cemetery and delivered the entire BLT to the airfield at Phu Bai. There, C-130s and C-123s waited with dropped ramps and props turning to deliver us to a place called Khe Sanh.

"Where the fuck is Khe Sanh?" Tony wondered.

What we were hearing was that some Marines were getting their asses kicked at Khe Sanh. BLT 2/3 was being sent in like the cavalry to save the day. In short order, in a frantic rush, Tony and I found ourselves stashed in web seating as our Marine-packed C-123 climbed into the sky and barreled north at thirty thousand feet. To help settle an anxious stomach, I twisted around to peer out the little window behind us. Like a tourist taking his first dry-mouthed airplane flight. Below, as far as I could see, green rolling mountains glimmered beneath the startling blue of the morning sky.

"Tony, look at how pretty this country is from the air."

Appearances could be deceiving, as we were to subsequently discover.

The Air Force crew chief, wearing a flight suit and a revolver belt strapped around his waist, hung onto a strap at the rear of the plane near its closed ramp. He stood spread-legged to balance himself against the sway and jolt of the fast-moving aircraft.

"Listen up, Marines!" he shouted. "As soon as this tailgate opens, I'll tell you to exit the aircraft. I will point in the direction I want you to go. Run to the stack of boxes you'll see off the side of the runway. Do you hear me?"

With that, the C-123 rolled over on one wing in a steep descent, leaving my gut at thirty thousand feet as the aircraft corkscrewed toward earth. It leveled out at the last minute and touched down hot on steel matting that planked the dirt runway. The ramp dropped even before the airplane came to a stop. For some reason, these Air Force guys were in a rush to get out of here. The crew chief waved his arms frantically and bellowed above the roar of reverse engines and air brakes.

"People, get the fuck off my airplane! Right the fuck *now!*"

I charged down the ramp carrying the Pig machine gun with a heavy pack on my back, Tony right on my ass and me on the ass of the guy in front of me.

"Damn it, people! Your *other* right!" the crew chief bellowed.

The airplane started to move again before the last Marine boot hit the ground. Tony and I stampeded with the others of Golf Company to a stack of boxes by the runway, which turned out to be crates of ammo and munitions.

From what I saw of it, Khe Sanh Combat Base more resembled an inner-city ghetto than a military installation. Or a rodent warren of bunkers, bunny holes, and trenches, most of it underground. Construction consisted primarily of sand bags, with everything bagged from the chow hall where you ate and the head where you took a crap to Charlie Med that patched you back together if you got shot up or took artillery shrapnel. Mud was the principal color. Even the steel sheeting on the runway was sinking into mud.

From the rush to get here I half-expected maybe the Alamo or the Battle of San Juan Hill. Instead, everything appeared deathly quiet. No signs or sounds of fighting. Anticlimactic. Like when we stormed Red Beach and found only a gull waiting for us. Except, here, even the gull was missing.

"Hey, you Marines! Get over here. We got chow waiting."

A big tarp provided shade for a long table laden with hot cans of Coca-Cola and piles of sandwiches, each made up of two pieces of white bread and a slice of bologna with a pickle on the side. A thin patina of red dust covered sandwiches, table, Cokes, and the weary-looking Marine mess cooks. Tony picked up a sandwich and attempted, unsuccessfully, to blow off dust. He shrugged and gave up.

"Maras, I got a feeling about this," he said, with no effort to conceal his sarcasm. "Something bad happens every time the Marine Corps feeds us this good."

CHAPTER FOUR

Saddle Up

ELEMENTS OF THE HARD-LUCK 9TH MARINE REGIMENT OCCUPIED THE rat warren of trenches, holes, and bunkers that comprised the Khe Sanh Combat Base. In its nickname, "the Walking Dead," the 9th displayed not only a certain blatant defiance but also the reason for its description as "hard luck." It had been the first outfit to come ashore in South Vietnam in March 1965 to conduct open land combat against the communist insurgency inspired and supported by North Vietnam. Until then, the war had been by proxy with the United States aiding the South while China and the Soviet Union supplied the communist North. For the past two years, the 9th had slogged all over I Corps accumulating casualties and adding to its reputation as the Walking Dead.

The newbies of 2/3 got our first look at these fabled warriors when several of them showed up with a forklift to transfer the boxes of munitions stacked by the runway to the ammo bunker. They bore that gaunt, mangy look of survivors, older than they should be and world-wise as they hustled about ignoring the cherry-cheeked FNGs—Fucking New Guys—who stared as though we had suddenly been slapped upside the head with a dose of reality. With my newly issued combat gear, I felt a bit envious of how tough and adapted these guys appeared.

"Holy Shinola!" Private Ronnie Boggs gasped. "Slap my tender cheeks and call me 'Boot Camp.'"

Tony Leyba seemed at a loss for words, a rare occasion. Besides, his mouth was full of bread and bologna. He chewed and swallowed before he finally got out, "I knew there had to be a catch when they fed us first thing we got here. Look at these guys. It's like they're here but nobody's home."

Colonel Pappy Delong and his battalion command element had flown in ahead of the rest of 2/3 to set up a communications/command network in one of the bunkers. The companies arrived one after the other on planes screaming in with power, dumping their human cargo, and screaming out again. Sergeant Crawford and Hotel Company exited the next plane behind Golf's and took their places around the field tables loaded with sandwiches and Cokes. As an old battle-scarred vet, Big Ed had a way of taking charge wherever he appeared. He considered the entire Marine Corps, not just Hotel and its Weapons Platoon, as "my boys." He ambled over to where I, Tony, Rainey, Kilgore, and several other "boys" were munching bologna and trying to look nonchalant as we struggled to make sense of things.

"What's going on, Sergeant?" I asked him. If anyone knew anything, Ed would.

He indicated several green peaks rising as part of a major hill mass about four klicks (kilometers) or so northwest of the runway. A small aircraft circled high above the hills, a single-engine Cessna referred to as a "Bird Dog" because it functioned as an observer to gather intel and as a pointer of targets in coordinated air and artillery strikes.

"The One-Niner needs our help up there on Hill 861," Big Ed said, designating it with a thick finger that slowly swept past to identify its neighboring peaks, 881 North and 881 South.

Hills were numbered militarily according to their height measured in meters. Farther north, Hill 1015 rose above the others in this sector of the rugged Annamite Range. It was known as Tiger Tooth Mountain because of its shape. Right now the green hills appeared quiet and peaceful. But suddenly I experienced a spooky premonition that we Marines were about to come face-to-face with whatever terror lurked up there waiting for us. I might have been even more unnerved had I known at the time the military history of the region.

Khe Sanh, in the far northwestern corner of South Vietnam, lay fifteen miles from the Demilitarized Zone (DMZ) that divided North and

South Vietnam and about seven miles from Laos. In August 1962 while the war was still an "insurgency," US Army Special Forces constructed a combat base on Route 9 at the site of an old French fort and dirt airstrip, the purpose of which was to train and incorporate local Montagnard tribesmen into a Civilian Irregular Defense Group (CIDG) to protect the local population and keep watch on North Vietnamese infiltrators. The Green Beret camp occupied a long, narrow plateau at the bottom of a bowl dominated by three hills—861, 881S, and 881N—that provided any enemy a perfect overlook, staging area, and artillery platform. Perhaps in hindsight the Berets might have selected a more secure location.

Nearby Laos afforded North Vietnamese communists their principal avenue of infiltration into the South. The Ho Chi Minh Trail—actually a network of trails—snaked out of North Vietnam to funnel communist troops and supplies into large, safe base camps in Laos and then on into South Vietnam. Tree canopies up to sixty feet in height, dense elephant grass, and bamboo thickets concealed the trails from the air.

In September 1966, Green Beret and Montagnard patrols discovered signs of increased NVA activity in the Northern provinces—freshly constructed base camps, cleared trails, rice bags, and other discarded equipment. In early October, 1st Battalion, 3rd Marines moved in to occupy the Khe Sanh Combat Base, the objective being to secure the old French airstrip, conduct surveillance and counter-infiltration operations, and, through superior US firepower, block the NVA's route west to Quang Tri City and the heavily populated coastal regions and make it costly for large enemy forces to advance into South Vietnam.

Increased enemy presence in the area confirmed what US Intelligence suspected—that the ruling North Vietnamese Lao Dong Politburo had concluded the time had come to "bleed [the Americans] without mercy [and] force the U.S. to accept defeat" in the same way legendary General Vo Nguyen Giap defeated the French at Dien Bien Phu.

This site of the French humiliation, Dien Bien Phu, lay west of Khe Sanh in the far northwestern corner of South Vietnam, along the border between the two Vietnams. As the Americans were doing now at Khe Sanh, the French in their occupation of the country after World War II established an armed outpost at Dien Bien Phu to interdict communist forces.

In early 1954, Giap's communist Viet Minh, as they were then called, methodically encircled the French stronghold and bombarded it from the heights while reducing the outpost in human wave attacks and choking off French ground and aerial resupply with antiaircraft fire and ambushes. The doomed outpost held out for nearly two months before it surrendered on 7 May 1954; the French subsequently withdrew their forces and went home.

Since the strategy worked against the French, General Giap, who was still in the insurgency business, now assumed it would work against the Americans.

In late 1966 and early 1967, under cover of heavy winter fog that shrouded the Khe Sanh region, the NVA began moving an entire regiment into the hill complex, where its soldiers proceeded to build a maze of heavily reinforced bunkers and artillery positions. Elephants were used to drag in heavy cannon. General Giap's plan of battle was to seize Khe Sanh and use it as a firebase for his 175s to pound "Leatherneck Square," that line of Marine fire bases along the DMZ.

From what we heard, the first indication of a large enemy force assembling in the hills came when a Marine patrol encountered the enemy and killed nine NVA regulars in early 1967. Among the bodies was that of an enemy officer whose satchel contained hand-drawn maps showing in remarkable detail Marine defensive positions at the airfield. Obviously, the North was preparing to launch a major offensive against Khe Sanh.

General Lew Walt, commander of III Marine Amphibious Force (MAF) and thus all Marines in-country, refused to believe reports of an enemy buildup. He flew into Khe Sanh.

"I want every Marine in the Recon Unit to come down here and tell me in person if he has seen an NVA soldier."

To his astonishment, the entire Reconnaissance Platoon showed up at his field headquarters.

"What the hell is this all about?" he demanded.

The platoon leader snapped to attention and saluted. "Sir, you said you wanted to talk to everybody who had personally seen an NVA. Well, sir, this is them."

"How do you know they were NVA and not VC?" the general asked.

"We shot and killed some of them, sir. I saw their rank epaulets, recovered information off the bodies that provided regiment and division. All the ones we've seen or killed up in the hills were wearing standard NVA tennis shoes, pith helmets, and camouflage or khaki uniforms. They were armed with AK-47 rifles, and there wasn't a VC cone hat among them."

Each Marine told a similar story. General Walt left Khe Sanh a believer—but his conversion may have been a little too little and a little too late. On 24 April 1967, while BLT 2/3 was slogging around the countryside in Operation Beacon Star raiding villages for VC contraband, a large NVA force ambushed Marine Bravo Company 1/9 on Hill 861, thereby prematurely triggering General Giap's offensive aimed at taking the high ground from which to lay siege to the combat outpost at Khe Sanh. Although Bravo was all but wiped out, survivors remained up on the hill fighting to hold on until relief arrived. This was the beginning of what became known as the Hill Fights.

General Walt pulled in 2nd and 3rd Battalions of the 3rd Marines to push the NVA off Hills 861, 881N, and 881S. And now 2/3 grunts consumed cold cuts and swigged hot Cokes at the airfield while we waited for something to happen. We didn't have to wait long.

The thunder of aircraft and jet engines jerked my chin toward the sky and lifted the short hair on the back of my neck as dozens of fast-movers streaked over the Combat Base in loud, alarming waves. Tony dropped a half-eaten sandwich, his mouth flew open, and crumbs dribbled off his chin as US airpower began a campaign of softening up 861.

"*Holy shit!*"

Echelons in *V*s by type—AD Skyraiders, Phantoms, A-4s—pounded the hill raw with napalm and bombs that made the ground tremble and the air vibrate, turning 861 into an erupting volcano. As one sortie swooped in and over, silver wings glinting back the midday sun, shedding ordnance like dandruff, a second wave dived into the melee of red-white explosions and boiling black smoke. The terrifying assault seemed to go on and on, filling the air with soot, smoke, and noise.

"It won't be 861 by the time they're through knocking twenty or thirty feet off the top," I observed, awed by the air show. "It'll be Hill 840."

Big Ed gave me a somber look. "They're bombing the gooks that almost wiped out 1/9 of the Walking Dead—and that's where we're heading."

It was one thing rooting out booby traps and taking occasional sniper fire from the scroungy little VC rice paddy villages, quite another to contemplate throwing ourselves into a volcanic cauldron on top of a hill that had previously all but consumed a company of Marines. Lieutenant Mac long-legged it among Third Herd and Weapons Platoon, carrying his M-16 with a pack on his back and his helmet strapped down.

"Ten minutes!" he announced. "Get ready to saddle up, people. We're going to war."

Response from the ranks sounded quite a bit more reserved than usual.

Nervous and frankly scared, I squatted and, to occupy my thoughts, doodled the first thing that came to mind on the top of an empty C-ration box. I had no idea where the phrase came from, only that it appeared in my mind: *For those who fight for life, it has a special flavor the protected shall never know.* In the opposite corner of the box I sketched a likeness of Tony reclining. My Mom always figured I might be an artist. She never figured on my being a Marine.

Later, I discovered that Navy Chaplain Ray Stubbe tore off the box lid and kept it as a souvenir of Khe Sanh. It eventually ended up in the US Marine Corps Museum at Quantico.

One of the other grunts, watching airpower work over 861, noted hopefully, "Man, there won't be anybody left up there by the time they're finished with it."

Sergeant Crawford glanced up and said with an ominous undertone, "That's what Marines thought about Iwo Jima."

CHAPTER FIVE

The "Big Picture"

FOR MORE THAN TWO THOUSAND YEARS OF THEIR EARLY HISTORY, THE
Vietnamese suffered under Chinese domination while struggling to
obtain independence or to maintain it once it was won. On at least five
separate occasions since the beginning of Vietnamese recorded history in
111 B.C., China either directly or by proxy ruled Vietnam, the two sides
batting the nation's independence back and forth like a ping-pong ball.
Each period ended in rebellion and civil war.

The 16th century produced an internecine struggle between two
opposing factions who each sought to rule Vietnam. The long brawl
between the Nguyens and the Trinhs resulted in their establishing a
precedence for partitioning the nation North and South. The Nguyens
created a government-in-exile south of the 17th parallel while the Trinhs
ruled north of the line. After fifty years of bloody and inconclusive fighting, the two sides agreed upon a truce that for the first time officially
divided Vietnam at the 17th parallel into two separate entities. They
would not reunite again until 1802, at which time they adopted Viet
Nam as the nation's new name. It previously existed under such names as
Nam Viet, Annam, and Tonkin.

Vietnam would remain thus reunited until the end of World War II.

By this time, the dominant influence in the region had transferred
from China to Europe. As early as the 1500s, European traders were
making inroads all over Asia, leading to the establishment of colonial
empires in India, Burma, Malaysia, the East Indies, and even China. By

1883, France had conquered Vietnam and made the nation its "Cochin China" colony. During the French colonization that endured, more or less, for well over a half-century, Vietnam relinquished much of its Chinese influence and began adopting Western-type culture, particularly in the cities where many turned to speaking French, dressing like Europeans, designing "modern" buildings, modifying the country's political structure, and accepting Catholicism.

The Russian Revolution of 1917 generated waves of communism that spread across parts of Europe and much of Asia, especially into China. Vietnamese seeking self-determination and freedom from French rule fell to the allure of the Marxist model. A young firebrand named Ho Chi Minh brought communism to Vietnam and pushed for revolution. France successfully contained his movement until World War II.

In June 1940, Hitler's Nazis rampaged through France, occupied Paris, and set up a French Vichy government loyal to Germany. The Vichy subsequently assumed power in Vietnam in alliance with Germany and Japan, but soon acceded to Axis demands and turned control of the entire French Indochina Peninsula over to Japan. Ho Chi Minh's resistance movement surfaced refreshed and intent on ousting both the Vichy French and the Japanese in order to import Chinese-style communism to Vietnam. Ironically enough, considering later developments, the US Office of Strategic Services (OSS), a forerunner of the CIA and US Special Forces, provided guerrilla leader Ho Chi Minh with matériel aid starting in early 1945.

In retrospect, what with all the chaos, Vietnamese emperor Bao Dai chose the wrong path in declaring Vietnamese independence under the protectorate of the Japanese, a proclamation that was to last only a few months before the Japanese surrendered following the atomic bombing of Hiroshima and Nagasaki. During that short period, the Viet Minh Nationalist Movement in Hanoi formed its Committee for the Liberation of the Vietnamese Republic with Ho Chi Minh as president. As soon as Japan capitulated and Bao Dai went on the ropes, Ho Chi Minh declared Vietnamese independence and the establishment of the Democratic Republic of Vietnam.

Britain accepted the Japanese surrender south of the 16th parallel in Vietnam while China was quick to perform the same function north of the 16th. In spite of Ho Chi Minh's having declared Vietnamese independence, England, concerned about preserving its own Asian colonial empire, permitted Free French troops to come back ashore and assisted France in regaining its previous status over Vietnam.

In Hanoi, Ho Chi Minh signed an agreement with France in which the French recognized the "free state" of the Democratic Republic of Vietnam within the Indochina Federation. This pact, which more or less divided the peninsula into a north and a south, endured for less than a year. On 19 December 1946, the Viet Minh launched its first guerrilla attack against French occupation. The "First Indochina War" would rage on for the next eight years.

Communist China began supplying Ho Chi Minh and North Vietnam in early 1950. In September 1951, the United States, which had supported Ho Chi Minh against the Japanese and the Vichy French during the World War, turned against him to provide economic assistance to South Vietnam, thus setting the stage for a proxy war between China and the United States.

The shock of France's defeat at Dien Bien Phu to General Vo Nguyen Giap in May 1954 bolstered French public opposition to the war. The First Indochina War ended when the French High Command and the Viet Minh's People's Army High Command signed a truce on 20 July 1954. While the Geneva Conference granted independence to Vietnam, it also officially partitioned the nation along the 17th parallel into a North Vietnam under the auspices of communism and a Democratic Republic of South Vietnam, much as Korea had been divided. The Chinese refused to gracefully accept the peace accords and partitioning; they continued pushing Hanoi to keep fighting in hopes that a final victory would reunite Vietnam under communism.

Despite the truce and partitioning, Ho Chi Minh left a well-organized network behind in the South to continue his campaign for a united Vietnam. As it became apparent that he could not gain control of the entire nation through political means, he opted with Chinese encouragement for a new radical method. In January 1959, North Vietnam's Communist Central Executive Committee issued Resolution 15, changing its strategy toward South Vietnam from "political struggle" to "armed struggle." Six months later, the first American servicemen were killed in South Vietnam when Major Dale Buis and Master Sergeant Chester Ovnard died in a communist attack on their Bien Hoa billets.

The CIA had attempted to provide a special forces role in Vietnam after the French left. It was mostly a low-level, low-budget covert effort that concentrated on stay-behind programs like the ones set up in Europe during WWII to seed resistance should the communists prevail. It was largely ineffective.

With John F. Kennedy's assumption of the US presidency, he became the nation's foremost advocate of combatting communism through counterinsurgency and unconventional warfare. He referred to the Cold War that evolved out of the World War as a "long twilight struggle leading to a new kind of war—revolution, people's wars, subterranean wars, multidimensional wars, slow-burn wars, war in the shadows [that required] a new kind of fighting force."

On its own, he believed, South Vietnam had no chance to ward off Ho Chi Minh's communists. The little nation's only hope of becoming a democracy free of communist domination lay in special warfare strategies and tactics in countering the North's guerrilla incursions.

US Army Special Forces, the Green Berets, followed the CIA into South Vietnam to train South Vietnamese troops in resisting Ho Chi Minh's insurgency. The US commitment to South Vietnam expanded from about seven hundred military "advisors" in 1961 to more than sixteen thousand in mid-1963. This "Second Indochina War" became a quagmire that incrementally drew the United States toward 1965 and its first deployment of US combat forces, the 9th Marines, for offensive operations.

That was the "Big Picture" of Vietnam; it was above my pay grade. About all I knew at Khe Sanh in the spring of 1967 was that the United States had somewhere around a half-million troops in-country, that a few thousand of us so far had been KIA, and that we were fighting at Khe Sanh because President Lyndon Johnson, who succeeded Kennedy after his assassination, didn't want the Combat Base to become another Dien Bien Phu. He subscribed to the "domino effect," which dictated we either stopped the commies here and now—or the next thing we knew, we would be fighting them in Tulsa and Indianapolis and Chicago.

Chapter Six

Take No Prisoners

THE COMPANY GUNNERY SERGEANT, GUNNY JANZEN, TOLD US THAT OUR aircraft had hit the enemy on Hill 861 with nearly a half-million pounds of bombs and napalm, that jelly-gas that burned like fires from the depths of hell and turned human beings into crispy critters within a matter of seconds. In addition, artillery batteries from the Combat Base contributed a thousand rounds of 105mm and 155mm to the pounding. It was like a tag team match. Arty roared and coughed and smoked. When it stopped, the fast movers thundered in to continue the devastation. On top of all this, B-52 bombers worked out with "Arc Light" strikes between the hills and Laos on any enemy NVA they could find trying to move in for the next curtain call.

The ground trembled. We ate our sandwiches. The prep assault against the hill went on and on. I kept thinking nobody could live through such a display of awesome and hellish power. Perhaps I was only *wishing* they couldn't. Tony even lost his Buddy Hackett and looked utterly scared. I doubted John Wayne was ever as terrified as we looked.

Finally, "Move out in ten minutes!" rippled through the ranks. We geared up, one eye on what we were doing—cinching packs and checking weapons, tightening helmets—the other eye on the erupting volcano still being worked over by aircraft buzzing around it like angry bees around a smoke pot. *We're really going up there!*

Hey, Jarhead, taunted this little bastard demon crouched on my shoulder, *you ain't seen shit yet.*

"I sure do pray, I *really* do, that they're all dead by the time we get there," Tony worried.

Under normal circumstances, a good Catholic boy would never have wished ill on another person.

"We knew this was going to happen when we enlisted," I pointed out.

"Maybe. But not like *this*. Maras, we could get killed up there."

I put on my best cavalier boot camp air. "No shit, Dick Tracy. What gave you your first clue?"

"You're not afraid, Maras?"

"Why, hell yeah, I'm scared. What do you take me for, a damned fool?"

Lieutenant Mac's thin face appeared more sunken and hard-edged than usual. "Leave your flak jackets behind," he ordered. "In this heat, you'll never make it up the hill wearing 'em."

It was shortly after noon. Temperature and humidity were both approaching triple digits. Sweat dripped from our every pore. Each Marine was packed-muled down with gear. I carried the 7.62 Pig on a strap with cans of ammo stuffed into my pack along with cans of C-rats, a spare canteen of water, an extra pair of socks, and miscellaneous other items such as a picture of my new wife, Linda. From my battle harness hung a .45 pistol in a holster, my K-bar field knife, pouches containing grenades, more ammo, emergency field dressings, compass, . . .

Tony was likewise encumbered, except instead of the machine gun he humped more ammo for the Pig, an M-16 Mattie Mattel, and a pack board containing rounds for Weapons Platoon's 3.5 rocket launcher. Kilgore or PFC Taylor or somebody else lugged the launcher.

Just before the battalion moved out in order by companies, Lieutenant Mac had one more thing to say: "Whatever you do, you're not to talk to the Marines you come in contact with who are coming down the hill. Roger that?"

That didn't make sense. Gene Kilgore provided a credible explanation. "They don't want us talking to them," he surmised, "because it'll scare the shit out of us if we know what's in store for us up there."

"Maybe I'll go take a dump now," Tony said, struggling to channel his inner Buddy Hackett.

Rough and colorful language was part of the camaraderie, the flavor of fighting men together, a rite of passage among men of arms.

"Fuck, fuck, fuck!" Tony exhaled forcefully. "There's going to be a party—and all the gooks are invited."

The party had begun two days before, on 24 April, when patrols from the 9th climbed 861 and walked directly into what appeared to be elements of an enemy regiment or division. Hard-core, well-trained, and well-disciplined NVA regulars supported by mortars and heavy artillery from bases in Laos and north of the DMZ and hardened to operating in rugged, jungle-clad mountainous terrain. They owned the turf and were precisely what Marine Recons had been trying to warn General Walt about for the past several weeks.

The war seemed to be taking a turn for the worse. There had been several other set-piece battles in Vietnam before now, such as Colonel Hal Moore's fight in the Ia Drang Valley, but primarily it had been like Nancy Sinatra singing, *These boots are made for walking—and they're gonna walk all over you.* American outfits were accustomed to splashing through rice paddies and walking right over ragtag bunches of Viet Cong guerrillas. They were not accustomed to being walked over themselves.

Now, the Marines of Bravo 1/9, what was left of them, were on their way back down 861 carrying their dead and wounded with them.

In classic infantry tactical formation, with Echo and Golf up front, Hotel trailing, and Foxtrot left behind in reserve, BLT 2/3 resembling a giant green caterpillar clawed its way up the steep eastern slope of 861 through jungle not nearly as postcard appealing as it had appeared from the air. Razor-edged elephant grass in the "clearings" nicked at exposed skin. Jungle growth snagged out packs and helmets. In some places, point men had to hack a path through the foliage with machetes, switching off to relieve each other every five minutes or so.

The relentless thunder of exploding bombs echoed off the green hills and howled down valleys and canyons. An occasional opening in the forest canopy revealed thick black and gray smoke percolating off the top of 861. As we approached, drawing near, I began to worry that the bombing might continue and we would march right into it. Gooks must really be dug in up there to survive all this and still offer to fight.

I overheard Tony breathing heavily on my heels. I glanced back. His round face was as red as a boil about to burst in the heat.

"Tony?"

"This sucks," he panted.

No worries as long as a Marine was bitching; it was when he *stopped* bitching that you knew his ass was dragging.

During a short rest break I had him remove his helmet while I poured water from my canteen over his head to cool him down. He shook his head like a dog emerging from a stream. Big, redheaded Navy Third Class Petty Officer Vernon Wike, otherwise known as "Magilla Gorilla," came along with his aid bag checking on the men. He was one of three Navy medical corpsmen assigned to Golf Company. The Marine Corps had no medical personnel of its own.

"Try not to waste your water," he cautioned. "There won't be any on the hill."

So this, I reflected, was what combat was like—jungle, sweat, heat exhaustion, humping impossible loads, gooks somewhere out there ready to pound us. . . . Nothing like what I expected. Hell, there wasn't even martial music and drums playing in the background.

"I'm good to go," Tony insisted, struggling to his feet as the battalion moved out again. "Say, Maras," he puzzled, "what do you suppose would happen if somebody gave a war and nobody showed up?"

It was something to ponder. Peace would break out?

Shortly, we encountered remnants of Bravo 1/9 straggling down the hill through and past us. They resembled zombies, all hollow-eyed, dirty, ragged, bloody, and silent with that characteristic after-battle thousand-yard stare that looked right through you and made you shiver. Men wrapped in bloody bandages served as crutches for those with mangled limbs. Those more able-bodied bore the weight of the dead and seriously wounded in ponchos. Blood leaking from makeshift litters left scarlet lines on the trail. These were the survivors and casualties of what had once been a proud company of Marines the size of Golf. I turned around in the trail, reeling under the full impact of reality setting in, and stared in horror at the backs of these beaten Marines disappearing downhill into the green morass on their retreat to the airfield. The Walking Dead, I thought, were aptly named.

The hammering of Hill 861 lifted as BLT 2/3 ascended, replaced by a sudden void of silence. We grew more cautious and alert for signs of enemy presence. Expecting combat, perhaps even anticipating it, we entered the lower bombing zone, a wasted moonscape of craters, splintered trees, burned grass, and bomb-ploughed earth. The only sounds were those of Marines breathing nervously, the crackling of fires still burning, flame-gutted trees toppling to earth. . . . The air tasted scorched and bitter in my throat. Tendrils of smoke seemed to curl up out of the earth itself. Blistering heat blew into my face and made my eyes water and my nostrils burn. A sudden feeling overcame me that this was what it would be like in a world devastated by nuclear war where no life remained.

Point platoon reached the crest by 1600, still a few hours before dark, and gazed down from the heights onto a vista of green, rolling terrain with 881N and 881S rising higher a short distance ahead on either flank. To our relief, at least to *my* relief, the NVA had withdrawn, taking their dead and wounded with them. Apparently, they hauled ass down the back slope either as soon as our bombardment began or while 2/3 was laboring up the hill to confront them. They left, however, ample evidence of their presence, and an ample presence it must have been—over three hundred interlocking bunkers, trenches, and mutually supporting fighting holes and spider traps. Some of the positions had been destroyed by pre-attack bombing and artillery, but many others were so well constructed in layers of logs and dirt that only a direct hit would have damaged them.

Bravo 1/9 Marines must have blundered into this hive where they fought savagely enough to run NVA soldiers off the hilltop. Battered and bleeding, they nonetheless occupied the hill themselves and held it against repeated enemy counterattacks while they waited for help to come. Much weakened and facing destruction if they remained, they finally began withdrawing this morning while BLT 2/3 was being jerked away from Beacon Star and dumped onto Khe Sanh. I wondered if maybe the wily North Vietnamese, having reappropriated the hill, might not have vacated the premises again *before* our artillery and planes began pyrotechnics. Had we perhaps been striking empty positions while the hordes reassembled and reinforced below and waited for their next victims to wander into the trap?

As the battalion repossessed the neighborhood and began setting up a defensive perimeter, word came down through the chain of command to be on the lookout for the bodies of four Marines that the 9th had been forced to leave behind.

"I guess they couldn't get everybody out when they broke contact," Lieutenant Mac said.

He and Gunny Janzen established Tony and me and the Pig in one of the NVA fighting holes that offered a field of fire downslope across one of the draws and ridgelines that separated 861 from 881S.

"Get set in, Marines," the Lieutenant hurried us along. "It'll be dark soon."

The connotation of that phrase—*It'll be dark soon*—was enough to pucker assholes all over the hill's mangled knob.

"Damn, Maras," Tony complained. "Couldn't you have picked a better penthouse? This one stinks like gooks."

I had never smelled a decomposing corpse before, but the stench in our hole was more than merely poor human hygiene. "I think somebody's real dead, real close," I decided.

The sun hung low, shooting its final rays over the tops of 881S. I didn't relish the prospect of spending my first night in the field with odor that foul. Tony kept watch while I wriggled from cover to take a look around. Sure enough, about ten feet away I spotted legs and fire-scorched boots protruding from a partially collapsed bunker. This was one of our guys; gooks wore tennis shoes.

"Holy shit!"

Tony scurried over. "What? What?"

We immediately summoned Lieutenant Mac and Gunny Janzen, who brought in Captain James Sheehan, who, in addition to commanding Golf Company, had been assigned as acting 2/3 commander in the field while Colonel Delong established an overall CP at the airfield. Everyone stared in horror at the mangled body, including Lieutenant Mac, even though he had seen men killed in battle before. "Big green shit flies," as we called them, swarmed the charred body. Enough remained of it for us to realize the Marine had been decapitated and his testicles stuffed into the throat of his separated head. The eyes were open and blackened by soot. His tongue lolled past his testicles and out of what was left of his lower face after rats and birds and the sun had gnawed on him. Lieutenant bars pounded into the chest helped Graves Registration identify the body as that of Lieutenant Philip H. Sauer of Alpha Company, 3rd Antitank Battalion, 9th Marines.

We subsequently learned Lieutenant Sauer, commander of a pair of ONTOS, had been a member of a thirty-man recon force climbing 861 ahead of the main body of Marines. An ONTOS was a medium-sized track and armored vehicle equipped with a 106mm recoilless rifle. Sauer split from the main patrol with three other men to scout out a good observation point on the hill and find a route to bring his vehicles to the top. None of the four returned. It appeared Sauer and the three Marines with him had inadvertently interrupted what may have been an overwhelming surprise attack on the Khe Sanh Combat Base. What followed was a brutal two-day fight on 861 that all but decimated Bravo 1/9.

Report of the discovery of the corpse and its condition spread rapidly across the hilltop. Attitudes hardened immediately, especially among the FNGs who had linked up with the battalion in Okinawa. The new grimness was almost palpable, a sudden thirst for blood revenge. This was no longer high adventure. This was *reality. War!*

"Kill 'em all and let God sort 'em out."

Resolve spread that the 2/3 would take no prisoners. Not after this.

"We'll shoot you ourselves if you let one of the motherfuckers live," became the general consensus. "These bastards are not *human.* They're savages and they don't deserve to live."

I found a Vietnamese banana knife dropped near Sauer's corpse. I assumed it had been used to carve up the lieutenant and the bodies of the other three missing Marines, which were located nearby the next day in a similar condition. I stuck the knife on the outside of my pack where

I could get to it and glared with a new fierceness down the hill in the direction the NVA had gone. I was a Marine trained on *how* to kill; after this, I *wanted* to kill.

The falling night wasn't nearly as bleak and scary as the darkness growing inside my soul.

CHAPTER SEVEN

Good Morning, Vietnam

A SEA KNIGHT HELICOPTER DROPPED IN AT DUSK TO PICK UP LIEU-tenant Philip Sauer's recovered body. As it lifted off again and banked sharp to get out of Dodge, some gook down the hill where the foliage started took a rifle shot at it. I detected the muzzle flash and felt tempted to unlimber the Pig and chew down the jungle on his ass. Except a machine gunner was not authorized to answer stray or probing fire without orders. It wasn't smart to let the enemy know where machine guns were located. Best to reserve them as a deadly surprise for when and if the enemy decided on a mass attack.

One of the mortar guys popped a 60mm round at the shooter. A puff of smoke drifted up out of the trees, after which everything went quiet again to meet the night.

"Maybe he's the only one left," Tony hoped. "Maybe the rest of 'em are back in Laos by now chugging brews and chasing *mamasan*."

My thoughts were elsewhere. I watched the chopper sail up and out and away over the purple-darkening hills and valleys. Back in the "Real World," there would be wailing and gnashing of teeth as a government sedan pulled up in front of a house in Omaha or Abilene or whatever town or city Sauer was from to deliver the sad news to parents and wife that their warrior had gone on to Valhalla.

Although no gook cadavers remained on the hill—the NVA must have carried them off when they departed—the stench of death poisoned the air we breathed. That was because bombardment of the peak had scattered parts all over—fingers and scalps, feet and hands, ears and chunks of flesh. . . . And blood. Blood blown in a splatter all over the hilltop to decay in the hot sun. The Vietnamese must have endured hell on this miserable hill. They deserved it, as far as I was concerned, after what they put Lieutenant Sauer and his team through.

When the breezes lay with nightfall, I heard Marines gagging, retching, and complaining.

"Damn! They stink!"

"You brush your teeth today, Morrison?"

"It's your ass you're smelling underneath your nose."

"Knock it off," NCOs snapped. "This ain't no church picnic, ladies. Get set for the night before you have gooks in your skivvies."

"Hell, Corporal, we don't wear no skivvies."

"If we get gooks, make sure they're females."

Banter like that, I recognized from my own reaction, provided a means of working off tension.

Night first arrived in the lowlands below the hills, slithering in like bruised reptiles before gradually creeping up the slopes. When I was a kid, Dad said there was nothing to fear about the night because there was nothing in the dark that wasn't there in the light. Dad was wrong. There *were* things out there in the dark to be afraid of. Most of the greenhorn Marines were like me, so scared we couldn't even spit. I doubt anyone on the hill slept that first night, even those who were on the sleeping side of 50-50 alert. Nail my eyelids shut and the nails would have popped right out.

We hunkered together for comfort in our holes like frightened rats, gripping weapons with white-knuckled fists, mostly listening for rustling sounds coming out of the night, imagining hordes of little yellow men in pith helmets massing out there for a Japanese-like banzai charge. In the darkness there was nothing to see except black unless you shifted your eyes upward to the stars.

If I were God, I thought, I probably would never have made people. Humans were such a contentious lot. I mean, cutting off people's heads and stuffing their dicks in their mouths. A lion or a bear might kill a deer, but neither would cut off the deer's penis or head to torture it or amuse himself. As God, I might have created platypuses and octopuses and giraffes, but never people. I wouldn't have made ticks and chiggers, mosquitoes and snakes either.

Tony thought God must have a dark sense of humor.

"Like a big Buddy Hackett up in the sky?" I said.

"Maras, anybody ever tell you you're strange?"

We stood elbow to elbow in our hole peering into the darkness, whispering so as not to attract attention from our NCOs or from any gooks lurking about.

"Look, so God makes people," Tony explained. "He makes 'em all different colors and where they speak different languages. Then he mixes 'em all together to see what happens."

"You say *I'm* the strange one? Tony, *you're* the strange one."

I thought God must be more like John Wayne. Tough and reliable and knowing just what to do to take care of things. What was significant about our whispered conversation was that it centered on the subject of *God*. God and creation and all they implied about life and death and eternity. When the men from Oklahoma returned from World War II, they brought back a saying: *There are no atheists in foxholes.* I was beginning to understand. I looked up into the night sky infinitely spangled with stars and planets, all serene and beautiful and so far away from the killing in Vietnam and its stench of death and dying.

About that time an enemy mortar round exploded inside the perimeter with a terrific doomsday crack and a blinding white ball of light. It had to be the Second Coming. And just when we thought the NVA didn't want any more fire from the sky and had packed up their shit and gone home.

Tony and I ended up piled on top of each other at the bottom of our hole. We remained like that, breathing hard as though from exertion, until it became apparent that the explosion was just a single harassing round to let us know the NVA were still out there and watching.

"Get off me, Tony," I said finally. "I didn't know you cared."

I clambered back to my machine gun. Tony kind of sniggered to cover his jitters. "Well. . . . Well, fuck!" he said.

The night passed long and dark. Except for every now and then a mortar shell arriving C.O.D. Probably from a stay-behind unit covering the withdrawal of the Main Force NVA and attempting to discourage pursuit. This was no Dien Bien Phu. Maybe the fight was already over, and we won. Without either Tony or me having busted a single cap.

We were still wide awake when dawn lightened the eastern sky over Khe Sanh and the night gradually turned to gray. The sun broke slowly over the misty green peaks of South Vietnam's most distant corner to reveal a scene of deceptive tranquility. Fine ephemeral mist lay down in the valleys between 861 and the other two hills of the triangle. The soft early light elicited a sigh from Tony.

"I gotta piss like a race horse," he said.

I broke open C-rats of fruit cocktail and pound cake for breakfast, emptied the contents into our canteen cups, and passed Tony one of the empty cans. I kept the other. We unbuttoned, filled our cans, and tossed urine out of our new home. It couldn't smell any worse than all the rotting gook parts scattered about.

"Good morning, Vietnam!" Tony cheered as he poured urine from the can. From then on it became part of our morning ritual: Wish Vietnam good morning while we pissed on her.

I wondered as I ate what Linda might be having for breakfast. She was staying with Mom and Dad and my little sister while I was gone. What with the time difference on the other side of the world, instead of breakfast she was probably sitting down at the dinner table with the rest of the family. Maybe I'd be joining them soon. The NVA might have messed up Bravo 1/9, but it seemed that when the Marines got serious and brought in the cavalry the gooks took off. If this was the best they could do, the war would be over by Christmas.

CHAPTER EIGHT

A Walk in the Sun

OUT THERE BE MONSTERS. NIGHTS ON 861 TONY AND I HUDDLED IN our miserable hole, and we half-expected dragons and fanged, two-headed demons to materialize out of the night to do to us what they had done to Lieutenant Sauer. Gooks were still *out there*, and they were out there in force. That seemed to be the general consensus of Colonel Pappy Delong and the I Corps leadership dug in at the airfield and trying to figure out what the NVA would do next. Uncle Ho and General Giap hadn't come this far to create a second spring offensive Dien Bien Phu just to pack up and go home at the first setback.

Every night, our artillery dueled with their artillery and mortars, mostly harassment and interdiction (H&I) fire. If anybody saw movement out there, if anybody *suspected* it, big guns from Khe Sanh and even bigger 175s from Leatherneck Square opened up to hurl a few rounds whose mighty explosions seemed to reveal the fiery soul of the universe.

The NVA responded in kind, H&I-ing us back. Officers cautioned troops not to get out of our holes after nightfall. If you needed to take a leak or a dump, figure something out.

"You're fair game if you're walking around inside the perimeter at night," Gunny Janzen warned. "Not just from gook mortars. Everybody's jittery and you may end up with perforations in your skivvies."

Nobody wore skivvies in the field, they gave us diaper rash, but he had made his point.

After H&I did its stuff, one of the C-47s we referred to collectively as "Puff the Magic Dragon" flew over to drop flares that, like little suns, lit up the terrain around us in an eerie, flickering approximation of daylight. Any NVA foolish enough to be exposed in the kitchen when the lights went on felt the Dragon's fiery breath. While only every fifth round from its 20mm cannon was a red tracer, the accumulative effect resembled the fiery tail of a dragon lashing back and forth. The sound it made was like the biggest ratchet in the world. Awesome sights and sounds for a good ol' boy from Oklahoma to witness.

I stood hip-shod at daybreak in our hole keeping a wary eye out for monsters over the Pig's heavy barrel when Gunny Janzen approached in that little sand crab run intended to keep a low profile against possible snipers in the green below. We called it the "861 Shuffle." Tony rested in the hole at my feet; he had stood our last 50-50 watch and felt groggy. Red dirt had already managed to grime into his utilities, and into mine. I needed a shave and a good hot bath.

"Warning order," Gunny said. "We're moving out in three-zero mikes."

Janzen looked as though he hadn't slept much either. At thirty-six years old, he was in fit shape, lean and mean with a square unshaved jaw underneath his helmet.

I blurted out the first thought that came to mind. "You mean—*out there?*" Then felt foolish as hell for saying it.

"What do you think we're doing out here, Maras? Kicking gook butt or pulling R&R?"

"If that's a choice, Gunny, . . ." Tony ventured.

The gunny sergeant rolled his eyes and pointed toward a green ridgeline below. It appeared to connect 861 and 881N. Thick fog covered it this early in the morning. That ridge, Gunny outlined in a hurried, condensed version of an OpPlan, was our intermediate objective on the way to a low hill mass farther on toward 881N, our ultimate target. From what I gathered, if we secured these three hills—861 and 881 North and South—we checkmated the NVA bastards right in their tennis shoes. Ho-Ho-Ho Ho Chi Minh!

"Muster with Lieutenant Mac's Third Herd," Gunny said, "and follow the boots in front of you. Mac will let you know if we need the M-60 up."

Gunny vaulted out of our hole and skittered on down the perimeter. Platoon leaders would provide briefings once we assembled to move out. I continued to study the ridgeline Gunny pointed out. Elements of the 9th that had replaced what remained of Bravo 1/9 when it pulled back had dug in on the ridgeline to hold it. Last night right after dark, they must have spotted movement between them and 881S and called in arty. Four or five 175mm rounds from one of the batteries at Leatherneck Square had scattered the gooks.

Maybe, if we were fortunate, today would be just another walk in the sun. We would walk over there, walk up 881N and 881S in a day or so, find nobody home, and that would be the end of it. The brass that played with our colored pins on maps would move BLT 2/3 back to our three boats to cruise around some more where we had hot chow and showers. There was a chance we might even venture south to Australia. That was the way to fight a war in comfort.

Although getting an outfit the size of a battalion ready to move out appeared to be little more than an organized clusterfuck, Captain Sheehan had it ready to go in surprisingly short order. Stay-behind elements that were left on 861 to hold and defend it watched as 2/3 Battalion along with supplemental companies from 3/3 and 3/9 dropped off the side of the hill.

Captain Ray Madonna's Hotel Company took point with Golf trailing in support. Golf had a fairly easy march compared to Hotel's breaking brush out front and tramping a three-foot-wide trail for us to follow that wended through chin-deep elephant grass and around clumps of trees and stands of bamboo that towered above our heads. My job was a simple one: follow the boots of the Marine ahead of me, like Gunny said, although in tall grass I switched from boots to helmets that resembled turtles swimming in a sea of grass. Within minutes of starting the hump to the ridge I was dripping with sweat that stung my eyes and soaked my utilities.

The long green caterpillar traversed the grass valley and pushed on toward the ridgeline with 881N and 881S rising ahead and 861 crouched to the rear. I noticed from below that the crowns of all three hills were denuded and stood out red-brown from having been shredded and ploughed up by artillery and air power.

Everything remained still as we left the grass and began climbing the ridge through heavy shrubbery and jungle, the only sounds being the clank of equipment, the grunting of straining men, and the swish of foliage swept aside.

"It's like in the movies," Tony pointed out. "You know the savages are waiting—but . . ."

"But it's quiet, *too quiet*," I finished for him.

The ridge leveled into a wide spot on top where elements of the 9th had set up to secure the high ground and establish a CP and jumping-off site for assaults on the two hills ahead and to our flanks. Bomb craters pock-marked the clearing while surrounding trees stood scorched and splintered from prior artillery assaults to drive NVA back and off the ridge.

A finger of the ridge plunged into a narrow draw that broke the ridge into two bones before it funneled uphill again to high ground on the other side. Captain Madonna's Hotel Company descended on point into the grassy draw while Captain Sheehan set his other companies in overwatch positions until Hotel's Marines were safely across.

Lieutenant Mac placed Tony, the Pig, and me on the lip of the ridge in an old shell crater to provide cover fire for Hotel were it needed. From our high vantage point we watched the drama play out like in a Roman coliseum as Hotel's column in staggered formation proceeded cautiously toward the opposite slope and the head of the draw. I noticed that the flexible whip antenna of the PRC-25 carried by Captain Madonna's RTO (radio-telephone operator) stuck up above the grass as a dead giveaway to the presence of a commanding officer. No wonder there were never enough officers to go around. First and second lieutenants kept getting knocked off faster than they could be turned out from "shake and bake" officer candidate schools. Attrition rates for junior officers in-country compared with the life spans of turkeys on Thanksgiving.

I nudged Tony and pointed. Sergeant Crawford spearheaded one of the point elements for the company. He crouched in the low-ready position while maneuvering through weeds, as alert and watchful as a pointer sniffing out quail or pheasant. Sticking close behind him came the civilian whose name was Bob Handy, a lean, rawhide-looking man we first thought to be a reporter but who turned out to be a CIA operative. He also wore jungle utilities and carried an M-16.

"You boys will do all right in a fight when it comes to that," Big Ed assured Tony and me. "Remember your training and don't do anything stupid."

Tony gave one of his best Buddy Hackett impressions. "Does enlisting in the Marine Corps qualify as stupid?"

Crawford's group of Marines approached the slope near the head of the draw, unaware that NVA had dug out a bunker complex on the forward slope ahead in the trees and were waiting to spring the trap. When hell suddenly erupted, I almost jumped out of my skin. The din was deafening and loud enough to awake the dead in Hong Kong—heavy 50-cal machine gun thump-thump-thumping, automatic weapons stuttering, mortars whumping, RPGs (rocket propelled grenades) whooshing from hidden sites on the slope and exploding in quick lethal flashes among Hotel's Marines. The effect was like a high-powered race car shooting off a starting line and going from zero to one hundred in a second and a half to crash into stadium spectators. My first terrified thought was that Ed and his "boys" had been trapped in the kill zone. I recoiled from the sudden violence, stupefied by it.

The gooks had not gone home after all.

CHAPTER NINE

Kill Zone

"MOTHERFUCKER! THERE'S ABOUT A MILLION GOOKS DOWN THERE!" Tony yelped.

Growing up in Oklahoma, kids sometimes amused ourselves by poking sticks into red ant hills and watching the critters scurry madly about seeking an enemy to attack. That was how the draw below the ridgeline appeared now—an agitated red ant hill but with Marines instead of ants tearing about searching for cover or somebody to kill. Those of us not in the fight and realistically unable to join it without charging into the kill zone ourselves watched helplessly as the fight below played out in real *unreal* time. The action was only a few hundred meters away. It was almost like viewing a John Wayne war movie from the front row.

We watched, stunned, as our fellow Marines dropped in the tall grass, not knowing whether they were hit or not, whether they might be dead. Grenades and rockets exploded among them while AK fire and an NVA machine gun raked through their ranks in a murderous crossfire. Screaming and shouting merged with the rise-and-ebb thunder of explosions and rifle and automatic weapons fire.

Our guys had been so close to the gooks before the enemy triggered the ambush that they could have kicked them in the balls, smelled their bad breath. The NVA were cunning that way. They had learned to get in tight during an attack in order to nullify our artillery, mortar, and cover fire. We dared not respond effectively without taking a chance of killing our own men.

47

Gunny Janzen appeared out of nowhere as he always seemed to do. He dived into our crater with Tony and me. He pointed to where the gooks were dug in among the brush on the far slope, from which the heaviest fire originated. I had seen some of our guys take to the ground and disappear into the grass not fifty meters in front of the enemy parapets.

"Maras, lay down cover on top of that slope," Gunny ordered. "Keep 'em high and be careful of our guys."

"Roger that, Gunny."

Until now, I had not experienced combat other than being mortared and that other time during Operation Beacon Star when the sniper with the 50-cal winged a shot at us, neither of which counted as *real* combat. After landing at Red Beach, the battalion had spent the following few days camped out nights in the cemetery or wandering around in the boondocks searching villages for contraband and looking for VC. When Sergeant Crawford and his boys stirred up enemy at the Catholic Church and it appeared a real fight might be brewing, our colored pins got abruptly moved to Khe Sanh. So far, I had only fired the Pig at range targets, never at live human beings.

As Gunny moved on to synchronize Golf's other machine gun crews, I took a deep breath and sighted down the barrel of the M-60. I saw nothing but thick brush and the indistinct flickering of muzzles in the foliage above and forward of our Marines. I squeezed the trigger and opened up the Pig for its first taste of combat, and for Tony's and mine as well. Not seeing anything definite to shoot at. Just shooting, feeling the satisfying recoil of the stock against my shoulder, the gun vibrating on its bipod and going *Da Da Da. . . . Da Da Da. . . .*

I fired in short bursts rather than lay on the trigger and risk overheating the barrel, pounding red tracers across the draw above the heads of Hotel's Marines and into the opposing slope. An M-60 could sure chew the hell out of things. Tony fed me a fresh belt of 7.62 and I gave the gooks another taste of Pork.

"*Yeah! Yeah! Hell, yeah!*" Tony cheered.

I caught a glimpse of Big Ed Crawford and Bob Handy the CIA spook scooting low through elephant grass on the western edge of the draw, dodging brush clumps as they maneuvered toward the Viet 50-cal machine gun thumping death into the trapped Marines. They and a few others were so near the gun that I dared not lower my aim to the NVA gun nest for fear of hitting them. I always figured Ed had gonads the size of basketballs; now I knew he did.

"Move to the left to flank the gun!" Big Ed yelled at Handy.

The NVA gunners hadn't yet spotted the two men closing on them. To Crawford's rear, Hotel Company's executive officer, whose name really was Hackett, sprang up from the grass the better to be heard above the bedlam.

"Pull back! Pull back!"

The 50-cal caught him full frontal bore, almost ripping him in half and slamming what was left of him back to the ground.

Captain Madonna took up the chorus from another part of the field. "*Fall back!*"

Crawford shouted counter instructions to keep his men from returning through the kill zone. "Shift left!" he called out.

A pair of well-camouflaged spider holes not twenty feet directly ahead of Big Ed and his sidekick suddenly flipped open their lids. An NVA soldier armed with an AK-47 automatic rifle popped up out of each one. Crawford barely broke stride in his headlong dash. Before either enemy could pull a trigger, he and Handy responded with bursts of 5.56 from their M-16s that slashed into the enemy soldiers' heads and upper bodies. A pith helmet spun high into the air and sailed off above the grass. The other soldier, confined in his hole, danced a restricted version of the spastic chicken, spraying blood in a pink cloud. He died with one lifeless hand sticking up wedged between the lid of his spider trap and its rim.

Spotting a discarded 3.5 rocket launcher, Crawford scooped it up, only to discover that a bullet had disabled it. And apparently its bearer as well, for the weapon was smeared with blood. He cast it aside regretfully; it would have been the perfect cure to the 50-cal still eating away at Hotel's Marines.

With Handy beside him and slightly behind, Crawford led their running, dodging advance up the slope toward the deadly machine gun that was doing so much damage. By now, they had attracted the attention of other enemy. AK-47s opened up on them.

Bullets slammed into Big Ed, blasting his leg out from underneath him and hurling his mangled rifle and other pieces of equipment into the brush and weeds. Tony and I, pausing to reload the Pig, saw him collapse out of sight like a dead man.

"Ohmigod, Tony! They've just killed Sergeant Crawford!"

Tony wailed back, "My God, if they can kill him—we're all gonna die!"

Such an overwhelming amount of fire. When the guy in Okinawa bashed his head into the shower wall to keep from returning to Vietnam, I remembered thinking, *How bad can Vietnam be?* I experienced a sudden sick feeling that I was finding out—and that things were going to get a whole lot worse.

Incredibly, Crawford was still alive in the grass and moving around. He crawled over to Handy and covered the spook protectively with his own body while the thumping of the gook's heavy machine gun continued to echo across the draw.

"Ed, if I don't make it back," Handy requested, "will you tell my wife what happened?"

The two men made a pact under fire. Big Ed would notify Handy's wife if the agent was killed, Handy would notify Ed's wife if Ed took one. Handy produced a ballpoint pen with which each of them scrawled his address and phone number on the back of the other's utility jacket.

"But we're not finished yet," Crawford vowed with the determination that had seen him through two previous wars.

"Ed, you're bleeding. We need to get you out of here."

"Not yet. Patch me up."

A bullet had perforated his upper thigh but appeared to have missed the artery. Handy hurriedly bound the bloody wound with a field dressing while elsewhere Captain Madonna's voice rose above the fray, still calling for the company to pull back. Big Ed realized that to retreat under this much fire would move his boys back through the kill zone and subject the company to even more casualties. The 50-cal had to be knocked out.

"Let's go!" he urged his stalwart partner.

The big sergeant relieved a fallen Marine of his M-16 as the two men wriggled forward on their bellies. The next time I spotted Sergeant Crawford, he and Handy were on their feet in thick brush at the edge of the draw. His tattered utilities looked black with blood from his upper thigh to his knee. He limped badly as he and Handy closed in on the machine gun, whose operators still hadn't seen them.

A khaki-clad figure flushed out of the bushes directly ahead. Crawford attempted to bring him down, but his commandeered Mattie Mattel jammed. He tossed it aside in disgust and drew his E-tool. An entrenching tool—a mini-shovel—was better than no weapon at all.

Crawford wasn't the only Marine on the battlefield suffering malfunction problems with the new M-16A1. Elsewhere, Corporal Gerald Pett's rifle jammed after he fired only eight or ten rounds. He rolled over in the grass and rammed a cleaning rod down the barrel, thinking a faulty round may have plugged it. The barrel was clear. No jammed bullet—just another unexplained malfunction.

He crawled around unarmed until he came upon a dead Marine, whose weapon he appropriated. It also jammed after a half-dozen rounds. He dropped his head on his arms and cried out, "Damn! We're all going to die down here!"

Crawford, armed only with his E-tool, was determined to let nothing stop him from silencing the NVA machine gun. Handy covered him with his still-functioning M-16, popping rounds at suspected enemy positions as the two men continued on their mission.

An NVA helmet appeared from a gopher hole not ten feet away. Crawford charged without breaking stride, swinging his E-tool. The Viet ducked and Big Ed missed his forward swing—but he caught his target on the back stroke. The sharp edge of the shovel in the hands of a strong warrior like Crawford exploded the man's skull in a mist of blood, brains, and bone fragments.

With that, the two Americans managed to eliminate the machine gun crew's flank security, which left the gun unprotected and vulnerable. The fight continued with bullets snapping and whining, green and red tracers interlocking like supersonic dueling fireflies on speed, the enemy

50-cal pumping heavy slugs into its trapped victims. Wounded Marines cried out, "Corpsman! Corpsman up!"

In all the noise and confusion, Crawford and Handy approached within fifteen meters of the enemy gun imbedded inside a thick embankment of logs, red dirt, and brush. The two men went to ground without being observed.

Captain Madonna was fast losing his company in this damnable draw. "*Pull back! Pull back!*"

Marines going into combat were customarily issued four frag grenades. Crawford always carried eight. "Boys," he said to us during train-up in Okinawa, "I learned the hard way in Korea how useful these things can be."

He demonstrated that now. He shifted on the ground to free his throwing arm and tossed the first grenade. It arced high in the air and plunged over the machine gun's defenses and directly into the nest. One of the gooks screamed a warning. Too late. A second grenade followed the first. They detonated on target one after the other in a red-white flash bright enough to sear unprotected retinas. Smoke curled out through the logs. The gun fell silent. What was left of two Vietnamese soldiers lay torn apart over their disabled weapon.

"*Withdraw! Pull back!*"

Only then did Crawford heed the order. Relieved from the pressure of the deadly 50-cal, the ambush's primary weapon now out of commission, Marines lunged to their feet and broke contact, scurrying back through the draw toward where the rest of the battalion held high ground on the ridge. Some of the Marines were shooting over their shoulders as they fled. Others assisted, dragged, or carried injured comrades.

With the ambush broken and space cleared between friendlies and foes, mortar, artillery, and automatic weapons support kicked in. Howitzer 105s and 155s from Khe Sanh were surprisingly accurate with a forward observer (FO) calling shots from the scene. Bursting shells and walls of flame engulfed the forward slope and the incline behind, which led on up toward the summit of 881N.

I laid on the Pig's trigger, pumping rounds into the conflagration, reveling in screams of pain and terror. Other Marines were now free to join in. Our ridgeline sparkled and rattled with discharging weaponry covering Hotel's retreat.

What was left of the battered company returned to the ridge. For many of those in Hotel, for *all* of us who joined up with the battalion in Okinawa, it was a cherry-breaking event, our first make-or-break combat with a determined and professional enemy. Nine Hotel Marines died and forty-three suffered wounds in that brief, vicious battle in the draw. There would have been much more damage except for the courage of Big Ed Crawford and Bob Handy, whose efforts shut down the NVA machine gun and allowed Hotel to escape the kill zone.

CHAPTER TEN

Rescue

THE NVA HAD DONE THEIR DAMAGE AND WERE RETREATING UP THE slope toward 881N to avoid further clobbering by mortars, artillery, and machine guns. In all the confusion, it was unavoidable that some of our wounded and dead were left behind in the draw. Captain Sheehan assigned Golf Company to cut down off the ridge and police up casualties while Echo remained behind to cover for us and hold off any NVA counterattack, though unlikely. The captain led the rescue operation himself. Although he was 2/3's commander in the field, he was not a man to stay behind while his men took the risks.

I slung the Pig on a shoulder strap ready for action as the company went on line to sweep the draw for our downed men, Tony covering me with his untrusty M-16. I had witnessed the carnage down there from our balcony seats on the ridgeline and still couldn't be sure all the enemy had fled. Every nerve in my body tingled with apprehension as the elephant grass closed around me like a cocoon, isolating me from the rest of the unit. I caught glimpses of Tony on my left through the grass and PFC Taylor, a 3rd Platoon squad leader, on my right, but other than them I could have been alone in a jungle of grass. I was no Sergeant Crawford, but nonetheless I was trained a Marine and a Marine did his duty.

Trails, many of which were blood-stained, wove through the grass at all angles where desperate and frightened men had fought, fled, cursed and died. Urgent shouts and screams of pain from the wounded rose above even the banging thunder of artillery and mortar fire that continued to chase the retreating NVA.

"Corpsman! Help me! Help!"

"Over here! We have a man down!"

Golf Company's three Navy corpsmen with their Unit-1 medical aid bags dashed around the draw, emergency-patching the wounded and calling on stretcher bearers to carry out the lifeless and those who could not walk. One stretcher bearer team hurried past me carrying a Hotel Marine whose shrieks of agony seemed to pierce the earth's core. One of his legs had been almost ripped off. Only sinews and skin kept him from losing his foot.

I glanced down in time to avoid stepping on a dead Marine who apparently expired where he fell, cut almost in two parts by the enemy 50-cal before Sergeant Crawford took it out. His body lay in a puddle of blood, torn-apart flesh, and leaking innards. I stared in horror. I had been to funerals before and seen dead people, but they were cleaned up and in caskets and looked more like mannequins than the people they once had been.

But now, within a matter of the past few days, I had witnessed what no human being should ever have to endure: Lieutenant Sauer with his head hacked off; now this Hotel Marine, whoever he was, exposed like fresh road kill. . . . I dropped my chin to my chest and closed my eyes for a moment against the grisly picture. Like maybe if I shut it out and tapped the heels of my magic red slippers together three times I'd be back in Kansas or Oklahoma with Aunty Em.

Captain Sheehan's voice boomed across the draw: "Get 'em and get 'em out of here."

Medevac choppers were flying into a clearing on the protected side of our ridge to evacuate casualties and bodies. Sergeant Crawford was already on his way back to the *Princeton's* sick bay and surgery by the time Golf finished its policing and returned to our previous position overlooking the draw. Tony and I missed the chance to say so long to him. Returning safely was almost like that old kids' game of hide-and-seek. Whoever was "It" had the discretion of calling in the game with "All outs in free!" Tony made a show of dropping to kiss the ground.

"I ain't going up there on that hill," he vowed, pointing to 881N looming above us.

Yeah. Right.

The air show was about to start. Captain Sheehan got on the radio with Pappy Delong at the airstrip. "Colonel, sir, I'm not sending my guys blind into an unknown area again when we know they're out there. We need artillery first, gunships, all kinds of stuff."

Heavy weapons men of 2/3 continued to lob mortar rounds across the draw into where the NVA had been. Clumps of smoke puffed out of the grass and brush where they impacted. They ceased only when the real show opened on Broadway and "all kinds of stuff" began working over not only 881N and the ridge leading up to it but also 881S.

It seemed every American firebase in the area, from Khe Sanh to Camp Carroll and the other bases of Leatherneck Square, opened up with 105s, 155s, and 175s to concentrate on the two enemy-occupied hills. Incoming shells looked and sounded like freight cars hurled through the air. Mountains trembled when they exploded. It felt like I was back in Tornado Alley, Oklahoma, with twisters blasting through.

The bombardment continued for the rest of the day and intermittently throughout the night while awed Marines hunkered on our little piece of ridgeline real estate as spectators to a drama relatively few people ever witness.

As night fell, Puff the Magic Dragon showed up during intermissions with his Gatling guns. Illumination flares lit up the terrain, flickering their weird shadows across draws and valleys to expose possible NVA massing for an attack. It was one hell of a night. None of us got much sleep, if any. Although only a few days had passed since colored pins jerked BLT 2/3 out of Beacon Star and deposited us here, it seemed we had been up in these heights for a lifetime already.

"Maras," Tony sighed fatalistically, "it was only this morning when we left 861, right? We didn't think there'd be any gooks left. We were wrong."

I nodded toward the erupting hills. "We're gonna be wrong again," I predicted.

The 9th Marines had paid a heavy price taking and holding 861. Hotel Company down in the draw had paid a similar price, losing 52 KIA or WIA out of a 110-man force; Captain Sheehan with Pappy's authorization sent Hotel back to 861 in reserve until it could be refitted and replacements brought in.

Gunny Janzen was the type of leader who never seemed to sleep even when he had the opportunity. He was always out circulating in Golf Company, checking on his men, encouraging us, asking us if we needed anything.

"How about a transfer out of this chicken shit outfit?" Tony asked, knowing it was not going to happen, just playing his Buddy Hackett.

Gunny flapped a hand toward the erupting volcanos lighting up the night sky with a strobe-like effect.

"We bombed the shit out of them gooks before," he said, "and they're still with us. They've dug in like rats. That means we're going to have to go up there and blast 'em out ourselves. It has to be done, boys, so get ready for it. We can't keep the gooks waiting."

Gunny moved on along the perimeter.

"Why can't we keep 'em waiting?" Tony wondered. "Just keep blasting 'em until these hills are flatter than the Sahara Desert."

I was starting to change my attitude about our being the baddest motherfuckers in the valley, the John Waynes who came here to kick ass and be home by Christmas.

"Maras," Tony said, "I got a feeling we'll *all* be the Walking Dead by the time we're sitting on those other hills."

CHAPTER ELEVEN

The Cherry Pie

WHAT I WAS DISCOVERING WAS THAT HUMAN BEINGS COULD BE SUR-prisingly adaptable, and resilient. The Vietnamese, for example. They took everything we threw at them—and they were still very much in the fight. BLT 2/3 dug in on that ridgeline, consolidated, and prepared to battle for the two hills. We adapted as well as they did and grew accustomed to the growl of war with a mixture of apprehension, high youthful hijinks, and boredom.

Boredom resulted from cowering in our holes waiting hours day after day for something to happen other than exchanging mortar rounds and artillery with the bad guys, broken by tense periods at night when we anticipated an attack. It all made for "The Longest Day," every day.

"We should have brought a deck of cards," I lamented.

"We had cards, I'd probably own your boots, love letters, and your children's grandchildren by the time we get out of here," Tony responded.

So, lacking anything constructive to keep us occupied, we hunkered on our ridge and watched the show—big guns and jets raining fire and brimstone on the hills and suspected NVA assembly areas. Bombardment of Hill 861 had not wiped out the NVA, nor apparently discouraged them. I doubted the incessant pounding of 881N and 881S would accomplish anything more than eradicating foliage and further pissing off the NVA.

On our ridge below 861 we dug holes and trenches and set out defensive Claymore mines. A Claymore was an evil slab of antipersonnel C-4 explosive packed with ball bearings that, when detonated, sprayed the forward area with a lethal fan-shaped pattern. These, plus grenades, rifles, and machine guns composed the extent of our defenses.

In the meantime, 861 to our rear was being transformed into a veritable fortress as Marines tasked with defending that key piece of terrain worked off former enemy positions to make it their "home." They filled sandbags to shore up collapsed bunkers and even established "shitters" from barrels cut in half; we on the ridge used cat holes. An outer barrier included rows of triple concertina wire anchored to a regular barbed wire fence and a swath of tanglefoot, a tautly stretched barbed wire laid out in a grid a few inches off the ground. Mixed into this maze were antipersonnel "toe poppers" to break hostile feet; "Bouncing Betty" booby traps that sprang up waist high when triggered before they exploded to shoot steel balls in all directions; powerful antitank mines; barrels of *fougasse* that, when set off, turned troops into crispy critters; improvised explosives fashioned out of 25-pound rolls of barbed wire packed with C-4.

Men could be devious when it came to killing each other.

Security and conveniences for Tony and me on the ridge consisted of our sandbagging the Pig into position to have it ready in the event of an attack while we carved out shelves in the walls of our hole to store extra ammo, grenades, and our rations. We arranged stakes at the four corners of the pit between which to stretch a poncho against threatening monsoon rains. Fortunately, as machine gunners Tony and I were exempt from dreaded OP/LP duty. Machine guns anchored strategic points in the perimeter. The hole Tony and I homesteaded overlooked a valley and a creek that ran between 881N and 881S.

"If they hit us," Gunny Janzen warned, "this is where they'll be coming through."

"A target rich environment," I acknowledged with more enthusiasm than I actually felt.

Nights as dusk approached, Rainey or Kilgore or Hill or whoever else drew the dreaded duty crept into the bush a hundred yards or so out front of the perimeter to hunker through the night in observation/listening posts ready to sound the alarm should we experience an NVA attack. Poor bastards out there in the night virtually alone. Gave me the shivers every time I saw them sneaking out into the dark, their only link back to us through the radio watch in the command bunker and clicks of the mike.

"If there ain't no jive, give me five [clicks]. Give me three [clicks] if you see."

Day or night, the enemy wasn't just sitting on his ass out there doing nothing. Random mortar barrages slammed us periodically and kept us close to our rat holes. Air or artillery was the best way to knock out the tubes, since they were ensconced on the military crest of an opposing ridgeline. For every enemy mortar destroyed, two more seemed to take its place. Which meant a lot of enemy soldiers were out there biding their time. An unsettling thought.

"*Incoming!*"

That clarion call initiated a desperate scramble for cover. First, you heard the distant *Whoosh! Whoosh!* Rounds leaving their tubes. You saw little black dots like flies on steroids climbing into the sky and then buzzing back down toward us. Most of the time, watching, listening, you could tell where they would hit. But you were a fool to depend totally on your senses. You had about ten seconds from *Whoosh! Whoosh!* to find a hole if you weren't already in one. I saw a guy in Foxtrot Company hesitate and as a consequence take a direct hit. All that remained of him for identification was his foot inside a boot, and that identifiable only because he had his metal dog tag laced into the boot.

More terrifying than mortars were Russian-made 130mm artillery. You heard the shells coming in like they were shredding the air. They made you dig deeper in your hole and catch your breath and hold it as though it might be your last and you wanted to keep it as long as you could. When the shells exploded, they seemed to blast a hole in the universe through which you caught a glimpse of eternity.

The arbitrariness of it all, who survived and who got hit, scared the shit out of you. Dig deeper, wear your helmet, run for cover, keep your head down—and you could still be wasted by a lucky shot or a piece of shrapnel. Indirect firepower made little distinction between the fool in the open and the good Marine with his head down. Luck was a major player.

Smoke and fire hung in the air during a shelling as corpsmen dashed from hole to hole in response to cries for help or merely to check on us. Golf's three corpsmen had more guts than a gut wagon at a slaughter plant. They might be Navy, but they were as much Marines as the rest of us.

Immediately following a barrage of three explosions, Corpsman Vernon "Magilla Gorilla" Wike dived into our hole on top of Tony and me.

"Everything okay?" he asked as we unscrambled ourselves.

"Yeah. How about the other guys?"

"A-Okay. Shells missed everybody."

Tony assumed a long face. "Doc, you need to send me home. I got fallen arches, a headache, cancer of the vagina, a bad case of the shits, and a racing heartbeat. . . ."

Wike's face lit up. "Great. Always wanted to do open heart surgery. I'll schedule it for this afternoon."

Tony, Magilla, and I had become fast friends, beginning at Camp Schwab. On Okinawa, the entire 1,300-man battalion lined up for gamma globulin inoculations prior to deployment. Made from human blood plasma, gamma globulin contained antibiotics that protected the body from diseases. It was a painful injection, like having motor oil shot into your veins. Tough Marines sometimes fainted with the needle stuck in their asses.

Three corpsmen in three different lines administered the serum in an assembly-line process. *Wham, bam, thank you, ma'am.* Tony and I managed to get into Wike's line.

"Doc, please don't kill me?" I pleaded.

"Just be quiet. Don't worry."

He called back to the supplies table for "more serum," a delay that provided him the opportunity to gently administer my dose while he waited. He did the same for Tony.

Wike was big, thick-chested, and redheaded. His muscles had muscles. Since he looked like the cartoon character Magilla Gorilla, Tony and I began to refer to him as such. He cornered us one day in the chow hall.

"What's this I hear you two are calling me?" he challenged.

I explained.

"Hmmm," he said, then grinned. "I like it."

He even began signing medical chits with his new nickname. It spread until every grunt in Golf Company used his adopted moniker.

Now, with mortar smoke still smudging the air, Magilla vaulted from our hole and headed off to check on Taylor and Rainey in the next position, calling back over his shoulder, "I'm offering a Magilla Gorilla special this week and this week only on ingrown toenails and hemorrhoids. Get in line early."

Bored during the day and nervous at night made sleep hard to come by. We fashioned beds out of scraps of whatever we could find—mortar ammo boxes, C-rat cartons, ponchos, or we dozed on and off crumpled in the dark bottoms of our pits. Waiting. The enemy made it less than easy to grab a Z or two.

We heard ghosts out there in the dark prowling and scurrying about like rodents or cockroaches. Felt their eyes watching, could almost see them in the bush below the ridge with their fingers on triggers. Frequent thick fog contributed to our trench anxieties. Random sniper fire from the distant jungle further added to the war of nerves, while enemy sappers under cover of fog and darkness moved to within forty yards of our perimeter. Out of the liquid dark emerged sounds of their activity—the slap of a rifle sling against the wooden stock of an AK-47, the high-pitched singsong tones of voices chattering in Vietnamese. Even *laughter*.

What kind of demons were we up against?

Marines yelled taunts and insults. "You yellow little cocksuckers! Come out and play if you got the balls!"

Here and there around the perimeter a Marine with frayed nerves fired off a burst from his M-16, his tantrum sometimes culminating with "Sonofabitch!" when his rifle jammed.

Hell of a way to fight a war. Guys who seemed to know said our weapons were manufactured by the cheapest bidders supported by political lobbyists in Washington. It was bullshit that they malfunctioned because of our own improper cleaning. The damned things were defective, and they were getting Marines killed. Sergeant Crawford once told us he never knew of an M-1 Garand or M-14 jamming in combat.

In between being mortared and pulling daily platoon-sized recon forays into the bush, guys managed to get together to kill time by chatting about girls, cars, and more girls, as young men will. We tried to avoid talking about returning home, as it gave us an empty, lonesome feeling to acknowledge how many Marines in these hills had been KIA and would never go home again—and that some of the rest of us likely shared the same fate. Down to a man, we all envied Jaggers.

Jaggers had a month left of his enlistment when BLT 2/3 hit Red Beach. Colonel Delong left him aboard ship to work Supply, since he was a short-timer.

"Lucky bastard," everyone agreed. "He don't know how lucky he is."

I had grown up listening to the tough Marines of my father's era, reading about them, and watching WWII movies. I wondered if that generation might have been tougher than we. Sergeant Crawford, who was about the age of my father, seemed to prove it. Word came back that his wounds were healing and he would soon return to action. The man was tough, *tough*.

"Maras," Crawford assured me once, "if Marines took a beach, they didn't give it up."

I tried to imagine what it must have been like. Later, I read about it in a book called *Two Fronts, One War*:

Iwo Jima was to be a 24-hour operation at most. The Navy had been working over the island for weeks, and were still at it. Battlewagons were spitting chunks of fire as transports pulled to anchor a mile or so offshore. Troops lined the rails of transports and watched the rest of the day and night as Navy guns and airplanes hammered the tiny piece of terra firma and smoke and fire roiled from it.

A cold drizzle fell. Just enough to keep Marines wet and miserable. Mount Suribachi, the 550-foot black cone on the island's southern tip, dominated the beach. It seemed to be waiting in ambush. Surely, nothing on this little hunk of rock and volcanic sand could withstand the beating it had taken.

Then why was it going to take three full Marine divisions—the 3rd, 4th, and 5th—to run the Japs off it?

*"Now hear this, now hear this!" blared transport PA systems.
"Chaplains will offer a moment of prayer before you board your landing craft. . . ." That was when you knew things were serious.*

How was that so much different than now?

The 3rd Marine Regiment, *my* 3rd Marines, carried the battle flag
from Iwo Jima and into Vietnam as part of our honor guard colors.
Would it carry the battle flag of the Hill Fights forward for a new generation of warriors to wonder about? It seemed every generation had its
war.

Tony shook his head. He suggested there might not be another generation after Vietnam if the world continued on the road to hell and the
Soviet Union and the United States started lobbing nukes at each other.

Screw it. Speculation like that was above my pay grade. The 3rd
Marines hadn't given up Iwo Jima. Neither would the 3rd today give up
861 and its sisters, 881N and 881S, once we took them.

We weren't always aware of it, but back in "the World" or "the Land
of the Big PX," which in Marine idiom meant the United States, Khe
Sanh made Walter Cronkite's *Evening News* and the nation's front pages
every day. It had become a political bone for dope-smoking hippies and
their "Hey, hey, LBJ! How many kids did you kill today?" From what
we understood, President Lyndon Johnson was determined to make the
Combat Base the turning point of the war, vowing, "We shall not, under
any circumstances, let Khe Sanh fall."

As the situation began playing out, we Marines were to find ourselves
trapped between the rock and a hard place, between Ho Chi Minh's
hammer and LBJ's anvil. Uncle Ho was hell bent on another Dien Bien
Phu; President Johnson was just as hell bent on winning here in I Corps
no matter the price Marines had to pay.

It became more difficult each day for Tony and me to maintain real
enthusiasm for our daybreak ritual of pissing on Vietnam.

"Good morning, Vietnam!" Tony muttered as he stood urinating on
a dirt pile.

I echoed the greeting.

There was fog this morning down lower. Tony squinted into it. Everything was quiet, so far. His round face went nostalgic. I thought he was thinking about his fiancée, Peggy.

Instead, he said, "Maras, remember the pie?"

We both chuckled.

"How could I forget it? You and Lappeguard ate it."

It was my turn to squint into the fog and remember Linda.

After boot camp and ITR, Tony, Don Lappeguard, and I went on to BITS at Pendleton for machine gun school. I brought Linda out so we could be together. We had been married no more than three or four months; the Marine Corps had kept us separated since our wedding during boot camp leave.

I rented a cheap little motel room on the beach at St. Ona Fre, just outside Pendleton's main gate. Sea lions bellied right up on the sand and barked to be fed. Linda was delighted; she laughed and laughed. Being from Oklahoma, neither she nor I had been this close to these beautiful sleek creatures with their big eyes and comical expressions.

One night, Linda baked a cherry pie and we invited Tony and Don out for a home-cooked meal. Linda had left the pie out to cool on the table. My buddies' eyes immediately fixated on it.

"Take it and eat it," Linda offered. "That's what it's for."

"Really?"

The Marines pounced on the cherry pie like two chickens on grasshoppers. They ate the whole thing while Linda and I watched and laughed.

"It was a good time," Tony reminisced as we buttoned our flies and headed back to our hole. It was no good thing to expose yourself long enough to present some sniper the chance to draw a bead on you.

Not long after the cherry pie, Lappeguard was assigned to the 1st Marine Division and we never saw him again. Linda returned to Tulsa to stay with my mom and dad. Tony and I went to the 3rd Marines and shipped out for Okinawa and Vietnam.

CHAPTER TWELVE

Dear John

TROOPS IN THE HILLS AS WELL AS DOWN IN THE VALLEY AT THE KHE Sanh Combat Base were almost entirely dependent upon air resupply. Enemy mortar teams had cut Route 9 between the air base and Cam Lo to prevent overland reinforcement. The arrival of a helicopter was always a welcome event. It approached by surprise, screaming in low and hot before the enemy could zero in on it. It had about thirty seconds to set down on our makeshift LZ, offload, take on medevac cases, if any, and get the hell out before enemy mortar rounds caught it like a sitting duck. Most of the time it hovered a foot or so off the ground while crews kicked out food, water, and ammo, and then it sprang back into the air. What really pissed us off was when the bad guys got lucky and blew up our resupply before we had a chance to get it off the LZ and safely into a hole. We were always short of everything. Troops groused that "nothing is too good for the troops, and nothing is what we get."

Choppers were a great morale booster when they brought in mail from home. An hour or so before dark one afternoon, a UH-1 "Huey" darted down out of the sky and kicked out a bag of mail. As it took off again, nose down and full bore for speed, I noticed huge boom box speakers attached to either skid strut. It must have been shanghaied into double duty; normally, a psyops (psychological operations) platform remained high and safely in the air over a battle zone to drop leaflets and broadcast enticements for the enemy to give up communism and join the South. The psyops people didn't like to get down and dirty with the hoi polloi on the ground.

PFC Gene Kilgore was Golf Company's duty "mail man" for the day. He scooted through Golf's positions delivering it. He had several letters for me from Linda and Mom. Since night was coming and Viet soldiers were on the move for their nightly hoedown, I stuffed the letters into my pack to wait for daylight to read and reply to them. Last time I wrote home, a warrior ant somehow got into the envelope and chewed up most of the contents before it reached Tulsa.

Tony slipped his letter into a cargo pocket. "It's from Peggy," he said. "Am I invited to the wedding?"

"If Linda brings a cherry pie."

Kilgore waved an envelope addressed to him. "There was this blonde at the San Diego USO with bazoombas way out to here. . . ."

Tony laughed. "Way out to *where*? She a cow or something?"

Kilgore feigned offense. "She sent me a picture. I was going to show it to you poor homesick suckers, but I won't now."

Kilgore was from Texas, short and stocky, a solid Marine. You could trust him with everything except your wife or girlfriend. He insisted no photo be taken of him smiling or laughing while in uniform. A Marine had to look *professional*. He was the A-gunner for Pelky's M-60 gun team and carried an M-16 with a see-in-the-dark Starlite Scope attached to it. The Scope was a classified item valued at about $3,000, or about two years' pay for a private. Its assignment to Kilgore attested to the trust officers and sergeants invested in him.

He also carried a thermite grenade with instructions to destroy the Starlite if he had to in order to prevent the NVA capturing it.

"How will you know when to burn it?" other Marines asked him.

"*I'll* know," he said with typical confidence.

Our mail/psyops Huey remained in the AO. I looked up when I heard it throbbing overhead. It circled wide and high up where sunshine still shone as its crew kicked out bundles of leaflets that drifted down onto enemyville like a big snowstorm. Each missile offered its bearer the opportunity to *Chieu Hoi* and change sides by simply presenting it to the nearest American or South Vietnamese. VC sometimes accepted the offer, but rarely a hardcore NVA.

The Huey's boom boxes began blasting music from the darkening sky to attract attention to the falling leaflets. Playing tonight and tonight only: the rock group The Animals and their hit song "We've Gotta Get Out of This Place." The incongruity struck a reaction from 2/3 on the ridge. Laughter broke out in infectious waves. Tony, Kilgore, and I laughed until tears came to our eyes. The NVA must have thought the Americans had all gone absolutely bugfuck.

Leaflets and music, however, appeared to have no effect on the NVA. During the day, enemy soldiers in groups numbering up to one hundred men in each were spotted on the move humping heavy packs and garbed out in their greenish-tan uniforms, sneakers, and pith helmets. More mortar and sniper fire than usual raked our ridgeline.

As night drew near, the enemy moved in close, flitting in rushes to evade the eerie green pulsating half-light of flares dropped from Puff or from artillery at Khe Sanh. The NVA were not yet serious about attacking us. They were merely probing, testing our weaknesses, attempting to pick off an LP/OP. But an attack was coming sooner or later. It was coming as predictably as hangover followed a drunk.

Marines responded with grenades and rifle fire. An occasional scream from a wounded enemy shattered the darkness. With excellent bedside manners, Marines shouted back, "Die, you cocksucker! *Die!*"

Action dwindled off into welcome silence as the eastern sky dawned out and the outline of the surrounding hills emerged out of darkness. Marines hunkered in our holes. Tony shook himself out of his turn at a catnap. He peered drowsily about, sniffing the air.

"Something stinks," he noticed.

"When was the last time you took a bath?"

"I smell *your* stinking ass, Maras, not mine. Have you ordered breakfast? I'll have an omelet with hash browns, toast, butter, and strawberry jam. Make sure the coffee is hot."

I rummaged through my pack and produced a pair of OD cans. "Ham and eggs," I offered, "or fruit cocktail?"

I tossed him the ham and eggs. He shook his canteen. "Half-empty," he said.

"I prefer to see it as half-full," I corrected. "Gunny said to ration water in case the choppers can't make it in today."

"Crimney, it's gonna be hot. Maybe we can lick dew before it dries up."

Private Hernandez from one hole over heard the discussion. "I got something you can lick, Leyba."

"Marines are crude bastards, Maras. You notice that?"

Hernandez chuckled. "We can't all be refined gentlemen like you, home boy."

Before Tony opened his can of breakfast, he and I enjoyed our ritual morning piss on Vietnam.

"*Good morning, Vietnam!*"

Tony opened his letter from Peggy while we ate. I saw his face darken as the sky lightened. He slammed his half-eaten can of ham and eggs against the trench wall, splattering it. His chin dropped to his chest. He looked defeated and somehow diminished as his thick body collapsed in on itself.

"Fuck! *Fuck!*"

"Tony?"

"The bitch!" he sobbed. "The two-timing, low-down, cheap bitch."

No need to ask. A Dear John. It happened all the time. Guys went off to war and the girls we left behind tumbled into the sheets with draft dodgers.

"Tony. . . . Tony, I'm sorry, man."

"Screw her."

He had had her name tattooed on his arm during boot camp Leave—a red heart with "Peggy" superimposed on it. He drew in a deep painful breath and lifted his head, sniffing.

"The world really *does* stink, you know that, Maras?"

CHAPTER THIRTEEN

Ambush

THE NVA AVOIDED SUSTAINED DIRECT CONTACT FOLLOWING HOTEL Company's brawl with them in the draw where Sergeant Crawford got hit. I shook my head in disbelief at word that Big Ed was eager to get back in the fight with his "boys." Wounded in Korea, now wounded in Vietnam—and he was *coming back* for more. Seemed to me he might be pushing his Guardian Angel's protection a bit too far. Even a cat only had nine lives.

"I get out of here alive," Tony fussed, "I'm going home and never coming out of my house again."

The sun glared at us. Sweating, we both removed our utility jackets down to green T-shirts. Tony rested his chin on his shoulder to peer unhappily at the Peggy's Heart tattoo on his upper arm. I saw how he was struggling to overcome his Dear John letter.

"Maras, loan me your banana knife."

"Huh?"

"I'm gonna skin off the bitch's name."

"Are you crazy?"

"Fuck it. Maybe if I'm lucky I'll get it shot off."

Truth be admitted, Viets weren't the only ones avoiding direct contact. The two sides were like boxers in the first round of a championship fight. Jabbing, feinting, probing, feeling each other out for the later rounds when the match got serious. Stood to reason that while we Marines conserved our resources and built up resolve, sending out frequent patrols to see if we could figure out what the enemy was up to, the enemy was doing pretty much the same thing. Rumors spread that, in spite of losses the NVA suffered during our near-constant bombardment of their hilltop redoubts, the North Vietnamese still had an entire division prepared to wipe us out in the hills and then move on Khe Sanh.

Likely the NVA generals had big battle maps of their own with colored pins to move around. I wondered if Alexander the Great and Julius Caesar had colored pins.

In spite of the heat, or perhaps because of it, mist lay thick by the creek between the two Wicked Sisters, which is what I took to calling 881N and 881S. It clung to forest giants like fiber caught in a cotton mill's teeth. While our big guns and air power may have denuded the hills, forest and grasses grew virulent and concealing down below. I compared our bombardment of the Wicked Sisters to going to a Marine barber and requesting he take a little off the top—and he chopped you off down to your ears.

"You all right, Tony?" I asked.

He still seemed in shock from his Dear John. Couldn't broads at least wait until we got out of combat before putting the screw to us?

"Piss on her," Tony said.

It was Lieutenant McFarlane's turn to run a daylight recon patrol down into the creek valley. Gunny Janzen came by.

"Maras, you and Leyba saddle up. You're going out with Lieutenant Mac. Meet up over at the Company CP."

Since Weapons Platoon was a company asset, weapons men could be assigned piecemeal anywhere within Golf Company. My pucker factor shot through the roof, providing we had had a roof for it to shoot through. Tony's expression remained unchanging and morose as we stripped down our packs to essentials, like water and ammo. At least he continued to function.

I slung the Pig on its combat strap ready for action and we shuffled toward the CP, keeping a low profile to prevent displaying ourselves against the skyline for the benefit of some eager-beaver downhill gunner. Tony pulled up short as we passed a swarm of green shit flies buzzing over what remained of a fighting hole the enemy must have dug ahead of our occupying the ridge. Not much left of it except a trash pit of logs, dirt, and debris on top of which Marines were tossing our own garbage—C-rat cans, empty ammo boxes, and the like. The stench Tony had been complaining about seemed to emanate from this location. It was stronger than ever. I was in a hurry to get on past it.

Curious, Tony kicked aside some dead tree limbs and jumped back, clasping his hand over his mouth and nose to protect against the noxious odor released. He pointed. There underneath all the brush lay the withered and rotting corpse of an NVA soldier, a little guy sprawled on his back gazing with empty eye sockets into the sky at Buddha or Happy Valley or whatever. The face had turned black. A colony of warrior ants was busily stripping off flesh and crawling in and out of cavities. A bamboo rat dining on intestines through a hole gnawed in the dead man's belly scurried off.

"*Holy shit!*"

"I told you something stunk, Maras."

Everything out here smelled like death, so strong sometimes when the wind blew in the right direction from off the Wicked Sisters that eating became nauseating. This guy's comrades must have overlooked him when they abandoned the ridge in favor of its opposing finger on the other side of the draw but still at the foot of 881N. The grisly sight made a hell of a send-off for a patrol venturing out there where this guy's live counterparts lurked and prepared to turn *us* into bait for rats, ants, and green shit flies.

Per SOP, machine gunners marched with the point element. We were needed for rapid response to a situation. Lieutenant Mac's 3rd Platoon was more or less home base for Tony and me. We were assigned to PFC Taylor's 1st Squad.

Normally, a sergeant or lance corporal served as squad leader, but a PFC had to suffice in the absence of more stripes. Taylor would be relieved of the responsibility once his replacement arrived, which, he was assured, should be any day now.

I was as nervous as a dog crapping peach seeds as the platoon, in staggered battle formation, moved down off the ridge toward the creek. No way could an element our size push through shrubbery and razor grass tall enough to slash our faces without making a trail the size of a freeway and sounding like rush hour traffic or, more appropriately in this setting, a gaggle of elephants.

I felt vicious little eyes watching us. I carried the M-60 with my finger on the trigger guard ready to spray anything that jumped up. I kept picturing Lieutenant Sauer with his head cut off and his dick stuck in his mouth. Rage replaced my fear. I experienced a certain clarity unblemished by lesser emotions, like a predatory fever.

Grass thinned out down near the creek, substituted by Tarzan-like rain forest. The creek was low as it waited for the next rain to gorge it with water gushing through the valley like opening a giant faucet. Enemy sign was everywhere—machete trails hacked through thickets; grass beaten down; cook fires; piles of fresh human feces; discarded or lost equipment. . . . The NVA were out here all right. And lots of them.

In combat, an outfit on the move suffered a grave disadvantage over a stationary enemy force that owned the element of surprise. All senses alert for danger, Mac's platoon moved slowly and cautiously, practicing noise discipline as best we could, looking around, sniffing the air. The platoon's best point man, a Spanish kid named Ramirez, took the front. I was fourth man back, Tony to my rear, and a few steps farther back came Lieutenant Mac and his RTO.

Even when you expected to be hit, it almost always came as a total surprise. One moment I could hear the sinister chuckle of the nearby little creek, the strident call of a bird, the rustle of rodents in the grass, my own breath. . . . The next moment everything exploded in my face.

Puffs of smoke and flickers of flame from the surrounding jungle. The zip and snap of rounds coming my direction sounded like whips cracking. Marines yelling and screaming in surprise, fear, and rage, responding to training by returning fire, our M-16s sounding a thinner, more rapid counterpoint to the throaty *Bark! Bark!* of the enemy's heavy-caliber AK-47s.

"*Ambush left!*" Lieutenant Mac sounding the alarm and a command simultaneously. "*Near ambush! Move!*"

SOP in a near ambush was to assault into it rather than go to ground, prolong the contact, and risk suffering more casualties. I wheeled toward the action, swung the Pig forward, and lay on the trigger, firing from the hip like John Wayne. Tony with his Mattie Mattel and me with the M-60 joined the mad charge into the very teeth of our unseen assailants. We functioned automatically, depending on training drills and raw adrenaline. Marines screamed and shouted like demons, every weapon on auto-fire. We crashed directly into the ambush, sending NVA soldiers fleeing for their lives. I continued pumping rounds into the forest, cutting down foliage until the gun clicked on an empty chamber.

"*Cease fire, Marines! Cease fire!*"

It ended as quickly as it began, my first combat firefight. I found myself breathing heavily from excitement. The pungent scent of gunpowder and exploding grenades hung in the air as our attackers got away, hauling ass uphill and disappearing toward 881S with no attempt at noise discipline. PFC Taylor and his point squad, Tony and I included, started to give chase. Lieutenant Mac called us back.

"That's what they want us to do," he warned.

When I stopped to think about it, this was not a classic ambush. These gooks were bait trying to lure us into chasing them into a trap laid by the real force. Fortunately, Lieutenant Mac was a combat vet and knew all the tricks.

"Good job, Marines! We kicked their asses. Now, let's pull back out of here. Keep alert."

The fleeing enemy left a dead man behind. Lieutenant Mac searched the body for intel before we withdrew. PFC Taylor appropriated the guy's pith helmet for a trophy; the dead soldier's buddies had already relieved him of his weapon and ammo to take with them.

Unbelievably, what with all the bullets in the air and grenades exploding, the platoon suffered only two casualties, one of them minor from grenade shrapnel, the other a young, new replacement private with a bullet flesh wound to his calf. Magilla Gorilla patched both men and fell into return formation with the wounded private hobbling and leaning on the corpsman for support.

"We were damned lucky this time," Magilla said as he passed by Tony and me.

Once we returned safely to the ridgeline, Tony and I resumed our machine gun watch looking downhill toward the creek where we were ambushed. I was still coming down off the adrenaline high of one of the most surreal days of my entire life. A couple of hours ago I was fighting for my life. Now, everything looked green and idyllic down there. The fog had dissipated, while fleece clouds drifted across an otherwise clear sky, parrots flew over. When you're nineteen, you think it's always going to be blue skies and that you'll live forever. It was a bit of a shock for me to realize I could have been killed, a reality I was going to have to get used to and accept.

Tony appeared to be considering the same philosophical riddle. Either that or thinking about Peggy. Both of us remained quiet and contemplative. Tony idly flipped pebbles toward the smelly dead guy in the rubble. A medevac chopper dashed in to pick up our young leatherneck wounded on his first day of combat. The chopper also flew in a replacement to take PFC Taylor's place as 1st Squad leader, 3rd Platoon.

After the chopper lifted off, the replacement checked in with Lieutenant Mac and introduced himself to 1st Squad before he began wandering about looking things over as casually as if he were on a stroll through the park. He wore an air of smug condescension that caused me to take him for a lifer ass-kisser bucking for promotion. He still had creases in his utilities, for God's sake.

"I am Lance Corporal Dye," he introduced himself. "You men look a bit lax."

I ignored him.

He wrinkled his nose. "What's that awful odor?"

"Dead gook," Tony supplied, not missing a beat.

Corporal Dye blanched. Clearly he was unprepared for what lay ahead.

"Your name is Die, huh?" Tony mused. "Who the fuck would have a name like 'Die' out here in this shit?"

"D-Y-E," Corporal Dye corrected tersely, and moved on.

Somewhat later, he returned with PFC Taylor to select a fighting position from which he might control his new squad. Unaware of the proximity of the dead enemy, he chose a vacancy near the corpse's brush pile. He discovered his mistake right away. He jumped back from the partly exposed corpse with a look of horror on his face. For a moment I thought he was going to upchuck his spaghetti and meat balls.

After a supreme effort to recover his composure, he sauntered over to Tony and me.

"I don't know your names yet," he said, "but I need you two guys on a detail to bury that thing. I can't live with the smell and the flies."

Tony was in no mood for his shit, what with his Dear John letter from Peggy and our being ambushed at the creek. "Corporal, we've been humping the bush all day," he snapped. "If you want that stiff buried, I suggest you take your little E-tool and bury him yourself."

So Corporal Dye buried the body. Tony and I watched him bravely trying not to retch while he scooped out a shallow grave.

Next day, not twenty-four hours after his arrival, he went out and down the trail on his first patrol and got himself killed. His body flew out on the same chopper that brought him in. His death was something else for me to contemplate: Fate. Perhaps it was Corporal Dye's fate to come all the way to Vietnam just to die. Perhaps it was also PFC Taylor's fate to remain as 1st Squad leader.

"Maybe we should have buried the gook for him," I decided.

Chapter Fourteen

A Good War

A MARINE NEVER ADMITTED DEFEAT. A ROUT WAS A TEMPORARY "strategic withdrawal." DIs pounded that truth into us from the first day a bunch of grungy *civilians* showed up to stand on the yellow footprints at R&O—Recruiting and Outfitting—to swear the oath to become Marines. They always placed the emphasis on victory and on *Semper Fidelis*—"Always Faithful."

"Today," declared the DI commander the day we graduated from boot camp with our buzz haircuts, suntans, and new attitudes, "you are *Marines*. From this point forward no one is authorized to call you 'girls,' 'pukes,' 'maggots,' or 'pussies.' From this point forward until the day you die, you are *Marines*. Never forget it."

Sir, yes, Sir.

The correct response always began with "Sir" and ended with "Sir." Your ass got reamed if you forgot it.

My ass felt reamed now in the hills as we lived minute by minute, hour by hour, not exactly contemplating defeat but letting it sniff around in the backs of our minds anyhow. It occurred to me that President Lyndon Johnson himself might be fearing a disastrous defeat in Vietnam. Newspapers, TV, and protesters were beating the hell out of him every day back home while here in the hills, these *dueling hills*, NVA batted us around like redheaded stepchildren and stained the hills red with our blood.

By now, the Wicked Sisters and their brood of ridges, knolls, and knobs were as familiar to us as our muddy boots while at the same time they remained as foreign as Vietnam had been when BLT 2/3 hit Red Beach just more than a week ago. Existing on the edge of living and dying meant we no longer claimed a past or a future, only a continuing present. The universe centered here. Nothing beyond existed. I wondered if I would ever see my wife again.

"Good morning, Vietnam!" became weaker and weaker for Tony and me during our morning ritual piss.

"Maybe we should have banged our heads against the shower wall in Okinawa," Tony suggested.

Mike Company 3/3's movement to set up a base at the foot of 881S from which to launch an assault on that objective provoked a confrontation with the NVA that we witnessed from across the valley. The company's three platoons started up the hill shortly after noon flanking each other in tactical combat formation. Apparently, they expected the North Vietnamese defenders to have either been crippled by prep air and artillery or to have fled. Instead, they ran into a shit storm when the NVA launched a furious first strike from all sides. It was not simply a head-butting skirmish with an exchange of shots before the gooks hauled ass. The ferocity of the fight echoed through the hills like the much-magnified sounds of a giant bowling alley. From the terrible cacophony of machine guns, mortars, RPGs, and small arms, Mike Company had poked up a large enemy element.

From 2/3's ridgeline, we looked across the creek valley and watched smoke billowing out of the jungle from grenade, mortar, and rocket explosions. It looked like a raging forest fire with all the cracking and popping that accompanied it. Word we received through frantic radio transmissions had our side getting its ass kicked and suffering casualties.

Kilo Company 3/9 descended from 861 as a QRF (Quick Reaction Force) and crossed over our ridge on its way to rescue Mike from near-certain disaster. These Marines rushing into battle were a grim-faced lot with prayers and other messages and names recorded on their helmet covers:

God Protect The Wise and The Foolish
Vietnam: I've Spent My Time in Hell

Margie
Donna
Paula

One of the drawn-faced grunts slogging past looked anxious but prepared with an epistle that began on one side of his helmet with, *Verily, Tho I Walk Through The Valley of The Shadow of Death, I Shall Fear No Evil.* . . . It concluded on the other side with, *for I'm the Meanest Sonofabitch in The Valley.*

On my helmet cover I had drawn a cartoon tiger sitting on its haunches behind bare human footprints representing the gook meal he had just consumed. In combat you went out of your mind if you didn't poke at the insanity that went on around you.

"At least they wrote their girlfriends' names on their helmet covers instead of on their arms," I pointed out to Tony. "You can always change covers."

"Fuck you, Maras. And piss on her."

Captain Jerald Giles and his Kilo 3/9 made the forced march to the base of 881S where the company joined the battle alongside Mike 3/3. In a brawl like this, you always wanted as many friends as you could get to show up with as many guns as they could get. Instead of retreating, the NVA maintained the initiative and kept up a steady pace of fire from several directions.

Marines crawled around in the bush on their bellies seeking cover. Bodies lay strewn all over the battlefield. It seemed someone was getting shot or fragged every minute. Screams of pain and fear counterpointed and accompanied the thunder of rifle and machine gun fire and explosions.

Orders came for Mike and Kilo to make a "strategic withdrawal." Bring out the wounded but leave the dead. Fog with approaching nightfall provided some concealment for the retreat, while Captain Giles's "danger near" request for supporting fires walked artillery directly up behind the horribly mangled Marines and kept the Viets from giving chase.

Kilo withdrew a few hundred meters and dug in for the night as the fog and darkness thickened. Captain Giles reported to his battalion CP that 881S was now clear of all *living* Marines. Mike Company, with a casualty rate that exceeded half the company, filtered on through Kilo to return to 861, carrying its wounded. This first approach to 881S cost 43 Marines killed in action and 109 wounded.

Mike Company had been decimated. Instead of stopping at 861, it had to be pulled off the line and sent back to the Rockpile via Dong Ha for an infusion of replacements. Foxtrot Company 2/3, which had been held in reserve, received a warning order to stand by at Khe Sanh for airlift into the hills at dawn. It would now be committed to the fight.

When I was a boy, I read the World War II classic *Up Front* by Bill Mauldin. I recalled a passage from it that went something like, "How a war is going depends upon what is going on in your particular area. No matter what is happening elsewhere, it's a good war if you're not being shot at."

Nobody was shooting at me for the moment. I had an uneasy feeling, however, that my "good war" was about to change.

CHAPTER FIFTEEN

The French Lady

WHILE MIKE AND KILO OF 3/3 AND 3/9 FOUGHT FOR THEIR LIVES ON 881S and withdrew, Echo and Golf of BLT 2/3 received warning orders to prepare to assault the other Sister, 881N. Hotel had withdrawn to refit after the fight in the draw, and Foxtrot in reserve would soon be assigned to rescue the units on 881S. Platoon battle briefings filled us in on what squads and individual grunts needed to know, no more. Our objective was the ridgeline and smaller hilltop on the other side of the draw where Hotel Company had been slapped back and Sergeant Crawford wounded. Take the little hilltop, consolidate, gear up to launch against 881N. Like everyone else, I was unabashedly apprehensive. I mean, hell, Mike and Kilo had employed an almost identical tactic against the other Twin. Should we expect a different outcome for Echo and Golf?

Two other items in the briefing stood out. First, for this action, however long it took, allotments of food and water must be cut to two C-rats and one canteen of water per Marine per day. Supply choppers were having a tough time getting through to us because of deadly NVA antiaircraft 51s staked out all over the hills. Taking a Marine's chow away from him was some serious shit.

The second stand-out item in the briefing concerned the acquiring of enemy intelligence. What was the strength of enemy forces in these hills? What units were here? What was their strategy? How were they managing to live through devastating air and artillery strikes and still have fight left in them? Native Bru woodcutters in the area, who knew every anthill, trail, and tree all the way to Laos, had tried to warn our colored pin pushers of the enemy's buildup. Marine brass sluffed them off. Now our strategists wanted more information, which meant taking prisoners. Captain Sheehan passed the word that Division was offering a five-day in-country R&R (Rest and Recreation) to any Marines who captured a prisoner for interrogation.

We were skeptical. Taking one of these guys alive was like entering a tiger's den to bring out the tiger. No one wanted to die attempting it.

"So," Rainey speculated sarcastically, "we walk up while they're shooting at us and say, 'Hey, Mr. Charles, want a cigarette?' And he gives up?"

It was a lot safer to kill 'em all and let God sort 'em out.

The big guns from Leatherneck Square supplemented by Army batteries from Camp Carroll and the Rockpile along Route 9, the 175s, pummeled the gooks with an impressive, earth-shattering wall of steel ahead of Golf and Echo as the two companies, separated by terrain, moved off our heretofore relatively safe ridge toward a new position on the multi-fingered ridgeline closer to the base of 881N. Fire and smoke boiled out of the trees in a constant booming rumble, the concussions from which rattled grass and tree branches along our passage. What I dreaded was when we would draw near our objective and its defenders. That's when the bombardment would lift to prevent shelling us along with the enemy. That was when the NVA could let loose and make things interesting.

"Poor bastards," Tony commiserated, meaning the enemy. "You gotta feel sorry for them."

I scoffed. "After what we seen they did to Lieutenant Sauer?"

Lieutenant Mac's Third Herd led Golf's advance across the wide draw toward the new ridge hill, Echo ranging somewhere on our right flank. As usual, Tony and I marched up front with PFC Taylor's 1st Squad and the point element, Ramirez as usual breaking brush and keeping his eyes, ears, and nose trained for NVA. The guy was a wild animal at sniffing the breeze and detecting them, like he had a sixth sense. We called him our "faithful Indian scout."

I kept the Pig ready to grunt on a short strap over my shoulder. I figured before this day ended we were apt to need all the firepower we possessed.

I checked on Tony. "You okay? Got your head on straight?"
Today was not a day to be mooning over a lost love.

"Piss on her," Tony said, by which I took he was up and running.

It was slow, cautious going across the draw and along the ridgeline toward the hill knob. So far, the NVA hadn't contested our approach. Probably conserving their strength and busy ducking our prep fires. Both companies pulled up short of the objective and set up defenses in a wooded ravine to wait for the pounding of the Wicked Witch to lift so we could proceed.

To our astonishment, a round-eyed female suddenly appeared out of nowhere with a Marine escort. Pretty and small-built, she wore safari clothing and a Marine helmet and carried a couple of cameras on straps around her neck. Someone explained she was a French photojournalist named Catherine from Paris here to cover the Hill Fights. The eye of every Marine in the vicinity locked and loaded.

Captain Sheehan had objected when informed by radio that she was coming out. Combat was no place for a civilian, especially a woman. It was primitive and dangerous out here. Colonel Delong gave him no choice; she would accompany the battalion into battle.

"I'll provide an escort," the colonel offered Catherine, "but I can't spare anyone to bodyguard you."

Captain Sheehan told her the same thing when she arrived.

"I can take care of myself, Captain," she responded. "I don't need my body guarded, except—" with a sense of humor, she added jokingly, "except perhaps from your Marines."

She proved a big hit, the highlight of the operation so far before the shooting began—an attractive female, *French*, no less, suddenly dropped into the midst of a bunch of young, virile Marines who immediately began posturing and looking brave for the pretty lady's cameras. A thorough professional, she was nonetheless charming and knew how to work her way into heads and hearts. The problem with women in combat, as Captain Sheehan saw it, was the male protective instinct. She could get Marines killed in their trying to shield her from harm.

One of the Marines was so awed by her presence that he forgot all about having ripped open the front of his trousers during movement.

Since Marines seldom wore underwear in combat—they caused rash and jungle rot—his privates hung innocently exposed.

"Chrissakes!" Gunny Janzen barked. "Turn around. She doesn't want to see your family jewels."

"It's okay, Gunny," the quick-thinking Marine retorted. "I'm a married man."

Even Catherine laughed. Laughter in this setting sounded totally out of place. Like a fart in church. This girl had balls to come out here, though. We had to hand her that.

Golf and Echo went on the move again once the artillery bombardment ceased, leaving the air saturated with smoke and smelling like a Fourth of July celebration. The silence that followed seemed more startling than the roaring explosions it replaced.

Still separated from each other, the two companies moved in the sudden quiet, each headed for its own sector of the objective. Lieutenant Hesser's 1st Platoon replaced Lieutenant Mac's 3rd on point. Another machine gun team from Weapons moved up; I wasn't disappointed at being cast further back in the procession. Again, like the giant green caterpillar, Golf climbed out of the ravine where we had temporarily sought refuge and struggled through thick foliage toward the ridge finger and its hill knob. Catherine roamed up and down the column, shooting up film.

With fog drifting in ahead of approaching evening, Captain Sheehan ordered Hesser to go for the goal. At the same time, he radioed Echo's Six to begin the attack from his kickoff point. Platoon Sergeant Santos led half of Golf's 1st Platoon up the left flank while Lieutenant Hesser took the other half right. Golf's other two platoons, the 2nd and 3rd, set up to cover Hesser and Santos. Catherine also stayed back.

Tony and I, still with Lieutenant Mac's Third Herd, dropped behind a felled tree to use for cover. We sprong-legged the M-60's bipod over the top of the log with its muzzle trained uphill into the tangle of brush. Both of us were ramped up, every sense hyper alert, eyes searching for movement in the smoke and fog gathering on the side of the knob.

Marines of 1st Platoon jackrabbited across the intervening gully and started up the enemy-held slope. It was slippery from fog and an earlier rain shower. Weapons clutched in one hand, they used their free hands to grab at bushes and small trees to keep from tumbling back down the incline. Men grasping for hand- and footholds grunted and cursed under their breath. Their equipment clattered. No need for noise discipline now. The enemy knew we were coming.

And the enemy was ready. What sounded like dozens of buzz saws cutting through cordwood suddenly broke out from higher on the knoll, followed by chaos among the attackers. Marines went to ground all over the slope as bullets snapped, whined, and popped through their ranks.

Echo Company on the hill's farther flank found itself in a similar situation. Their stay-behind elements, as with Golf's, laid down a blistering barrage of cover fire to take pressure off our men and pin down defending NVA forces. In all the excitement, I burned through a full belt of 7.62, sweeping the Pig back and forth and spraying rounds into an enemy whose presence was marked only by flickering muzzle flashes in shadowed timber. The Pig emitted a satisfying deafening growl as it ingested rounds and spat out the seed with deadly intent.

"Feed me, Tony!" I yelled above the melee, indicating that the gun needed a fresh belt.

Next to me behind the log, sprawled on his belly, Tony expertly primed the machine gun with new ammo. High on adrenaline, we functioned together from training and drill like a machine, all thought vanished except for a primitive reptilian core that demanded satiation in death. *Kill! Kill!*

Tony slapped me on the shoulder. He pointed and added in a high, shrill rush of words, "Something moving in the bushes up near the top, to the left."

"I see it."

I burned up another belt in controlled three-round taps to let the gun cool down from overheating. I had gone through my first belt with a single trigger pull. Movement in the bushes ceased.

"Did you get them, *mon ami?*" asked a voice, distinctively French and distinctively feminine.

Catherine was suddenly *there*, next to me behind the log. She had one eye glued to her camera viewfinder and was busily snapping the shutter.

"Lady, maybe you oughta move back," Tony suggested as enemy fire honed in on us and began eating at our barrier, sending wood chips flying.

"Good idea," she decided, belly-crawling rapidly back the way she came.

"Be a shame for a pretty girl like that to get all shot up," I noted.

Fog rapidly crept into the lowlands on little cat feet, as the poets like to say. Smoke from the previous bombardment and from flames in the foliage further decreased vision. Firing dwindled off from both sides, as if in acknowledgment of approaching nightfall and the terrors it contained.

Captain Sheehan apparently hadn't expected such stiff resistance. Anyhow, because of that resistance, it was too late to attempt further taking of the hill knob tonight. He ordered both companies under his command to break contact and withdraw to the ravine in our rear where we went to ground to wait for another attempt in the morning.

The gooks seemed just as ready as we to call it a night. The battlefield fell eerily silent while night crept through the valley, leaving only the disfigured top of 881N glowing in weak, dying sunlight.

It was going to be another long, tense night. After Gunny Janzen came around to emplace machine guns on likely avenues of enemy approach, I left Tony manning the Pig while I adjourned to some nearby trees to relieve myself, looking around first to make sure Catherine wasn't nosing about with her camera. My taking a leak on the battlefield would look striking on the front page of the *Tulsa Tribune*.

Enough daylight remained that I spotted the dead uniformed NVA soldier just before I urinated on him. He lay face up in the weeds, all blackened from the weather and beginning to shrivel and decay as though melting into the earth, teeth showing in a death rictus, eye sockets already cleaned out by warrior ants taking home the bacon.

By now I was becoming accustomed to running into corpses. I moved to one side to finish my business, feeling nothing for the dead guy other than hoping he took others with him when he went to Hell. One thing though I couldn't help considering: *Is this what will happen to me? Is this what I'll look like?*

CHAPTER SIXTEEN

Wounded

It was a restless night in the ravine. Golf and Echo companies had been lucky in today's brief encounter. None of our people were killed and everybody walked back out of it with only a few suffering minor wounds that Magilla and the other Docs patched up without need of a medevac to send them to the rear.

The crunch of twigs, a whisper of moving branches, the scurry of some small creature through the weeds put everybody's nerves raw and rubbing against his backbone. Stationed at the buttress of a rain forest giant with Tony, I struggled to suppress panic alarm in the motor response areas of a very tired nervous system, to control a natural instinct to breathe too fast and too shallowly. Fear, I scolded myself, was a handy warning system, nothing more.

Muscles ached, eyes stung, skin and clothing were caked with sweat and dirt. My ears rang from today's explosions and I dared not trust my hearing as I strained to distinguish monsters in the night from the harmless sounds of nature. Imagination was a terrible thing to waste—and none of us was wasting it. A number of times, unable to sleep during our 50-50, either Tony or I heard the tiger-heavy noise of men stalking us through the forest. A pattern to their movements—*Step, step, pause. . . . Step, step, pause.*

"Somebody's out there," Tony whispered, his breathing fast and sharp.

"No, no. It's your turn to sleep. I'll keep watch."

"Sleep? You gotta be shitting me, Maras."

So, together we stared into the long night, eyes wide.

Elsewhere, guys with less discipline and more imagination, unable to restrain their natural impulses for self-preservation, beguiled by threatening movement in the surrounding jungle, would toss grenades that split apart the night. Somebody else would blast off with an M-16. That brought platoon leaders up and shouting their fool heads off.

"Cease fire, damnit! Cease fire!"

How was a guy supposed to get any sleep with all this racket, providing, of course, he was inclined to sleep?

"Maras, do you ever pray?"

"Not much before," I admitted. "Now I pray every day."

Like the old World War II guys said, there were no atheists in foxholes. "God," I promised, "I'll never take life for granted again—"

If You'll get me out of this. That last part went unsaid. I just *thought* it. You don't bargain with God or fate.

Exhausted, we finally catnapped on and off in turns. Tony opened one eye to greet the dawn.

"Good morning, Vietnam!" he managed half-heartedly as he got up on his knees to piss in place against our tree.

The sun broke over the misty green peaks of the Wicked Sisters of the North and South. Last night's thick blanket of fog engulfed all but the tops of the hills whose foreheads stuck up above in soft early light that helped cover blemishes and damages inflicted by prep fire.

Back home, on a morning like this, the most important decision I might have to make was what to have for breakfast. "Mom, let's have eggs and bacon. No, make that oatmeal."

Linda and I hadn't lived together but for our honeymoon and those few weeks we spent in the motel on the beach at Pendleton where I attended Basic Infantry Training and where she baked a cherry pie.

Of course, at home, decisions weren't about life and death. My next-door neighbor wasn't apt to take a pot shot at me with his deer rifle, nor was the Neighborhood Watch Committee organizing to overrun the block and eat my brain.

For those who fight for life, I had scribbled on the C-rat carton at Khe Sanh the day BLT 2/3 arrived in these hills, *it has a special flavor the pro-*

tected shall never know. That *special flavor* was becoming more difficult to define as the Hill Fights dragged on. It was becoming . . . *bitter.*

Warplanes stacked up in air space over Khe Sanh as prepping fire against the hills resumed. Aerial bombing blasted the tops and sides of both 881S and 881N, shaking earth and sky and making trees rattle against each other like skeletons. Artillery followed as planes cleared the AO. The hills absorbed a total of 166 aircraft sorties dumping over a half-million pounds of ordnance and 1,500 artillery rounds.

At 1015 hours, Captain Sheehan received orders from Colonel Pappy to commence the operation, our objective once again the hill knob on 881N's northeastern slope. The 1st Platoon, Lieutenant Hesser's, led off again. Tony and I tagged along as a machine gun team with PFC Taylor's 1st Squad in Lieutenant Mac's 3rd Platoon. Taylor still resented Corporal Dye's failure to live long enough to take over his responsibilities.

"He would have to go and get himself killed," Taylor fussed.

Golf Company moved easily but cautiously along the narrow ridge that led toward the hill knob. To the right the ground fell away into Crawford's Draw, to the left it began to swell into 881N.

Hand signals flashed. Damn, it was a scorcher of a day, geared down as we were with weapons, ammo, packs. I was soon sweating like a pig, no offense to the Pig. Tony trailed along, puffing from exertion and the weight of 3.5 rocket rounds he carried. Over to our left, I spotted Rainey and Kilgore with his Starlite-mounted M-16 sneaking along in a half-crouch, weapons ready, eyes big and glaring beneath their helmets. You bet they were scared. We were all scared. We were also *Marines*, and we would do our job.

War in Vietnam was nothing like the world wars of I and II with their large-scale operations of thousands all hitting a beach at the same time, or taking a town or an island, or seizing a range of hills. Here, there was a feeling of isolation in relatively small units moving more or less separately. I knew that Echo was off to our flank, but I had no idea which flank nor what it was doing. Same thing with units at 881S. While BLT 2/3 was tasked with taking 881N, other outfits, probably elements of the Walking Dead and perhaps our Foxtrot 2/3, were assigned to 881S. Aside from when air and artillery worked over the hills, I experienced war as that portion of it that occurred immediately around me and my squad or platoon. In that aspect, battle for the individual Marine in Vietnam was very personal and confined.

Tony was a bulkier man than my lean 150 pounds. He soon drained his canteen. I still had half of my water left. I offered it to him during a break. I was afraid he would become dehydrated again. He licked his dry lips and shook his head.

"Damn, Tony. Take it. What, you think I got syphilis or something?"

He swigged and handed the canteen back. "Better ration what's left, Maras, or we'll be sucking the dew off toads."

Golf entered an area of thick woods and dense brush. During the last break, Lieutenant Mac's Third Herd Platoon had relieved Hesser up front of the company. Our point man, currently Lance Corporal James Boda, who was giving our faithful Indian scout a break, forged a path through the woods and soon came to the edge of a small clearing, on the other side of which rose the hill knob just below our taller objective. He halted and took a knee to scan for the enemy.

"Maras, I got a bad feeling again," Tony mentioned.

"Probably indigestion from the spaghetti you copped off me."

Boda stepped into the clearing and rushed to the far side with 2nd Squad right behind. PFC Taylor's 1st Squad emerged next with Lieutenant Mac and his RTO, Bill Vlasek, Tony, and me. We footed into the clearing like mice scampering across a barn floor, followed by 3rd Squad bringing up Tailend Charlie.

Tony's "bad feeling" was right on again. Suddenly, a violent blast of AK-47 and automatic fire erupted from the vicinity of the knob, catching many of us in the open and cutting through our ranks like through a crop of field cane. Marines dropped, riddled with lead. I yelled at Tony to follow me to cover while other guys went to ground where they were.

Bullets whip-snapped around my head. Some gook had spotted my machine gun. I hit the dirt only a few paces into the edge of the woods, but kept going, crawling on my elbows with the Pig cradled in my arms and Tony still in my wake, rounds snapping and whining above our heads and chopping off green foliage that showered down on us.

Vlasek, Lieutenant Mac's RTO, was one of the first to fall, a bullet in his temple. The lieutenant stripped the badly wounded and unconscious man of his radio and took cover among the gnarled roots of the nearest tree. PFC Tom Huckaba overheard McFarlane radioing Captain Shee-han, whose command element traversed back and forth between Golf Company and Echo.

"Skipper, I got a number of wounded up here. My radioman's down."

"Don't worry, Mac," came the calm response. "We'll get you out. We're calling up the sixty mike-mikes."

While a 60mm mortar crew moved up, Lieutenant Mac's 3rd blasted back at the knob with everything we had, even though the brush and trees made it impossible to select targets. Still, anything was better than lying on the ground sucking our thumbs and waiting to be slaughtered. I let loose the Pig and kept squeezing the trigger to burp out three-round bursts that avoided overheating the barrel. I carried a spare in my pack, but this was no time to burn out a barrel and have to try to replace it.

"Yeah! Yeah!" Tony cheered, blasting away with his M-16 in between feeding me ammo.

While 3rd Platoon kept the enemy occupied, Golf's other two platoons seized the opportunity to charge across the clearing to enter the fight. Lieutenant Hesser's 1st Platoon moved into a nearby patch of woods on a rise off to my left that had been previously plowed up by artillery. Lance Corporal Bill Roldan's Mattie Mattel jammed. Instead of dropping to seek cover, he bent over to work on the rifle's cocking lever. An NVA shot him through the chest and he collapsed.

Lieutenant Hesser darted forward and dragged Roldan out of the line of fire while shouting, "Corpsman! Corpsman up!"

From the corner of my eye, I observed Magilla Gorilla, unarmed except for a .45 pistol strapped to his waist, spring from cover and head toward Roldan with his aid bag. At close to two hundred pounds on a six-four frame, he provided a prime target. A year ago he was playing high school football in Phoenix, Arizona. Now, he dodged through a hail of enemy fire clutching his bag like it was a football and he had goal to go. We regarded our Navy corpsmen as angels of mercy who responded to the sounds of guns while everyone else ducked for cover.

Magilla skidded up to Roldan on his belly, already unsnapping the cover of his aid bag to get at his bandages. At the same time, Catherine the French photojournalist ran forward and dived into a shallow shell crater nearby from which she proceeded to capture on film a series of images that would become some of the most famous of the Vietnam War. They showed big redheaded Vernon Wike on his knees in the middle of a fierce firefight bandaging the unconscious Marine.

The following photos showed him looking up with rage and sorrow etched on his face as Roldan died from the bullet that had pierced his heart and lungs. Wike grabbed his dead friend's M-16 off the ground, cleared the jam, and, roaring at the top of his lungs, jumped up to charge the hillside.

I happened to glance his way. "No, Magilla!" I yelled. "*No! Get down! We need you!*"

Someone else noticed what was going on and bellowed a second warning, "Don't do it, Doc. J.K.'s been hit over here and needs help."

That caused Magilla to pause. Duty came first over personal vengeance. Wike ran back to render aid to Lance Corporal J.K. Johnson, who lay crumpled and semiconscious on the ground while bullets cracked all around him.

My attention returned to the ongoing battle, attracted by unnatural movement in shrubbery not one hundred meters to my front, almost down my throat. A bush appeared to open and close. I recalled the spider traps during Hotel Company's bloody contest in the draw. NVA fighters were masters at the art of camouflage. But I had this guy dead to rights, with the operative term being *dead*. I felt a certain cold anticipation as I paused to wait for the bush to open again and its tenant to show himself.

I hovered over the Pig, sights centered on the bush. Presently, the leaves parted. A pith helmeted head and shoulders appeared. In a rush of adrenaline and satisfaction, I laid on the trigger and burned through a half-belt of 7.62. The guy's chest fluttered with black starbursts. His body launched backwards, electrified, his arms and legs flailing in what appeared to be attempted flight.

Except he wasn't going anywhere, ever again.

This was my first confirmed KIA. In most firefights, everybody was shooting and no one was certain of who killed who. But this time, I was face to face with the guy. I saw scraggly hair on his chin, one of his eyes larger than the other, a small scar on his cheek—and I squeezed the trigger and watched him die.

I felt nothing for his death except a slight elation that he would kill no more Marines.

"I wasted his ass," I said calmly to Tony.

He was calm in return. "I know. I saw."

Time has no meaning in a firefight, is somehow truncated. A battle that lasts for an hour might seem two minutes—or two minutes feel like a day. This one ended in a series of artillery explosions before 60mm mortars could go into action on our behalf. Both the enemy's big guns and ours opened up simultaneously and stomped geysers of fire and destruction all over the slope. Our artillery from Khe Sanh tried to kill the enemy out only a few hundred meters in front of us and save our asses. The NVA's big guns from over by Laos attempted to kill us and save *their* asses. Our lines were so close, perhaps even mingled here and there, that it was difficult to tell whose shells were killing whom. What a fucked up mess this was turning out to be.

I felt no fear. What I felt was sheer *terror* as deadly shrapnel buzzed and cut through the brush, indiscriminately seeking targets on both sides. Out front, exploding shells walked directly toward Tony and me, step by step. And like Nancy Sinatra sang about her boots, they were gonna walk all over us.

I grabbed Tony. "Get the hell out of here. Follow me!"

The look in his eyes—early signs of shock.

"Tony? Damn it!"

"Yeah, yeah. Go!"

The two of us scooted through the grass like a pair of lizards on amphetamine, not knowing where we were going. Just *going*. Anywhere but here.

Old soldiers and Marines always said you never heard or saw the round with your number on it. They were wrong. I heard the shell coming in like an elephant trumpeting and blistering as it hurtled from the sky. It thudded to the ground where Tony and I were lying not two seconds ago. It shook the earth when it exploded. I became like a flea trying to hold onto a dog shaking itself after coming out of the water.

What felt like the blast from a furnace nearly ripped off my arm. Or so I thought. I yelped with sudden excruciating pain. Tony cried out in almost the same instant.

"*I'm hit!*"

My first thought was of the rotting dead gook I almost pissed on in the trees. Man, I hoped nobody saw me looking like that.

CHAPTER SEVENTEEN

Get on the Chopper

IF IT WAS YOUR TIME TO DIE, IT WAS YOUR TIME. DEATH COULD COME right out of the sky and kill you in an instant. Apparently, this wasn't my time. Nor Tony's. We lay together in the grass where we had fallen and assessed our wounds while bullets and shrapnel continued to saturate the air over our heads. With overwhelming relief I realized I still had my arm and other parts.

A shrapnel fragment had first struck my 781 web gear, slicing the strap, before it lodged just above my elbow. The piece of steel glowed red hot and cauterized the flesh around it, staying most of the bleeding. The wound still hurt like hell, and bled a little more when I snatched the fragment out of my arm, burning my fingers and prompting an involuntary stream of curses.

Tony groaned. "This is no time to blaspheme God," he warned.

Surprising how calm a man could be when wounded, as long as it wasn't deemed life threatening. Your poor body might be riddled from hostile intent, but fellow Marines weren't likely to coddle you and let you stew about it. Man up. Keep a stiff upper lip, you're not dying.

Tony was hit in the outer thigh. It bled like a sonofabitch, saturating his utility trousers. We quickly ascertained, however, that no vital vein or artery was involved. I ripped open a battle dressing and applied pressure to the ugly gash.

"I guess we got Purple Hearts coming," I mentioned. "Peggy'll change her mind when you come home a wounded hero."

"Piss on her."

Corpsman Lloyd Heath must have seen us take the hits. He rushed over. After patching us up, he decided our wounds were serious enough to warrant our going to the rear and a pre-designated casualty collection point. We slithered on our bellies to a thicket of trees that provided some protection near the clearing we crossed before everything started. A couple of other Marines were already there, one shot through the meaty part of his back, his torso wrapped in OD bandages, the other lying on the ground with blood oozing through lips already turning blue. Appeared he had a sucking chest wound and would have to be evacuated immediately if he was going to survive.

Tony and I exchanged looks. These guys were our buddies since Okinawa. And now—?

"Damn!" I exhaled, the expletive all but drowned out by the sounds of battle. "*Damn!*"

Corpsman Heath looked me right in the eye for emphasis. "Maras," he said, "you and Leyba get out of here while you can. It's gonna get much worse in these hills before it gets better. Your wounds are enough to get you out. Here are your tags."

He affixed casualty "Get out of Dodge!" tags to our jackets. More cries for help rose from the direction of the hill knob.

"I have to go," the corpsman said. He dumped bandages in Tony's lap where he leaned against a tree. "It's a flesh wound, Leyba. Put more pressure on it and tie a knot in the crevette. You'll be fine."

Then he was gone back toward the sound of guns. A few minutes later, while we were still contemplating what came next, Gunny Janzen crab-legged through the trees seeking volunteers to help bring out the other wounded and escort or carry them down the ridgeline to a clearing that we might use as an LZ for medevacs. Tom Huckaba and Dennis Johnson were with him.

"We'll go," I volunteered. It just came out, no pre-thought involved. Afterwards, I chastised myself for being some kind of fool to go back out there after we had barely escaped with our lives.

Tony shot me a "What the hell?" look.

Gunny hesitated. "How bad?" he asked, indicating our injuries.

"We can do it," I said. "We'll be flying out on the chopper anyhow. We need to make sure some of the other wounded guys go with us."

He nodded solemnly. "You're good Marines," he said.

My elbow throbbed something awful and threatened to lock up. Tony was limping. Nonetheless, the two of us plus Huckaba and Johnson zig-zagged toward the knob where the ambush occurred and our company corpsmen had more casualties than they could cope with by themselves. Cries and screams for help resounded throughout the brush. It was a matter of picking out a cry and rushing toward it while at the same time dodging bullets snapping past our heads.

Private James Golden was the first casualty we came upon. He had taken a round in the spine and seemed paralyzed. Tony and I took him while Huckaba and Johnson scrambled toward another summons for help.

One of the corpsmen had already patched up Golden and left him for us to carry out. His eyes full of pleading and suffering stared inward as Tony and I, keeping low, rolled the private into his poncho, gathered up the ends in an emergency litter, labored to our feet, and headed for the collection point carrying the fallen Marine between us. Through the lead and steel hailstones, dodging and ducking. Not knowing if we would make it or not.

Huckaba and Johnson brought in another casualty, whose face the poncho covered. I didn't look to see who it was, nor did I ask. I didn't want to know. Not now. Tony and I headed out again.

Get past this. Get through this alive and we're outta here.

"Maras, I thought you'd have learned by now not to volunteer for anything in the Marine Corps," Tony scolded.

He didn't mean it. If I hadn't offered our services, he would have. Somebody had to bring the WIAs to safety. Besides, Tony and I were best buddies and partners. We did everything together—slept together, bitched together, fought together, were even wounded together.

By the time we collected our casualties, Captain Sheehan was calling off the assault for the second day in a row. The enemy force apparently proved much larger and stronger than anticipated. First off, he called for our artillery to cease fire. Mixed together like everyone was on the battlefield, shelling might be doing as much damage to our own men as to the enemy.

The company broke contact with platoons covering each other in another "strategic withdrawal," leaving our dead out there where they fell. Four or five that we knew of. Maybe more. The urgency now was in getting our WIAs out. Elements of Echo Company had secured the LZ in the clearing. Medevac choppers were on their way in.

PFC Vlasek, Lieutenant Mac's radioman who took a round through the temple at the start of the ambush, was still breathing, but just barely. A hoarse, disconcerting sound. Magilla Gorilla had wrapped his head up like a mummy's, leaving only openings for his eyes, nose, and mouth. Tony and I slung our weapons across our backs and hoisted him in his poncho and started back with him from the casualty collection point to the medevac LZ. By this time the fight at the knob was pretty much over, leaving only scattered rifle shots in residue.

Storm clouds had been gathering for most of the day beyond the hills. Flashes of lightning stabbed out of the roiling skies as the column of walking wounded and those carried in makeshift litters wended our way across the clearing and down the slope and over to the ridgeline for medevac pickup. Golf Company guarded our rear in case the NVA might not have had enough and attempted to pursue.

A light rain started falling, making footing even more precarious. Wind rattled in the trees, but wind was a big improvement over the previous rattle of bullets. The sky darkened to almost night. Thunder rumbled. Lightning struck the remains of forest giants on top of the hills.

I figured the storm was God's way of saying He had seen enough of this shit.

My one good arm, Tony's bad leg, the walking wounded hobbling along reminded me of the *Yankee Doodle Dandy* skit in school where kids bandaged like soldiers of the Revolutionary War shuffled along to the beating dirge of drums.

Tony and I were breathing heavily under the weight of our load, the further awkwardness of our wounds and keeping Vlasek's IV bag aloft on a stick and the line free and open. I slipped and fell on a wet upgrade, dumping our unconscious patient out of his poncho and into the mud. His mummy bandages slipped off to reveal his face as we lifted him back onto the poncho. Tony jumped back.

"Oh, God!"

I had witnessed unimaginable horrors in the brief time since 2/3 landed at Red Beach, of violence and madness, of men mangled, brutalized, and slaughtered. Sergeant Hard during Vietnam training in Okinawa had tried to prepare us.

"You're going to see things," he said. "Horrible scenes. Dead men. Some of them your buddies. But remember one thing: You are Marines. Marines don't quit. Marines *can't* quit."

Lee Marvin the movie star, he said, was a Marine during World War II. "I knew I was going to be killed," Marvin said. "I just wanted to die in the very best outfit. There are ordinary corpses—and then there are Marine corpses. I figured on the first-class kind and hitched up."

Frozen in horror, Tony and I stared at what remained of Vlasek's face, stared while thunder banged across the sky, lightning strobed, and a few guns still cracked from the bad place we left behind. Hardly enough remained of the young Marine's face to recognize him. Just a red, gory mass of tissue and bone fragments from the temples down, a monster mask out of which breath rattled and blew bubbles of bloody fluids.

Tony, all choked up, murmured, "Maras. . . . Thank God we're getting out of here."

I heard a chopper coming in. "Let's get him to the LZ."

Tony prayed all the way. So did I. "Lord, please? Let him die."

No way would he survive, not with gray brain matter dribbling from his skull. I wouldn't want to live like this. A vegetable. Neither would Vlasek. A compassionate God would let him die.

We got him to the chopper as it came in fast, whipping rain showers with its rotors, hovering a foot or so off the grass while we loaded casualties aboard. Magilla Gorilla was there.

"Get on the helicopter," the crew chief ordered, looking directly at Tony and me. "You've got your tags."

I hesitated. Magilla came over. "Get on the chopper," he encouraged. "You two have done your part. Now save yourselves."

I had that fabled million-dollar wound. All I had to do was climb aboard that aircraft and Tony and I were out of here.

Still, I hesitated. Tony looked anxious. Sergeant Crawford wouldn't have left with such a puny wound. I thought of Captain Sheehan, Bill Rainey, Ramirez, Burnham and Kilgore, the Gunny, Lieutenant Mac, Magilla and Heath. All of them. Staying behind, being Marines while I bailed out on them. *Semper Fi* had to mean something.

"Maras?" Tony's voice quivered.

I drew in a deep breath. Damn! I was about to do the dumbest thing I had ever done in my entire life. I tore the casualty tag off my jacket and handed it to Magilla.

"Take it. I've got my gun. I can still shoot. I'm going back. See you later, Tony."

Tony couldn't believe it. "What? Maras, you stupid bastard."

I headed down the ridge to where Golf was digging in again for another night and another try at the hill tomorrow. Not looking back, the Pig slung forward for possible action. Above the ominous rumble of thunder, I overheard Tony saying to Magilla, "He'll never make it without me. I have to go with him."

We returned to the fight together, walking side by side, our utilities stained with our blood and the blood of others, not talking as the gathering storm lashed at our faces, gale winds shrieked in the trees, and thunder sounded like the bombardment of enemy hills.

We heard later that Vlasek died before the chopper reached the *Princeton's* sick bay.

CHAPTER EIGHTEEN

The Green Parrot

"WE COULD HAVE CAUGHT THAT CHOPPER OUT OF HERE." TONY WAS limping, I was cradling my arm. But we made our way through the building storm to link up with the battalion. "Both of us—stupid!"

I couldn't dispute Tony. I wanted to get out of here as badly as he did. But what brand of men would we have been to desert our brothers-in-arms when they needed every shooter they could get for what lay ahead? I was beginning to understand why Sergeant Crawford kept returning to the battlefield.

I had seen how they were, Sergeant Crawford of Korea and the World War II vets of my pop's generation. They didn't talk much about combat itself, the dying and killing, when they got together at reunions. That wasn't what they missed, wasn't what they lost when their wars ended and they went home. They missed that special bond forged among them in the crucible of war, a brotherhood attachment that they clung to and would continue to do so for the rest of their lives. You couldn't explain that kind of connection to someone who had never experienced it.

Johnson, Huckaba, and some of the other able-bodied who had helped wounded to the medevac pickup LZ hadn't expected Tony and me to return with them. They left the LZ and went on ahead to where the battalion's two remaining companies were digging back in at our old position on the flat ridgetop below 861. It was there that Tony received his Dear John from Peggy and he and I found the dead gook.

A light rain continued, soaking our utilities and bandages and caus-ing our wounds to sting. Wind picked up, whipping foliage into a frenzy. Heavier monsoon rains were on the way. Presently, with temperatures still high, we sweltered in the steaming heat. That was bound to change after nightfall when the mercury plummeted. Why couldn't they give a war in a more pleasant climate?

Exhausted from our wounds and the exertion of toting casualties off the battlefield, Tony and I collapsed in a thicket where we wouldn't easily be spotted. We sprawled out on the grass and lost ourselves for a few moments gazing up through jungle canopy at black boiling patches of storm scuttling overhead. Terrific bolts of lightning that sounded like exploding mortar rounds jolted us back to reality.

Tony exhaled wearily. "Maras," he confessed, "I couldn't have left either—not unless they carried me out."

"I know, brother."

Above us, a large green parrot flew toward the recent battlefield. It struck me as somehow out of place, this beautiful, iridescent bird in its otherwise idyllic and familiar setting, and what was it doing? Flying toward war.

"Don't go that way!" I warned, but only under my breath in case some gook might be lurking about.

Tony's eyes followed the parrot's progress on its path to 881N. "Stu-pid bird."

The clouds coalesced into a full tropical storm. Water washed off the cartoon tiger on my helmet like a waterfall in front of my eyes and poured down the back of my neck. Hail pounded the helmet, sounding the way it did falling on the tin roof of a barn. Gale-force winds slashed through the forest with the roar of ocean waves. Jagged lightning bolts bayonetted trees, lighting up the terrain and cracking like artillery.

Garvin and Hughes out on OP/LP seemed surprised to see us. "We heard you two bought the farm."

"Price was too high," I replied.

Lightning struck nearby, making nerve endings tingle. "God's pissed off at us," Garvin decided.

"Can you blame Him?" Tony grumped. "*I'm* pissed off at us."

Gunny Janzen was even more astonished at our return. He was up pacing with concern over Captain Sheehan's delay in returning from the battlefield with his CP element. Lieutenant Brian Jackson was assigned to the CP as FO—Forward Observer—whose duty it was to direct artillery fire onto targets. Everyone accused him of calling friendly fire in on top of us, which wasn't the truth but which nonetheless damaged his reputation because every Marine knew the most dangerous man in the world was a second lieutenant with a map and a radio. Gunny thought Sheehan might be late due to Jackson's having turned up missing during the artillery exchange and presumed to be dead or injured.

"Welcome home," was all Gunny said to Tony and me when he saw us, after shaking his head in disbelief.

Hell, Tony and I found it hard to believe ourselves.

He seeded us and the Pig into the perimeter to cover a likely enemy avenue of approach. By now we were both soaked and shivering. Our hole was the same one we had occupied previously; but the old homestead needed some improvements. It hadn't been raining before.

"Maras, you put up a poncho over the hole and I'll dig a rain trough around it to divert some of the flood," Tony suggested.

"Keep your eyes peeled," Gunny warned as he hurried off.

"Reckon the gooks'll be out in this weather fucking with us?" Tony wondered.

"Would you be?"

Using the razor-sharp banana knife, I cut some bamboo stakes with which to tack down the four corners of a poncho over our hole, leaving a machine gun port open downrange. Tony couldn't dig fast enough or deep enough with his E-tool to redirect the flow of water and it continued to rush into our hole. Wind popped and snapped the poncho roof and kept jerking up stakes.

While we struggled with our abode, other Marines around the perimeter were likewise digging in and trying to erect shelter from a cold, dark, miserable night. The only thing that could make it worse was for the gooks to come out and start fucking with us. Maybe lightning would strike them.

Finally, I managed to stake down my poncho and Tony accomplished all he could with his E-tool. I slid underneath the low canvas roof and splashed into freezing rainwater already up to boot-lace level. We bailed frantically with our helmets but made little headway as rain continued to drum down in monsoon sheets and wash over the top of our pit in waves.

I gave up. "You going to bed first, or shall I?"

"You're bullshitting me, right?"

Bullshit and black humor were what kept us sane.

Dennis Johnson dropped by begging for cigarettes. "No food, no cigarettes, no water—"

"No *water*?" Tony splashed a hand in the overflowing drainage ditch he dug around our hole.

Johnson scoffed. "You ain't gonna drink that stuff, are you? Gooks have been shitting in it. You could catch something and die. Now, about that cigarette? Me and Huckaba tried to split our last one, but the rain melted it."

I didn't smoke and had already traded off my little C-rat packs for choice C-rats. Tony used his last butt when we took our break up the ridge where we saw the parrot.

Disappointed, Johnson peered out into the darkness from beneath our poncho roof, reluctant to venture out again into the weather.

"You know," he mused, sounding sad and, I thought, lonely, "I think God must be crying. He's as sick of this as the rest of us."

It came as no surprise to me by now that servicemen at war turned to thoughts of God to help them reason through chaos, madness, and so much death. Few are not in some way or in some degree touched by the supernatural as they struggle for understanding, comfort, and protection.

I had not considered myself particularly religious while growing up. I rarely attended church. Sunday school had been hit and miss. But not a day passed under fire but thoughts of God and life and death and eternity intruded. What did it all *mean*?

Maybe it didn't mean anything. Marines in Vietnam had a phrase used to dismiss confronting difficult and hard-to-understand concepts. "It don't mean nothing," we said.

It don't mean nothing.

If that were true, then why were we here? Why were we killing and dying—and for what?

It don't mean nothing.

Soon, water in our hole rose above our knees, forcing us to stand up rather than sit down where cold, muddy water could lap at our chests. We stood and waited for daylight, or for the crazy gooks. Whichever came first. I had never been so miserable in my life.

Gunnery Sergeant Janzen waited until Captain Sheehan and his CP, along with Lieutenant Jackson, who had been found, returned safely before he wrapped himself in a poncho and crawled into a shell crater. In spite of freezing rain, hail, and wind, he lapsed into the deep sleep of the chronically exhausted. Water had risen to his shoulders when he awoke at dawn.

"If the gooks had got me," he told everyone, "I'd have at least been put out of my misery."

CHAPTER NINETEEN

The Watch Continued Running

"VIETNAM! I'VE HAD ABOUT ALL THIS SHIT I CAN ENJOY!" CAME A CHAL-lenge from within the perimeter.

Gray dawn found the storm moved out of the AO. Its soaked and wretched victims were cranky and tense. Distant thunder rumbled from the departing storm.

"Fuck you back very much!"

Gunny Janzen interceded. "Knock off the bullshit."

Everything looked slow and desultory in the morning gray. Even Doc Magilla seemed uncharacteristically depressed as he made his rounds. The only words he uttered while he changed dressings on my elbow and Tony's thigh were, "Heath gave you two birds a chance to get out of here and you blew it."

"Where is Heath?"

Magilla took a deep breath and blew it out again, puffing out his cheeks. He looked old and tired.

"We went back out there while the fight was still going on to get more wounded. He's still out there. Lloyd didn't make it back."

What could you say? It occurred to me that I knew very little about Lloyd Heath. Not where he came from, his family, nothing. Just enough to say, "Hey, Doc. How's it hanging?" Although we considered him and the other Navy corpsmen as much Marines as any of us, they played by different rules. Their mission was not to kill people, break things, and take ground. Theirs was to save Marine lives. Any way they could. Heath tried to save Tony and me by tagging us for medevac with what turned out to be minor wounds.

Doc Magilla issued us tubes of antibiotic ointment. "See you don't get infections," he said before moving on.

I stopped him. "Magilla?"

"Maras?"

No words came. We just looked at each other. He understood. How could you ever properly thank these guys? He nodded and moved on.

Marines were so miserable from last night we were in no mood to take shit from anybody today. A bunch of pissed-off Marines waiting to be turned loose bore ill for the enemy.

On the other hand, the gooks were probably just as pissed off as we were. What was that verse from the Bible? Something about rain falling equally on the righteous and the unrighteous.

I knew we had to go back out there, back into the abyss. Our colored pins were no doubt being moved even now. To avoid another Dien Bien Phu, we were saddled with the task of running the NVA out of these hills and occupying them ourselves. That meant casualties. Casualties had to be expected and accepted. You looked into the abyss, I remembered reading somewhere, and the abyss looked back at you.

Doc Heath was missing and, I feared, another of us who may have fallen into the abyss.

We received warning orders. The best I understood about the "Big Picture" was that we were attacking two objectives simultaneously this morning. Golf would take on the same knob from yesterday and the day before. Echo would move off to our left flank to seize and hold another small hilltop on another ridge across the valley from us. Once secured, the two knobs could be launch pad for assaults against 881N proper.

Further delay, went the reasoning, allowed the NVA to reinforce their positions and thus more difficult to dislodge. We had hurt them and seized the initiative. The enemy knew we were coming back, they knew where we were coming from, and they should know who they were dealing with. Marines could not be stopped for long.

Again, arty and air prepped the two objectives. We were becoming so accustomed to the routine that even fire and thunder delivered by bombs and shells gave the gray morning a distant lazy look. Smoke hung in the now-still air like a dirty cloud.

Finally, Captain Sheehan issued orders: "Saddle up! Move 'em out!"

Lieutenant Mac's Third Herd Platoon took point for Golf Company, with Ramirez our "faithful Indian scout" in the lead and PFC Taylor's squad, including Tony and me, backing him. One of our tasks, should we have the opportunity, was to recover our dead who had been left on the field yesterday. Except for Doc Heath, the missing were all Lieutenant Mac's people. He insisted his platoon be the one to make the recovery.

Out into the forest we went, down once more into Crawford's Draw, up the opposite slope and across that same cursed clearing below the rise of the knob where we had been ambushed less than twenty-four hours ago. Sounded like a SciFi thriller: *The Rise of the Knob.*

Prep of the knobs lifted as we approached. Apparently, somebody decided not to do any more "enemy close" scenarios that subjected us to the possibility of friendly fire. The fight started once the arty stopped. Today became a replay, a continuation of what had gone before.

In a bush fight, each man felt almost isolated within his individual war. You saw only what happened immediately around you. Everything else was mostly sound—cries and shouts, screams when somebody got hit. *Crack! Crack!* of rifle shots. Ripped-cloth *Tat Tat Tat!* of machine guns. Sudden *Whump!* of a grenade, RPG, or mortar round landing, its signature of smoke rising out of the weeds and underbrush. It was, in a practical sense, like the blind fighting the blind.

A battlefield was so damned noisy. Plus: "*I'm hit! I'm hit!*"

"Relax, man. They're just dirt clods."

"Doc up!" A cry out of the bedlam that made me feel sick, knowing a Marine had taken one.

The crack and pressure of slugs passing near my head almost took my breath. *Damn! That was close!*

Panting like a marathon runner, sweating like a pig. No offense to the Pig.

A bullet whacked my pack, knocking me to my knees and exploding my last can of chicken noodle soup. Now, *that* pissed me off.

"I'm okay, okay," I assured Tony, regaining my feet and continuing on the wild advance toward the knob, firing the Pig from my hip John Wayne style, lighting up groups of bushes while Tony sprayed any likely enemy hidey hole with his M-16.

I wondered if John Wayne had ever been in actual combat. Sacrilege! Bite my tongue!

Over on one flank, Corporal Richard Schmitz came upon what he took to be an abandoned bunker until he spotted movement. Thinking a wounded gook might be inside and perhaps anticipating capturing a prisoner to win Pappy Delong's promised R&R, he rolled into the end of the trench that made up part of the bunker.

I overheard him shout, "Drop your weapon! Drop it! Come on out! *Chieu Hoi! Chieu Hoi!*"

Captain Sheehan also heard and knew what Schmitz was up to. He yelled at Schmitz, "No! Get back!"

These guys we fought weren't VC guerrilla types. They were hard core down to the bone and would sooner cut out your throat than fuck with *Chieu Hoi.*

"Let's go!" I called out to Tony. We raced through the weeds to contribute our machine gun to Schmitz's dispute. To hell with John Wayne, this was what Sergeant Crawford would have done.

The gook bunker consisted of a trench about chin deep, eight feet long and two feet wide with a cave-like bunker carved into one wall. Schmitz was hugging the wall next to the cave entrance and shouting out for its occupants to surrender. The barrel of an AK-47 thrust from out of the hole and blasted into the Marine's chest, splattering blood and flesh.

Schmitz's combat buddy, a private named Coleman, saw Schmitz disappearing into the bunker's tiny mouth, being dragged inside like the earth was eating him. The gooks probably intended to use him as a shield or a hostage.

Enraged beyond rational thought, Coleman leapt into the trench and grabbed his friend's boot in a deadly game of tug-of-war.

The dark mouth of the hole lit up with another burst of AK fire as gooks inside shot across Schmitz's body, striking Coleman in the legs. The heavy slugs slammed him back against the wall and to one side where the bunker occupants would have to show themselves in order to finish him off.

Although bleeding profusely and in severe agony, Coleman wasn't about to give up on his buddy. He grabbed a boot and returned to the task of trying to pull Schmitz free.

Sergeant Santos, who reached the scene seconds before Tony and I appeared, threw himself on the ground at the lip of the trench above the bunker. He was a tough lifer Marine on his second combat tour in Vietnam. He stretched over into the trench, grabbed Coleman by his battle harness and manually yanked him up and out of danger, depositing him in the grass.

"They got Dickie in there!" Coleman cried. "*Corpsman up!*"

The gooks were wily enough to stay hidden deep inside the bunker and out of sight to wait for another Marine to show himself. Like rabid rats in a tunnel, these guys weren't going to be any Marine's R&R ticket.

I flopped down on my belly at the end of the trench where I might get an enfilade shot at the hole without exposing myself to those inside. I trained the Pig's snout on the entrance but held fire for fear of hitting Schmitz. His body, now still and undisturbed, lay mostly inside the bunker with only his feet showing.

Santos lay sprawled next to me. "Cover me!" he said.

He snatched a rope off his gear and dropped into the trench where he quickly tossed a loop around Schmitz's extended foot and attempted to pull him free. NVA inside the hole opened fire, muzzle flashes flickering to light up the entrance. None of the rounds struck Santos since he remained out of their sight against the trench wall, but he was so near the entrance that muzzle fire burned his face. Giving up on rescuing Schmitz in this manner, he sprang out of the trench and went to his knees on the thick earthen roof of the subterranean den. It was clear to him and to us that Schmitz was dead.

"Gimme a grenade!" he demanded.

I freed a frag from my belt pouch and tossed it to the sergeant. He slammed it over the side of the trench and into the den. He rolled and flattened himself on the ground.

"Fire in the hole!"

The grenade exploded with a muffled *Karump!* Flame shot from the bunker's mouth. Santos reached out a hand for a second grenade. I pitched it to him. He transferred it to the bunker in the same motion.

A fortunate call, that second grenade. Subsequently, while retrieving Schmitz's body from the wreckage, we found the corpses of two NVA soldiers. One of them appeared to have sat on the first frag to save his buddy. Had Santos not sent in a second grenade to finish the job, the surviving gook would likely have added to his personal body count when the next Marine attempted to retrieve Corporal Schmitz.

The difference between living and dying, as this incident proved, could be a matter of seconds, of good and bad decisions made instantaneously.

"Okay," Santos said to the men of his squad, "get Dickie out of there and bury the gooks with another grenade. May they rot in Hell."

It had become obvious by this time that we faced not a major resistance but instead a small stay-behind element whose job was to delay us until the main force withdrew further up 881N to reconsolidate and bring in replacements from Laos and the Ho Chi Minh Trail. One thing we acknowledged by now: These guys were not going away. They were not guerrillas employing hit-and-run tactics. They were professionals. I wondered if the NVA had Marines.

Tony and I waited with Sergeant Santos' men to cover them with the Pig while they attended to Schmitz and the bunker. Captain Sheehan ordered Golf to ascend the rest of the steep slope to the top of the knob, which it did without further resistance. In the meantime, Echo was well on its way to controlling the other knob. Surprisingly, no more firing came at us. Apparently, the bad guys were pulling back after having delayed us. Golf Company lost two Marines killed in the skirmish and nine wounded.

We located our four dead left behind in yesterday's action. They were all together in what appeared to be a last stand gone horribly wrong. Tony and I and some of Santos's squad members came upon Lieutenant Mac, Captain Sheehan, Doc Magilla, and a couple of other Marines standing with their helmets off and their heads bowed in a field next to a grove of thorn trees. Lance Corporal Jim Boda, PFC Andy Carter,

PFC Jim Hill, and Navy Corpsman Lloyd Heath lay in a cluster where they fell. I joined the living around the dead, all of us silent and grieving. My injured elbow suddenly began to ache, as though reminding me of how Doc Heath tried to save Tony and me from all this. In the end, he couldn't save himself.

I had chatted with Jim Hill only this morning. Now he too was dead.

"Maras," he had said to me, "what do you reckon it'll be like when we get home again? I can hardly remember home. It's like it was another life."

After a pause, he added, "*If* we get home again."

Hill would never go home.

A cleaning rod stuck out the barrel of Carter's weapon. It had obviously malfunctioned. Hill's weapon also jammed. When he went down, he appeared to have been trying to force a stuck cartridge from the chamber of his M-16 with the Bowie knife he always carried. Lieutenant Mac picked up the knife and studied it a moment before he sighed and handed to Magilla. "Here, Doc. Remember this day."

Doc Wike looked at it, shook his head, and also sighed before he passed it on to one of the other grunts, a newbie who had arrived on Okinawa with Hill. "Jim would have wanted you to have it," he said.

The newbie nodded solemnly and accepted the big knife.

Magilla stood over the KIAs for a long time. A big man just standing there with his head lowered, his shoulders shaking, lips moving in silent prayer. Tears streamed down his cheeks. The Doc took the deaths of his friends personally.

"They didn't stand a chance," one of the Marines said bitterly. "Their M-16s malfunctioned."

"Fucking McNamara." This from a PFC in Santos's squad who had been at the trench where Schmitz died.

Rumors had circulated freely since we were issued the weapons in Okinawa that Defense Secretary Robert McNamara held investments in Colt, the company that designed and manufactured defective M-16s. It was further rumored that he and other politicians were making a profit off the war and the blood of soldiers, sailors, airmen, and Marines in Vietnam.

"*Fucking McNamara!*"

Surely there was enough evidence by this time to prove something was badly wrong with the design of the rifle.

I knelt on both knees next to Heath's body. I didn't know him well, would never really know him now as other than the brave and compassionate man who ran to the sound of guns and attempted to save those harmed by them. His eyes were open and fixed staring up into the sky as into another world.

It struck me odd that Heath was dead here, his spirit gone, but his watch continued to run. How long, I wondered, was eternity?

CHAPTER TWENTY

The Pond

ONCE ATOP THE KNOB, WE DISCOVERED DOZENS OF WELL-CONSTRUCTED bunkers, fighting holes, and trenches arranged for interlocking fire. Looking back over what seemed an interminable distance to where the top of 861 stuck up at the other end of the ridgeline, I couldn't help succumbing to a sudden feeling of isolation. It occurred to me that the NVA may have employed an ages-old strategy of "isolate and destroy." Brilliant move to sucker us out here, cut us off from our control and supply anchor, and trap us against the base of 881N, which swelled up out of the jungle above our heads.

We hadn't *driven* these guys out. *It's a trap! It's a trap!* But nobody listened to a nineteen-year-old FNG private. These guys would be coming back in force to collect rent. I could almost *feel* them out there waiting for full dark.

Our officers established a hasty night perimeter, taking advantage of the enemy's abandoned bulwarks. As usual, a machine gun being a critical defensive weapon, Tony, the Pig, and I were assigned to cover a strategic point. On 50-50 alert with listening posts sent out in all directions, Marines settled down for another in a series of long, restless, scary nights. The fighting hole I shared with Tony was virtually a replica of every other hole we had occupied since that long first-day march from the Combat Base at Khe Sanh to 861. Mud at the bottom of it from last night's rain sucked at our boots and reeked of an odor somewhere between spoiled food—gooks relished fish heads and rice and a sour fish sauce called *nuc mam*—and unwashed bodies. We were decidedly in a low-rent district.

Across a wooded lowlands from our knob, Echo Company likewise dug in on their ridgeline hill following slight resistance. Both companies now prepared to kick off when ordered to assault and seize 881N. When a job just had to be done right, call the Marines.

Golf's knob was relatively flat on top, its timber shredded and splintered and strewn about. Edges sloped off on three sides and rose on the fourth into the mother hill. Near where Captain Sheehan set up his CP lay a large crater the size of a small pond. Judging from the green scum on the surface, it had been here for quite some time. Recent rains had filled it to the brim and attracted new swarms of mosquitoes.

Only emergency medevac choppers braved NVA fire to get in to us; a pair of Sea Knights managed to drop down fast and hover at the top of the knob long enough to pick up the wounded and our dead, among them Heath, Hill, Carter, Schmitz, and Boda. Mortar rounds landed on the LZ moments after the choppers sprang back into the air and barreled balls-to-the-wall for the *Princeton*. Trying to bring in resupply choppers seemed too risky. As a result, most of us nursed the few drops of remaining water in our canteens and hoarded our last cans of Cs. It was so bad that heavy smokers were trying to barter off their last Camel for a John Wayne chocolate bar.

The mosquito crater-pond provided the knob's sole source of water. For all we knew, it bred all manner of bugs and microscopic critters to play havoc with our systems and give us the running shits, or worse. Still, it was better than licking dew off bamboo leaves and toads. Tony and I and a few other Marines were replenishing our canteens from the crater, ignoring the odor and the pond's green-brown sickish tint, when Magilla came around passing out halcyon purification tablets.

"No telling what's in that stagnant water," he cautioned. "It's probably full of napalm, and no telling what else."

Gene Kilgore swished scum aside and dipped his canteen into the water. "Napalm kills stomach worms, doesn't it?"

Magilla shrugged and dropped a tablet into his own canteen before he filled it. What the hell? A Marine had to have water.

Kilgore picked up his M-16 with attached Starlite scope and started back to where Captain Sheehan assigned him to night-scope the terrain.

"Still got your thermite grenade?" Tony needled.

Kilgore grunted and patted his harness pouch. He took seriously his responsibility to destroy the scope if we were ever overrun.

Tony and I returned to our hole while darkness and fog crept eerily up out of the lowlands. My elbow ached from the shrapnel wound. I tried to ignore it. Tony rubbed his injured thigh. Neither of us wanted to be the first to collapse in the bottom mud to try to sleep while the other kept watch. It was difficult to decide which would be more miserable—sleeping in the mud or grabbing a few winks standing up.

I shook my canteen to make sure the halcyon was well distributed. Squinting and mentally holding my nose against the smell, I unscrewed the top and took a deep swig. Immediately I gagged on something foreign that felt like a soft length of squirmy plastic that almost went down my throat. I retched water and a two-inch leech all over Tony.

"You reckon there's any protein value in a leech?" was all Tony said.

I vowed not to drink from the pond again; I was lying to myself and knew it. Wait until the sun came out again and temperatures spiked at about one hundred.

Night was a time of angst and reflection. The Marines of Golf felt stressed by the deaths of our buddies. I kept seeing Heath's watch running, mocking, keeping time while time had ended for him. Tony and I opted to stand up again to sleep, leaning against the side of our rat hole in the enveloping night, each of us deep in individual thoughts and fears.

"Maras, do you suppose you see it coming and know you're about to die?" Tony asked in a subdued voice. "You think Lloyd knew he was going to die just before he died?"

"I don't know, Tony."

Echo Company, less than a couple klicks away across the lowlands from Golf's position, came up on the commo net to report activity in its area—"sounds of heavy digging" out front of the lines. Every unit in the vicinity of the three hills went on full alert when Kilo 3/9, Mike 3/3, and now the recently added Foxtrot 2/3, all of which remained stalemated at the bottom of 881S, looked across from their angle and confirmed NVA swarming around the bottom of Echo's knoll and farther up the ridgeline.

They spotted enemy soldiers in groups of fifty or more humping large packs as they appeared and disappeared in and out of fogbanks. Kilgore with his Starlite further corroborated their sightings. It appeared Echo Marines might be in for a long night.

Tension mounted. Something was about to snap.

"Relieve each other and try to get some rest," Gunny Janzen advised, passing along our lines. "This may be our last chance to sleep tonight."

I nodded at Tony. "Go ahead. You first."

He failed to sleep. So did I. Finally giving up on it, we hunkered gunner and assistant gunner wide-eyed next to each other staring into threatening darkness where Count Dracula and his minions lurked.

"Quiet."

"Yeah. Too quiet."

About midnight I began nodding off in position over my machine gun. Sleeping with the Pig.

"I'll wake you when the pizza comes," Tony remarked. "I ordered out. A supreme with anchovies."

"Anchovies give me indigestion."

"Especially if gooks deliver it," Tony said.

My eyes closed. I bumped my helmet off the Pig. Tony's sharp cry of alarm snapped me awake. "*Motherfucker!*"

In the distance, across the lowlands, a green star cluster flowered bright above Echo Company, followed by the eerie tooting of bugles, both common NVA signals launching a ground attack. Sergeant Crawford, while we were in-training at Okinawa, told stories about how the North Koreans used bugles during their mass human wave charges.

"If that sound doesn't pucker your asshole," he said, "your pucker is worn out."

My pucker factor puckered up completely as Echo's hill erupted in strings of bright explosions. Rifle and machine gun fire surrounded the knob and twinkled like hundreds of lightning bugs. The roar, crackling and rumble of the commencing fight carried across the intervening valley and slapped us upside the head. Captain Sheehan received a message from the battalion S-3 whom he had seeded in with Echo.

"Golf Company could be next on the NVA hit list."

Platoon leaders and sergeants fast-legged along the perimeter to pass the word to every fighting position. "The gooks are hitting Echo. We're back on full alert. We could be next."

CHAPTER TWENTY-ONE

A Night of Imposters

THE NVA APPARENTLY PLANNED TO END THE HILL FIGHTS IN ONE fell swoop by striking against one of our two battalion positions at 881N. By attacking Echo, they may have expected Golf to strip out its own men to send across the valley to Echo's aid. NVA elements held in reserve would then ambush our people in the lowlands while others assaulted Golf's diminished defenses on the knob.

Pappy Delong wasn't going for it. "Hold tight," he instructed Captain Sheehan. "Help for Echo is on the way."

That meant Golf did little but wait and watch the nonstop light-and-sound show of exploding shells and flares and crisscrossing red and green tracers. We used red: *they* used green. The NVA threw everything at Echo except Ho Chi Minh's outhouse. The battle resounded throughout the hills, reflecting vividly against fog and a low bank of clouds left over from the rain. It was a spectacle none of us was likely to forget.

Impotent rage engulfed the Marines of Golf Company. Our sister company might be getting overrun and we could do nothing about it.

The gooks' favorite tactic during an attack was to get in close and hug the line in that narrow buffer zone between the Marine perimeter and the wall of support provided by air and artillery that dared move no closer for fear of wiping out our own people. That meant the fight was mostly at close quarters, face to face. So near and personal that opposing sides yelled and screamed insults at each other.

"Marines! Tonight you die!"

"Fuck Ho Chi Minh!"

Just like in the war movies—except actors in movies rose up from the "dead" after a scene, slapped each other on the back, and went out for coffee together with John Wayne.

While snipers positioned on ridges to the north and west of Echo popped away—"They're in the fuckin' trees!"—NVA infantry scampered about outside the perimeter tossing grenades, killing Marines, attempting to penetrate Marine defenses. Battalion standing orders dictated that in this kind of situation everyone should hold fast; anybody up and about was fair game since it was often impossible to distinguish friend from foe in the dark.

Company corpsmen took extreme risks to reach the wounded who, along with felled enemy soldiers, thrashed about in the grass screaming and sobbing for help. Ignoring the danger, corpsmen crawled or ran to them, calling out desperately to verify their identity so our own guys would not shoot them: "Marine coming through! Coming through!"

NVA wearing Marine uniforms they had stripped from dead 1/9 leathernecks at the start of all this added to the confusion. Glimpsing a Marine uniform illuminated by exploding grenades darting through the chaos caused some defenders to hesitate on the trigger and in that hesitation pay the price with their lives.

Enemy soldiers wearing Marine gear to cause confusion broke through Lieutenant Cannon's 2nd Platoon sector and rampaged inside the perimeter, shooting and hurling grenades, executing those already wounded.

"Gooks inside!"

"Motherfucker! There's thousands of the little bastards!"

"Shoot 'em! *Kill 'em!*"

Sergeant Bob Powell led his squad racing across the top of the hill to fill in the gap in Cannon's line. An enemy 50-cal machine gun opened fire from a crew that had approached to within fifty meters to provide cover for the marauders. It cut down Powell and most of his squad.

Radio traffic from Echo's CP grew desperate: "We need help if we're going to hold. They're all over us. We need anything you got. It's 'enemy close.' Do you read? It's 'enemy close.'"

Something had to be done. And quick! Even if the solution posed a hazard for Echo's Marines. Colonel Delong authorized Mike Company over below 881S to enter the fray and fire its Howtars 4.2 wheeled mortars across the valley in an attempt to relieve the pressure on Echo. Desperation increased to recklessness. As one Marine put it, "Better to die by friendly fire than gook fire."

Echo's FO on the knob passed instructions to Mike and radio-walked exploding shells "enemy close" up the slope to within fifty meters of Echo's perimeter. I felt like cheering every time a bright burst revealed tiny stick figures in the distance getting blown to Hell.

Puff the Magic Dragon appeared in the sky overhead, circling, circling, raking its red neon wash of cannon fire through the attackers below in a visual display as dazzling as an alien flying saucer working a giant death ray. Although only one out of every fifth round was a tracer, the red groove they cut through the night appeared as a solid moving bar from sky to earth.

Gunny Janzen went around to Golf's machine gunners and assigned areas into which we were allowed to shoot to provide Echo further assistance. He pointed across the lowlands to where Echo Company's hill boiled with fire and smoke.

"That's where Echo's dug in." He lowered his finger to point into the darkness below. "There is where you can shoot if you see movement."

"Do you see movement?" I asked Tony after Gunny left. It was too dark over there to see anything outside the little hill's flaring core.

"Yeah, yeah! I see 'em."

That was all I needed. Tony kept the M-60 fed while I goosed the Pig into action, stabbing tracers in red supersonic bee flights across the lowlands and into the lower part of Echo's hill. I couldn't tell if we were doing any good, but it felt good doing it. Judging from the rattle of other Golf machine guns, we were all feeling good about doing it.

Echo fought on and prayed for sunrise. The battle began to subside when the first signs of morning broke the eastern sky. Generally, North Vietnamese liked to fight at night when they were not such ready targets for air and artillery. Stunned Marines, those blood-splattered, hollow-eyed, exhausted survivors of the night's battle, still held the knob when firing ceased and the sun rose.

About eighty of the enemy dead littered the ground around Echo's perimeter. An equal number may have been dragged away. Unexploded mortar shells, cartridge casings, and other debris trashed the area, while blood from the enemy dead and wounded soaked into the red earth. Echo had also suffered in the night's fighting: twenty-six young Marines paid the ultimate price and would be making their final journey home in government-issued wooden coffins draped in American flags. Another eighty-four were wounded. It was BLT 2/3's worst night since the Hill Fights had started.

The NVA dropped back out of sight and out of range to lick their wounds. In the quiet that followed, CH-46 helicopters soared in above the sun-tinted bloodied hills to recover our dead and wounded. They received minimal hostile fire. It was so soon after a major battle that all either side wanted was to find somewhere safe to recuperate.

Colonel Delong ordered Foxtrot Company to relocate from the bottom of 881S, where it had been part of the defenses, to Echo's battered knob to fill in Echo's personnel gaps pending replacements. Echo Marines, greatly diminished in numbers with a casualty rate of well over 50 percent, were too spent to leave their holes. Foxtrot assumed the nasty business of burying NVA corpses in a common trench before they began to stink.

Golf had avoided being hit during a miserable night on alert anticipating marauding NVA to practice their tactics on us. As the sun brightened and burned off night fog, renewed breezes dissipated smoke and haze over Echo's hill. The quiet that followed was almost as shattering as last night's bedlam and violence.

Tony heaved a sigh of relief as we scrounged in our packs for breakfast and heat tabs with which to boil water from the mosquito crater-pond for coffee. Tony thought maybe we should have saved my leech for seasoning. He sighed again, weary from lack of sleep, and lifted his eyes up to the sky from the depths of our rodent den in the ground.

"Good morning, Vietnam!" he managed, almost worshipfully, like a prayer of Thanksgiving.

Chapter Twenty-Two

Premonition

Echo Company, along with its support, threw everything we had at the gooks and set them back on their heels. The company suffered in the attack, but it dealt out more misery than it absorbed. The enemy's brutal thrust revealed not only the NVA's determination and overwhelming troop numbers available for combat, but it also exposed the tenuous hold BLT-2/3 had clawed into the base of Hill 881N. Perhaps just as significantly, it revealed the tenuous hold each of us claimed on life.

Marines never gave up clawing, however. And we learned from our environment. For example, the caper the gooks pulled by donning Marine uniforms to penetrate Echo's perimeter. Echo turned the tables on them by saving a few Vietnamese stiffs from the mass burial, putting Marine helmets on them, and propping the bodies at strategic locations inside the perimeter or outside as fake OP/LP watches. The objective was to draw fire and provide advance warning of further attacks or probes.

In the dark, about the only way to identify friend from foe was the distinctive silhouette of the Marine helmet compared to the pancake-like NVA pith helmet. The ruse of those several corpses rigid from rigor propped about after nightfall like scarecrows in a corn field was a bit macabre, but it worked.

The NVA wasn't ready for another heads-on fight after the blooding they took. Best they could do the following night was launch a few probes to test Marine resolve and keep up the pressure. The first foray occurred about an hour after sunset when a squad-sized NVA element crept up on what it took to be two "foolish Marines" out almost in plain sight on perimeter watch. They were decoys, of course, which the gooks discovered to their detriment when they opened fire.

Marines overwatching the decoys with machine guns and M-16s on auto mowed down the attackers, having seized this advantage over the enemy once he exposed himself.

An hour later, another enemy squad "ambushed" an "OP/LP" at the edge of the woods outside the Marine perimeter. Again, a Marine overwatch was waiting. The situation reminded me of a little ditty composed by 9th Marines operating out of the Da Nang area.

Eighteen gooks in a free-fire zone,
Last one hit goes home alone.
These fucking gooks will never learn. . . .

The gooks did learn, of course. At least they learned caution, even if it took them most of the night and a bunch of casualties before they figured it out.

"Hey, hey, you Hos want to try that again!" Marines taunted. "We need some fresh gook bodies. You keep shooting these up."

Echo and Foxtrot on their little hill and Golf on ours dug in to hold on while pin pushers in the rear reorganized and reoriented rifle companies for a final push on the Wicked Twins. Fresh troops from the 26th Marines arrived at Khe Sanh, choppered in from Phu Bai to provide security assistance to 2/9 at the airfield—or, we supposed, to be available as reinforcements in the event BLT-2/3 got chewed up on 881N. LBJ must have thought the bloodshed worth it—and Marines weren't going to give up on him.

B-52s stalked the sky seeking concentrations of the enemy infiltrating from Laos or crossing the DMZ. The distant thunder of exploding bombs reverberated through the draws and valleys like an ill wind that rattled leaves on trees. Artillery at Khe Sanh, the 105s and 155s, kept up H&I into areas where enemy might congregate. Even bigger guns, the 175s from Leatherneck Square, along with fast movers in the air, took their turns at bombarding the Twin Witches. Ploughed-up red earth at the tops of the two larger cones reflected back sunlight and appeared as though the hills themselves were bleeding.

Surely, to endure all this and keep coming at us, the gooks must have nine lives like cats. Either that or we were fighting ghosts.

Snipers contributed to the war of nerves by taking pot shots at us from the surrounding jungle. We learned to keep our heads down so that they did little damage except to our psyches. We went around constantly pissed off, vowing to rain death and destruction on the sneaky little bastards at the first opportunity.

You gotta get yourself a weapon,
An automatic weapon. . . .
'Cause every night when you're a'sleepin',
Charlie Cong comes a'creepin'
. . . All around.

Gook mortars were worse, but we had more success against them than against snipers. The *Whump! Whump!* of rockets leaving tubes down in the woods pinpointed their location for our 60mm mortar teams to respond in kind. The rest of us utilized the three-second interval between the *Whump! Whump!* of the firing and the *Boom! Boom!* of the explosions to dive deeper into our holes before hell fire rained down from heaven and stomped blossoms of flame back and forth across our little knoll. We jeered back at the gooks whenever our 60mm guys scored.

"Lord, Lord?" Tony beseeched from the bottom of our hole during a particularly heavy bombardment. "Lord, let me make it through all this and I promise I'll stop cussing forever."

The shelling stopped. We looked at each other. "The Lord must have heard you, Tony."

Minutes later: "*Incoming!*"

A shell exploded so near our position that it splattered mud and rock down on top of us.

"Son of a bitch!" Tony erupted. "That one was too fucking close!"

We looked at each other. Tony shrugged.

Since the enemy couldn't be allowed free run in the hills to plan more mischief and move up more troops and guns, Marine combat patrols went out constantly to gather intel and keep the NVA nervous and unsure. Most of the time the gooks avoided direct contact in order to nurse their resources and wait for another opportunity to attack. On our hill redoubts we reinforced bunkers and trenches, cleared fields of fire, and cleaned weapons. We still had problems with the M-16s.

One of the guys decorated his hole with a bouquet of orange fire poppies and golden eardrops, which grew only after intense fires. Gunny Janzen shook his head in amusement, but warned, "Don't get too comfortable. We still have to go up there."

He pointed at 881N, which overlooked our small first step on the way to the summit.

I looked up at the hill, the bitch, and thought, *This is going to be bad. Really* bad. Our guys were dying, more buddies were going to die. Hill and Doc Heath and Schmitz and the others—all gone. Thinking about them only made us feel sorry for ourselves. Thinking about *not* thinking about them while thinking about surviving made us schizophrenic. So, a man compensated with bravura and bullshit and macho bluster. You had to make yourself believe you really were the meanest sonofabitch in the valley.

Dying? Dying was the easy part. Not to let your buddies down while dying was the hard part.

Gene Kilgore struggled with that part. He experienced premonitions of his own death. "I know how it's going to happen. I shut my eyes and I see it in detail."

His thin face appeared pinched and drawn beneath his helmet, accentuated into the haunted look of a concentration camp survivor by the beard he hadn't shaved since 2/3 joined the Hill Fights. We all looked that way by now.

"See," he said, "in this dream we're on patrol and we're going through a draw, just like it was when Hotel and Sergeant Crawford got hit. I actually hear it happen—the shooting and awful screaming. I realize I'm the one doing the screaming. *I'm dying! I'm dying, guys!* I look down and what I see is me lying there dead."

"Oh, man. Come on. . . ." Tony said.

"I'm dead. Just dead. Like Doc Heath and the others."

No matter how we, his buddies, tried to cajole him out of it, he remained convinced he hadn't much longer to live. He even knew what he wanted inscribed on his tombstone: *PFC Gene Kilgore. A US Marine Who Died For His Country.*

"Did you thermite the Starlite first?" Bill Rainey cracked, attempting to lighten the mood. That produced nervous laughter. Even Kilgore smiled.

CHAPTER TWENTY-THREE

Dog Biscuits

DUE TO INFREQUENT RESUPPLY, WE STILL DREW WATER FROM THE scummy shell crater. After a mid-afternoon mortar shelling, I left Tony on watch while I grabbed our canteens—"No leeches this time, Maras"— and scuttled across the top of the explosion-riddled knob to the pond. Magilla, Jacubowski, and Gunny Janzen were at the watering hole on the same errand. Instead of kneeling at the water as usual to fill up, the three stood eyeing the crater with open revulsion. I approached cautiously.

"*Holy*—*!*" That was as far as I got.

We had been drinking from the pond—only to discover now that it served as a grave for dead gooks. Not just one, but *three* of them. What we figured was that an aerial bomb or one of the big 175s from Leatherneck Square must have landed right on top of an NVA fighting position, burying its occupants at the bottom of the crater. Rain came down and filled the depression. After a few days, the corpses produced gases and had now floated to the surface. They were all face down, with their backs humped out of the water and covered in a green-scum crust. Pieces of rotted flesh slewing off the corpses left greasy rings in the algae. Jacubowski retched from the overpowering stench and fled back to his hole with his canteens empty.

"It's all protein," Gunny remarked with tired sarcasm.

Pollution of the pond made resupply more critical than ever and made us almost entirely dependent on helicopters as a lifeline. Chopper pilots had big balls. Hell, their balls had balls. CH-46 Sea Knight medevacs and smaller Sikorsky UH-34s varied their routes to stay unpredictable and avoid enemy antiaircraft fire from guns studded on valley walls along Route 9 that led into the Khe Sanh area. They chopped about and snaked into our stronghold from various approaches to fool the gooks. But there were only so many ways in. Each arriving flight became a magnet for NVA guns. Aircraft arrived with windows shot out, bullet holes punched in cowlings, hydraulic fluid leaking.

Those nervy flight crews won our undying admiration and gratitude. We might go hungry and thirsty, but we knew they'd deliver as soon as they could make it through. You had to believe that if you were wounded, somebody would come get you and fly you to an aid station where you had a chance. Medevacs were our angels out of the sky who made valiant efforts to reach our hills through hell and brimstone and sometimes through zero-degree visibility because of fog and rain and darkness.

A chopper had about thirty seconds to get in, offload supplies and mail, pick up casualties and perhaps outgoing mail, and get back out again before enemy mortar rounds began falling. Coming in one morning with fresh water and supplies, a chopper suddenly appeared running hot with tracers cutting the air all around as it air-skidded onto a tiny makeshift LZ on a 45-degree slope near the pond. While its wheels hovered a few feet off the ground, it dropped the ramp to allow crew to dump off cargo and rush any wounded or dead aboard.

"*Incoming!* Get the hell out!"

"*Go! Go!*"

I ran out, jumped on the outside step to the cockpit and handed the pilot a note home I had scribbled on a B-3 unit lid.

"Will you mail this for me?"

"Don't worry about it. We'll get it out."

My note read: *Mom. Linda. Whatever you hear about what's happening, I want you to know I'm still alive.*

Little things matter under difficult circumstances. The successful arrival of a resupply mission was always cause for a celebration. Gunny tapped me, Tony, Kilgore, and Bill Rainey to meet the next Sea Knight as it galloped in and pulled up hard on one of our crude landing zones. We always had two or three designated LZs so the enemy wouldn't know which one was in play and pre-target it.

The big green bird settled in with a blast of downdraft so loud it demolished rational thought. A tall kid with big ears caught my attention among the helicopter crew kicking out C-rat boxes, jerry cans of water, and cans of ammo and grenades. I did a double take as I recognized Jaggers, the short-timer Colonel Delong left behind on the ship to work Supply. He had survived the deadly ambush that sent 2/3 back to Okinawa to refit and pick up replacements. Pappy didn't think it fitting to send him back into combat after that since he had only weeks remaining on his tour. But here he was, right in the thick of it with only days left in the 'Nam before he shipped back home.

Spotting us, he stood straight inside the body of the chopper and began waving and shouting above the rotor roar: "Hey, guys! It's me. Jaggers."

He jumped out onto the ground to hug his old buddies.

"Vietnam can kiss my ass in two more days!" he shouted through all the noise and bustle. "Two days and I'm outta here. I seen Sergeant Crawford on the ship. I understand you guys have really had it bad. I see every fucking day somebody is dying. I heard Doc Heath got it, and Jim Hill, and—"

"Yeah, but we're killing their asses too," Tony shouted back.

The helicopter crew, in a hurry to get back in the air, shoved supplies out on the ground. Tony, Kilgore, Rainey, and I tossed the boxes and cans into a nearby shell crater to get them out of the line of mortar fire.

"*Incoming!*"

"*Oh, shit!*"

Boom! Boom! Boom! Three shells landed in quick succession, bracketing us. One long, one short, and . . .

Jaggers dived for cover among the offloaded cargo we had transferred into the crater. That was where the third round landed. Hardly enough of him remained to identify. The in-and-out pressure of the explosion popped his face like a balloon. The chopper leapt into the air and left the remains of our old comrade with us. The next medevac would have to take him out.

Afterward, I retrieved Jaggers's brain from the rubble when we policed up his parts. Unabashed tears streamed down my face. Vietnam had popped the ass of another Marine and sent him on his final journey home just two days before he was scheduled to DEROS out.

Following that kind of blow, the men of Golf needed a pick-me-up. But even that came with a certain cruel irony.

Most of the offloaded cargo made it through the explosion relatively intact, although scattered all over the landscape. From among the debris we recovered a large care package sent by some stateside civilian organization to share a little home cheer with the troops. It was addressed generically to *U.S. Marine Corps, Vietnam*, but had somehow found its way to us. Care packages normally contained cookies and cakes and candies and other goodies, along with personal care items like shaving cream, soap, and paperback books.

Gunny delayed opening it until the next morning to allow our grief over Jaggers to subside. An outfit in combat had to hold tough and move on quickly. Otherwise, it fell apart.

Gunny performed the unwrapping honors with agents from each platoon present and anticipating the grand unveiling of our windfall. Cookies and cakes and candy all around. Tony and I represented Weapons Platoon.

Gunny Janzen ripped apart the big cardboard box, it having hardly been damaged at all by the mortar explosion. He flipped open the top and froze. Everyone stared in stunned disbelief. The box contained *dog biscuits*. Along with a note from antiwar protestors in Oceanside, California: *You guys are animals, you might as well eat like animals.*

A disappointed Marine expressed the resentment that all of us felt: "Piss on 'em. And fuck California."

Tony and I tried some of the biscuits. We figured they'd clean our teeth. Not bad—and they in fact did clean our teeth.

"They won't hurt you," Magilla said. "They're probably good for you, but they might make you start barking."

We shared them with the rest of our fellow animals.

CHAPTER TWENTY-FOUR

The FNG

BEFORE THE OLD COMBAT VET SERGEANT CRAWFORD WAS HIT AND medevac'd out, he left us with a dire warning about what to expect fighting in these hills. The Hill Fights, he predicted, would rank alongside epic Korean and World War II battles like Pork Chop Hill and Tarawa. The war in Vietnam, he explained, had been waged in some form or another since World War II, but had heated up out of the Cold War following the 9th Marines' landing at Da Nang. Marines were the first combat troops to arrive; we would probably be the last to leave.

"We may be fighting in this shit hole ten years from now," he said. "We can take these hills, but we won't hold them."

"Then why are we fighting for them?" I asked.

"Because that's what we *do*."

That was what *real men* of his generation did—and, to a lesser extent, perhaps, of my generation. Especially if you were from Oklahoma or Texas or some other rural state and not from San Francisco or Berkeley where long-haired, dope-smoking hippies whimpered and whined and sent dog biscuits in care packages to the battle front. We heeded the call of our country when it needed us. *Uncle Sam Wants You*, and all that. Just like our fathers and grandfathers had done.

Before shipping off to Marine Corps training and then Vietnam, I had rarely traveled out of Oklahoma. Some folks said Oklahoma, Arkansas, Missouri, and surrounding states had barely escaped from the nineteenth century. We were protected from the outside world in many ways, isolated in the center of a nation where people only went if they had a real good reason to go. Like a death in some remote branch of the family or something. Growing up, I knew farm people who didn't have electricity or know how to use a telephone.

Living in Tulsa made me a city kid, but in many ways Tulsans were as provincial as our country bumpkin cousins. I barely knew anything about Vietnam before I enlisted. Certainly I couldn't have found it on a map. My first vague awareness of its existence and America's involvement with it occurred with the Gulf of Tonkin incident. I was a sophomore in high school, too busy with school and parties and girls to pay much attention. After all, Oklahoma was a long way from Vietnam.

President Johnson said dirty Red Communist North Vietnamese attacked one of our destroyers in international waters. The "little yellow bastards" would have to pay for it. The by-God Marines would make them pay.

I graduated from high school at eighteen years old and enlisted in the Marine Corps on a deferred program that allowed me to hang around Tulsa for the rest of the summer with Linda and our school chums before reporting for duty. I knew I was headed for the 'Nam when I enlisted. The recruiter told me so.

Linda protested. "Bobby! Don't do it!"

I brushed her off, but then came home on boot camp leave and married her. I figured she could use my $10,000 federal life insurance payout, even though I felt confident that guys like me never got killed. We came home decorated heroes. Like Audie Murphy, Lee Marvin, and Ed Crawford.

Now, in the hills, I no longer felt that certain about anything. Guys like me *did* get killed. War was nothing like what I expected from watching John Wayne movies. It was filthy and brutal and nasty and you watched your buddies die in random, equal-opportunity combat. No stirring background martial music playing, no electrifying oration about God and dying for Mom's apple pie.

Perhaps my making judgment on the conduct of the war was a bit like a house mouse appraising the human occupants whose scraps he lived off. Nonetheless, it appeared to me from my nineteen-year-old private's perspective that the NVA's General Giap held the master plan for winning the war while we merely reacted. We were lured into Giap's and Uncle Ho's stronghold to die for a worthless piece of real estate that hardly anybody wanted. Into the same hills where the French had met *their* Dien Bien Phu.

Maybe what it all boiled down to was that LBJ had thrown us into the fire and now he didn't know how to pull our chops out and save face at the same time. But what the hell? I was nothing but a common jarhead grunt, part of a colored pin on a battle map, a pawn on the Big Chess Board at the Pentagon and White House.

I cleaned and oiled the Pig to keep my mind occupied. It seemed that waiting to fight, rather than combat itself, might be the toughest part of war. The sun beat down on our hole and was so bright I squinted whenever I looked out into enemy country. Tony stripped off his utility jacket, revealing the "Peggy" tattoo on his upper arm. It caught his eye and brought back memories. I saw it in the way his face collapsed in on him and made him look much older than a kid just beginning his adult life.

He squatted in the dirt on the floor of our "penthouse," his head turned, chin resting on his shoulder, eyes fixated on the tattoo.

So *this*, I pondered, this affable Buddy-Hackett-character-turned-warrior was the "baby killer" we kept hearing about from antiwar protestors back home who mocked us, chanted their senseless ditties, and sent us dog food. Isolated as we were in Vietnam, we still picked up some news from letters, hometown newspapers in the mail, and rumors. None of it made sense. It was like the nation was going hog crazy, what with black people rioting in the cities, students occupying college administration offices, and leftwing radicals bombing police stations and staging at airports to spit on returning soldiers and Marines, sailors, and airmen.

"Ho, Ho, Ho!" they chanted. "Ho Chi Minh's going to win. How many babies have you killed today?"

Sonsofbitches! What did they know shit about anything?

We were dying over here while these spoiled brats remained oblivious to everything except toking a joint and dissing "the Man." Let them get shot at, see their friends die. See what they thought then. Would they still run off to Canada and hide?

"Faster than ever," Tony predicted.

I couldn't seem to shake the sight of the monster mask Vlasek's face became before Tony and I put him on the medevac to die on the way to Charlie Med. I kept seeing what was left of Jaggers's face with his brain knocked out of his skull, leaving one eye and almost nothing else. Grisly images that threatened to haunt me from now on.

I was beginning to understand about previous combat vets who sometimes, right in the middle of a sentence, suddenly went slack. One second they were with you—and then suddenly they were just *gone.* Reliving some horror, recalling old buddies who never made it back.

Frank Sousley, a fun-loving Kentucky hillbilly boy, was the same age as I was now when he died on Iwo Jima. He was one of those depicted in the famous "Raising of the Flag" Iwo Jima memorial. When the War Department sent out the telegram to tell his mother that he was dead, it went to the General Store in the little crossroads of Hilltop. A barefoot boy ran the telegram to his mama's farm. Neighbors living a quarter-mile away heard her screaming all night.

In my mind, I saw Jaggers's mama screaming. And Heath's . . . and Jim Hill's . . . and Vlasek's . . . and Boda's . . . and Carter's . . . and Schmitz's . . . and Roldan's . . . and . . .

"When it's your time," Tony moped, "God's finger comes down out of the sky and squashes you like a bug."

Choppers, when they got through, brought infusions of replacements for our decimated ranks. One of the fresh-faced Newbies whom Gunny assigned to a neighboring position in the perimeter dropped over for a visit. I didn't bother asking his name. He was a down-home, aww-shucks kind of FNG who, like the new kid in a preppie high school, just wanted to fit in with the cool crowd and be accepted. Difference was you could take a new kid in school under your wing, become friends, and not worry about his getting knocked off tomorrow or the next.

This Cherry hunkered down with us. Tony ignored him. I continued cleaning the Pig. I didn't intend to be mean, to be cruel. It was just that we had lost friends KIA out here in these hills and weren't eager to make new ones to lose.

"Whaddya want?" I finally asked.

"N-nothing. I mean—"

We were of approximately the same age, but I felt years older than the fresh-faced FNG I had been not so many days ago when BLT-2/3 landed at Red Beach. Older, wiser, more wary while growing a crust around my soul to protect it.

"I don't want nothing," the Cherry repeated, ready to flee.

"Look, you're new so you don't know yet," I counseled. "This is how it is: Do your job and don't expect to make friends. We're your brothers, but we don't want to be your friends. Believe me, kid, it hurts too much. Do you understand?"

I felt like a bully for telling him the truth.

The poor little fucker looked scared to death and about to cry. He nodded once, quickly, and scrambled away.

"Do you think you might have been too hard-ass on him?" Tony said.

What did I know? I was a lowly grunt in a mouse's hole. For days now—or had it been weeks, years?—we had fought to wrest these hills from the NVA—and the NVA refused to let go. It was like Tony contemplating his "Peggy" tattoo. Torturing himself. Likewise refusing to let go.

He put his jacket back on to hide the tattoo. "Piss on her," he said.

He looked at me. "Maras, don't you dare get yourself wasted."

We stood side by side in our hole and gazed out over the enemy's kingdom of monsters, death, and destruction.

Chapter Twenty-Five

The POWs

Obnoxious odors corrupted the air on our hill knob. They clung to our utilities and spoke of dead gooks in the clutter left behind after prep fire demolished the enemy's bunkers and fighting holes. It occurred to me, more house mouse philosophy, that while we continued to bombard the tops of 881N and 881S, there was nobody up there. Like with this knob, the gooks pulled out of the kitchen when it got too hot.

Then they returned to harass, ambush, mortar, and fuck with us, knocking us off a few at a time. A war of . . . What was the word? *Attrition*. That was their strategy. To take these hills was only bait to lure us out here in *their* neighborhood where we were vulnerable. All the fighting for the Wicked Sisters was not going to be on top of the hills. It was taking place down here on the ridges and lesser hills and in the jungled valleys.

I bounced my theory off Tony and PFC Taylor. Tony shrugged.

"What difference does it make whether we die down here or up there?" Taylor challenged.

"And a good Vietnam morning to you too, Sunshine. I think I'll go take a piss on that note."

"Piss on *her*," Tony suggested, subconsciously indicating the "Peggy" tattoo he now kept concealed beneath his jacket.

I retreated into the perimeter where little mounds of dirt marked where guys dug little holes for their shit and covered them back up. I took a leak on the ground, not bothering to dig a cat hole. Dead gook smell masked any odors of urine. Besides, how much longer were we going to be here anyhow? It wasn't like we were homesteading waiting for spring to put in a crop.

None of us, not even officers and sergeants, showed any inclination to search for dead NVA and bury them proper. If by *proper* we meant dumping corpses in an unused trench assholes to belly buttons and pushing earth over them. We could live with them on the knob as long as they were dead.

Another boring, uneventful day passed. *Uneventful* described a day when we took only a few mortar and sniper rounds. Darkness slowly crept in, bringing with it the greater terror of the night when Charlie went a'sneakin' and a'peekin'. Parents back home told their kids, "Kids, there's nothing out there in the dark to hurt you."

They had never been to Vietnam.

In the dusk just before the sun disappeared for the night, hopefully not forever, Tony and I in position with the Pig stared into the gathering gloom, prepared to loose the M-60 on tonight's probers and no-gooders.

Movement, although slight, attracted my attention. A shifting of shadows about thirty meters out front and outside the perimeter, from a mound of broken earth that remained from a collapsed gook bunker. I nudged Tony with my elbow and nodded at it. He nodded back that he saw it.

While we watched, mesmerized, rubble gave way and an open hand slowly emerged, as though of a ghoul rising from a grave. Definitely a Twilight Zone moment. Everything except the eerie background score.

Spooked, Tony and I fixated on the hand as it seemed to sniff its surroundings, twisting in various directions like a submarine periscope. Instinctively, as though fearing it really *could* see us, we ducked down so that only our startled eyes showed between the top of our hole and our helmets.

A second hand appeared, mate to the first. My trigger finger found the Pig's sweet spot, but I held fire. Instead, fascinated, we watched as slowly, very slowly, the hands lengthened into arms, followed by a thatch of black hair and dark, frightened eyes staring directly at me.

"*Chieu Hoi?*" the head pleaded. *Chieu Hoi* stood for "open arms," which was how we were supposed to greet defectors.

"I think he wants to give up," Tony whispered.

Conflicting thoughts raced through my head: Jaggers's brain, Lieutenant Sauer after gooks carved him up with the banana knife. . . . Communist fanatics who gave no quarter but now, like with this guy, apparently expected quarter. Tony sensed my mood. He touched my arm. It was quivering with tension.

"Five days R&R," Tony reminded me softly.

I held fire as the guy cautiously clambered from his den, hands high above his head, still looking directly at me, into my eyes. Creating a jolt of one human being recognizing another.

"*Chieu Hoi?*"

To our surprise, two more gooks followed the first out of the ground, their hands likewise reaching for the night's first stars. They must have been buried all this time inside what was left of their bunker. Maybe even watching us through air holes they had scrabbled out, waiting for their comrades to return, overrun the knob, and rescue them. Hunger and thirst must be finally driving them out.

Making up my mind—after all, I couldn't just *murder* them, no matter what they might have done—I motioned for them to approach. I kept the Pig ready for action in case this was some kind of evil gook trick.

These were the first *live* NVA I had encountered up this close. Gray-green uniforms bagged on their slight frames. They were bare-headed, slack-faced from fright, with nervous eyes and trembling lips. What astonished me was the realization that these guys were actual human beings rather than apparitions in the night, evil reincarnate, zombies capable of atrocities so horrible as to defy imagination.

They appeared so weak from malnourishment that their feet shuffled through the red dirt like those of very old men. One appeared injured. He cradled an arm caked in dried blood against his chest. He stumbled and almost fell. His comrades caught him.

"*Chieu Hoi?* Please?"

"They don't look like much, do they?" Tony whispered.

What sprung to mind was the thought that they weren't so very different from us. They were very young. Back somewhere they had mamas and daddies and perhaps wives and children. They worked their rice fields or whatever, trudged home at dusk to eat their meager meals in grass hooches, bedded down with their women, laughed with their children. They probably didn't want to be out here anymore than we did.

Communism. That was the demon that drove them, lashing them with a promised utopia if they went out and killed capitalists. Not for God, since commies didn't believe in God, but for Uncle Ho and Karl Marx. *Utopia? Right!* They continued to live in grass huts and eat fish heads and rice while they waited for a promised paradise that never came.

"I feel sorry for the little bastards," I admitted when some of the other guys came over to take a look for themselves and Captain Sheehan and Lieutenant Mac took the prisoners off our hands.

"Maras, Leyba. You guys did good."

"The Colonel promised five days in-country R&R for prisoners," I noted. "There's three of them. One is mine, one is Tony's, and the third belongs to Private First Class Taylor. Now where's our R&R, sir?"

"You'll get it," Captain Sheehan assured us. "But nobody leaves until these hills are secure."

"Or until we're all dead," Taylor responded with sarcastic false cheer.

CHAPTER TWENTY-SIX

Pencil Dicks

ECHO COMPANY, OVER ON ITS OWN LITTLE HILL ACROSS THE VALLEY, grew uneasy about its isolated circumstances. During the major NVA attack on its people, gooks had run wild inside the perimeter, killing twenty-six Marines. Although reinforced by Foxtrot, the Marine leadership on the hill was concerned about another enemy buildup and a second attack. Sergeant James Marden was dispatched with a patrol to sweep the northeastern slope of 881N to determine the presence and strength of enemy in the area.

Due to the distinct possibility of enemy contact, Echo's command issued an unusual order, directing Marden to recon the hill by fire rather than by foot, which might trigger a deadly ambush. Marines almost never used such an incautious tactic. But the sergeant shrugged his objections aside and placed his patrol on line to ascend the slope.

Whenever the patrol approached any unusual feature, such as a clearing with thick undergrowth on the other side, Marden gave the order to fire at will. Rifles crackled and spat flames as the line marched against any suspicious terrain feature.

Shortly after these maneuvers commenced, every single M-16 in the patrol malfunctioned at almost the same time. It could have been a disaster of unprecedented proportion had the NVA known what was going on and had been listening when our radio traffic went ape shit. Guys were justifiably pissed off.

"They send us out here with these pieces of shit when they *know* they're junk! Why don't they just issue us clubs and bows and arrows and get it over with?"

Marden requested machine guns, mortars, and M-79 grenade launchers prep his front to cover his men while they cleared their weapons. It was a jumpy bunch of Marines who continued the patrol, especially when they came upon enemy sign. NVA bunkers and spider holes festooned the vicinity while wooden firing platforms for mortar tubes dotted the reverse side of a nearby ridge. Clearly NVA were still in the area, watching us and preparing for the next confrontation.

Miraculously, Marden and his men made it back safely to Echo's lines with coordinates of their discoveries. Artillery raked the area to destroy enemy construction.

On Golf's hill, I patted the stock of my trusty M-60 when news of the mass M-16 jam dribbled out onto the line. "I think I'll call her Ol' Faithful from now on," I decided.

"*Her* and *faithful* never go in the same sentence," Tony said. Buddy Hackett had never been moody like this before the Dear John letter.

That same afternoon, an escort from Colonel Delong brought out a CBS-TV News crew by helicopter to film the war. I wasn't impressed. Both were pencil dicks, one tall and wasted, the other a shorter version. A jittery duo with their pressed-together lips and nervous eyes that bounced around in their heads like balls in a pinball machine. A Marine dropped a piece of rusted tin he was using to floor the bottom of his hole against standing in the mud. Both "combat correspondents" flung themselves to the ground where they lay shivering and shaking like a pair of Chicken Littles waiting for the sky to fall on them.

Gunny Janzen watched them. "Disgusting," he scoffed. "Damned disgusting."

The French journalist Catherine had had more balls than the both of these clowns put together. Maybe CBS-TV ought to send their crews to her in Paris for training.

Officers and NCOs passed among the troops ahead of interviews by the Pencil Dicks. "Don't say a word to the press about our M-16s, not a word. That's an order."

Tony opined the order sounded like a political CYA, Cover-Your-Ass. Maybe from McNamara's Defense Department, or even the White House. Everyone knew you couldn't trust politicians. They'd feed Marines to Ho Chi Minh if necessary to cover their own dirty butts.

I overheard the Pencil Dicks debating whether they ought to chance a visit to Echo Company while they were already here out in the field. I could tell both wanted to be back at Khe Sanh before darkness fell. They must have known the NVA didn't much care for fighting in the sunshine. We had taught them the inherent risk of fucking with Americans when our formidable artillery and aircraft could be marshalled.

"Is it safe?" the Pencil Dicks asked Gunny Janzen.

"Gentlemen, you're in a war zone. People shoot each other in war zones."

The Pencil Dicks were nothing like Catherine. They opted to expose some footage of us in our holes and then go back.

"What we should have done," I said, "is tell them how fucked-up our M-16s are—and then send 'em out on a patrol."

A warning order came down from those on high who pushed around our colored pins. Companies of BLT-2/3 should prepare to assault 881N upon receipt of further instructions. It was about time. That set off a flurry of activity as men cleaned weapons, gathered ammo, sharpened knives, prepared their rucks, and wrote last letters home. I scribbled a note to Linda to let her know what was happening, but asked her not to worry Mom and Dad with the details. Tony took out a note pad and looked at it for a long time before he folded it again and stuck it back in his pocket. Gunny came around gathering mail to send out on the next chopper.

"Maras?" Tony said. "Whatever happens, promise you won't leave me out there?"

"Fuckin' A. We're buddies. But what's with you, man? You're sounding like Kilgore. You having premonitions too? I know you're not having bad dreams because we're not getting any sleep."

"Don't run it in the ground, Maras. I'm just saying, don't leave me."

"You on your period or something?"

"Why shouldn't I be? I think my leg might be infected. What about your arm?"

I flexed my elbow for him. It still twinged a little from where the shrapnel cut me. Otherwise, good to go.

"Better talk to Magilla," I advised, "and get some more pills and salve for your leg."

"That's not it, Maras. I think I want to go home."

I nodded in understanding. "We'll all go home when this is over," I said. "Twenty years from now, we'll be like the old World War II vets sitting around the VFW sucking suds and telling each other war stories about the Hill Fights."

"You know something, Maras? When I get home, I want to get dementia or Alzheimer's or whatever it's called and forget all about this shit."

I admitted he had a point.

CHAPTER TWENTY-SEVEN

America's Living Rooms

"WE ARE NOT, REPEAT *NOT*, GOING TO BE DEFEATED AT KHE SANH," General William Westmoreland, overall commander of troops in Vietnam, was soon to declare as the base itself came under siege. "I will tolerate no talking or even thinking to the contrary."

I was no military strategic expert. Hell, I was just a nineteen-year-old kid fresh out of high school and thrust into events that would impact American society for years to come. But I had a brain and I had a personal stake out here in the hills that almost none of our critics back on the home front could claim. There was one damned big difference between getting shot at and watching your buddies die and marching your fat ass through the streets carrying antiwar signs and spitting on our guys in uniform when we came home. One thing I swore: when I got off that Freedom Bird in the U.S. of A., the first sonofabitch who spat on me or called me a "baby killer" was going to get knuckles in his chops and have trouble spitting on the next GI.

Like most Marines, I took *Semper Fidelis* to heart. Always faithful to God, country, Mom's apple pie, and each other. Still, General Westmoreland or not, the little house mouse I channeled refused to stay quiet. It appeared to me that events in both Vietnam and the United States were conspiring against the general. And against us.

The way I saw it, four critical factors were arrayed against us, the first one right here in Vietnam.

Marines landed at Da Nang two years and one month ago full of piss and vinegar. We stormed ashore confident of kicking communist butt in a few short months and then going back home to ticker-tape parades and flags waving. Marines secured the Da Nang sector, followed by the first big American drive in August 1965 that crippled a Viet Cong regiment.

Two months later, a US Army division crushed three NVA regiments in the densely jungled Ia Drang Valley near Pleiku and prevented communists from sweeping out of the Central Highlands down to the populated coasts. This action, which cost the North Vietnamese two thousand casualties against American losses of three hundred, demonstrated the effectiveness of using helicopters in mobile warfare. Air Cavalry.

Things started getting bogged down fairly quickly after that. Vietnam was an entirely new kind of war for US troops, posing a challenge unlike any America had faced before. Fighting on *their* ground always gave the enemy an advantage. They got to call the shots.

There was also the matter of the enemy being *communists* with the communist disdain for human life. After all, Comrade Stalin deliberately starved to death over ten million of his own Soviet citizens during the Great Famine in the 1930s just to make a point and bring the peasant kulaks to heel. Commies seemed always willing to sacrifice two thousand troops in order to kill three hundred Americans, as at Ia Drang.

Realizing they would surely lose if they fought on American terms, the North Vietnamese chose to create their own conditions. While Americans possessed superior firepower and mobility, the Vietnamese were light and nimble. Fighting them was like a heavyweight boxer in a ring with a quick lightweight who ran circles around the big guy while bleeding him to death with a million cuts. The System Analysis Office at McNamara's Defense Department revealed how communist forces controlled the pace of action, as well as the size and intensity of combat engagements.

U.S. forces entering a remote area were anything but secretive about it, our insertions advertised by massive helicopter movements and artillery and aircraft prep fires that provided the enemy plenty of time to plan and react. Ready to move at a moment's notice, the enemy evaluated the situation and decided to fight only if they fancied their chances. Otherwise, as fast and flitting as shadows or ghosts, they split into smaller units to regroup later at a more opportune time.

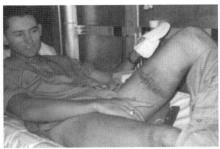

Bob Maras (left) and Gene Kilgore in the only known photo of Kilgore actually smiling while in uniform. He had a premonition that he would die in combat—which later came true.
ROBERT MARAS COLLECTION

Bob Maras in sick bay aboard USS *Princeton* with wound sustained along the DMZ a week after the Hill Fights ended.
COURTESY OF TONY LEYBA

Bob Maras (left) and Sergeant Ed Crawford at a reunion thirty-five years after the Hill Fights at Khe Sanh. COURTESY OF KATHY CRAWFORD

Larger-than-life bronze of three warriors of the Vietnam War who seem to be guarding and overlooking "The Wall" that lists the names of more than 58,000 servicemen who died in combat.
CHARLES SASSER COLLECTION

Bob Maras (left) and R. J. Todd, whose body remains missing in action. COURTESY OF TONY LEYBA

Bob Maras (right) and Private Bill Rainey aboard CH-46 helicopter after being picked up after Red Beach. ROBERT MARAS COLLECTION

BLT 2/3 in force on Red Beach in Vietnam.
ROBERT MARAS COLLECTION

Private Bill Rainey in a Vietnamese village after the Red Beach landing prior to BLT 2/3's sudden withdrawal and insertion into Khe Sanh. ROBERT MARAS COLLECTION

Marine movement to contact during the Hill Fights. UNITED STATES DEFENSE DEPART-
MENT

A Marine "medevac" helicopter arrives to evacuate the wounded and dead during
the Hill Fights. UNITED STATES DEFENSE DEPARTMENT

Bob Maras with M-60 machine gun,
"the Pig," during the Hill Fights at Khe
Sanh. ROBERT MARAS COLLECTION

This dramatic photo shows Golf Company corpsman Vernon "Magilla Gorilla" Wike treating LCPL William Roldan while under fire. Roldan died shortly after this photo was taken. COURTESY OF CATHERINE LEROY

Tony Leyba (left), Maras's AG on the machine gun and close buddy, with an unidentified member of Golf Company who had just been wounded. ROBERT MARAS COLLECTION

Marines of Bravo Company 1/9 carry their dead down from Hill 861 after first contact with NVA that led to "the Hill Fights" at Khe Sanh. USMC

Lieutenant Andrew "Mac" McFarlane, platoon leader of 3rd Platoon, Golf Company, who referred to himself as the "oldest second lieutenant" in the Marine Corps. USMC

Golf Company Gunnery Sergeant William Janzen (center) with Golf Company commander Captain James Sheehan (right) aboard ship on their way to Vietnam. ROBERT MARAS COLLECTION

Golf Company 2/3 Marines prepare to assault ridge knob below Hill 861. Bob Maras is on the right, as indicated by the arrow. ROBERT MARAS COLLECTION

Bob Maras test fires a 3.5 rocket launcher aboard the USS *Ogden* prior to insertion into Vietnam combat. COURTESY OF TONY LEYBA

Bob Maras aboard USS *Ogden* en route from Okinawa to Vietnam.
ROBERT MARAS COLLECTION

B-52 bombers with their "Arc Light" raids against North Vietnamese Army forces helped prevent another Dien Bien Phu at Khe Sanh. UNITED STATES DEFENSE DEPARTMENT

Official USMC photo of Bob Maras.
USMC

Bob Maras packing gear for deployment from Okinawa to Vietnam in 1967. COURTESY OF TONY LEYBA

Bob Maras (right) and Private Bill Rainey aboard the USS *Ogden* en route to Vietnam.
COURTESY OF TONY LEYBA

USS *Princeton* (LPH), a member of a three-ship convoy that transported BLT 2/3 to action in Vietnam. UNITED STATES NAVY

USS *Ogden* (LPD) underway for Vietnam as part of a three-ship convoy transporting BLT 2/3. This was the ship that Maras called home during the voyage. UNITED STATES NAVY

The VC and NVA, as we discovered in the Hill Fights, initiated more than 90 percent of all firefights. Even when we went looking for the NVA, it was *they* who invariably found *us*. Rarely were they ever taken by surprise.

The classic NVA pattern of battle waited until one of our platoons or companies pushed out from its FOB—Forward Operating Base. Somewhere out there in gook land the unit walked into a carefully prepared ambush, as Hotel Company had done in the draw. The first sign of the enemy came from a hail of machine gun, rifle, mortar, and artillery fire.

Captain Sheehan called it "damned frustrating." So why did we keep doing the same thing over and over expecting different results?

The second factor that lined up against the war and, by extension, against those of us fighting it was the national media in America. Vietnam was becoming the most-reported conflict in the history of warfare. Reporters were already on the beach popping camera flashbulbs and shouting questions when the 9th Marines sloshed ashore at Da Nang. Since then, hundreds of news people from nations around the globe were swarming to this little shit hole of a country, most of them critical of our involvement. Talking TV heads and pundits of every stripe, print or otherwise, were starting to chatter about "winning all the battles but losing the war."

Walter Cronkite, the "most trusted man in America," brought TV images of blood, gore, and brutality to America's living rooms every evening. Mothers recognized sons being slaughtered a world away. People in the United States, from President Johnson on down, seemed obsessed with Khe Sanh and were helping turn it into one of the most headlined and controversial battles of the war, what with every commentator with a mike comparing it to Dien Bien Phu. Letters we received from home—when the mail got through—dripped with anxiety. *Are you okay? We're praying for you. Oh, God! Let it end!*

We responded in a general way to ease their worries, like when I replied to Mom and Linda: *I'm still alive and fine.* I hadn't told them about my having been wounded.

Nothing beat this kind of mass exposure to turn the stomach and change hearts and minds.

The third factor involved the *youth*, not only in the United States but also in Europe, and the growing number of antiwar organizations. Out in these bloody hills without TV and Walter Cronkite, we still received news about the home front via mail and newspapers from our families and friends. I suppose people thought we wanted to know what was happening—but hearing about it while we were being shot at only served to increase our angst. It seemed the nation and the world was unraveling around our ears and abandoning us. The dog biscuit care package said everything about what they thought of us.

While the 9th Marines were getting mauled on Hill 861 before BLT 2/3 arrived for the fight, a group of US Quakers sailed a yacht into Haiphong Harbor loaded with thousands of dollars' worth of medical aid for North Vietnam. Marines of Echo Company on their hill below 881N were fighting for their lives at the same time British philosopher Bertrand Russell conducted a mock war crimes tribunal in Stockholm to condemn the United States for atrocities its troops were allegedly committing in Vietnam. In New York and San Francisco, antiwar protests drew as many as two hundred thousand marchers.

"Our *youth*, our young people, are trying to tell us something." That was the chatter, the rallying cry for protesters and peaceniks. Hell, the majority of grunts in these Vietnam hills were *youth*. The "baby killer" branch. No one was listening to what *we* thought or felt, especially not the press that came out to watch and film us dying. I kept thinking we served as mere props for agitators back home, proof of war crimes and imperialism and all that.

The "counterculture," the "hep generation" and their protests were *in* this year of 1967 while many of *us* were *in* Vietnam. We fought for our lives while "flower children" with their two-finger peace signs—I had a finger for them—responded to Harvard professor and LSD champion Timothy Leary in a "youth revolution" to "turn on, tune in, and drop out." Hallucinogenic drugs and free love, flower power, and peace. Long hair, beads, psychedelic love vans, idleness, pot, and dirty bare feet. Draft card burners and draft dodgers, hippies and pampered Columbia students.

They rejected all the values I had been brought up on. Time-honored values like honesty and decency, patriotism and love of country, courage and freedom. None of what was happening outside made sense viewed from a muddy red dirt hole on a remote hilltop in Vietnam surrounded by a vicious enemy that wanted to kill us, cut off our heads, stuff our dicks in our dead mouths, and conquer the world for communism. No matter what, I refused to believe efforts to stop communism and free people from its oppressive clutches were unjust.

Politics presented the fourth factor. Politicians were beginning to respond to and cave in to the other three factors. Secretary of Defense Robert McNamara, who had been a staunch advocate of the war after the Gulf of Tonkin incident, gradually became disillusioned until by the time of Khe Sanh he was recommending the United States cut back its efforts against the communist encroachment into South Vietnam and pursue diplomatic measures.

For all his determination to triumph at Khe Sanh, President Johnson nonetheless extended diplomatic feelers to Ho Chi Minh. Secretary of State Dean Rusk revealed that North Vietnam had so far turned down at least twenty-eight US proposals for peace talks, a stand bolstered no doubt by Moscow and Peking stepping in to ship war supplies and matériel to Hanoi, making the war a proxy war for the forces of communism. Commies thought they were going to win. They did not negotiate. Communism was "the wave of the future." Ask any peacenik.

Former Eisenhower vice president Richard Nixon warned, "This apparent division at home is prolonging the war." At the same time he considered campaigning for the presidency on a platform of ending the war and "bringing our boys home."

General Westmoreland seemed to be the only one who had not lost his resolve. On 28 April 1967 with the Hill Fights still raging, he addressed Congress to declare that the United States would "prevail in Vietnam over the communist aggressors with the resolve, confidence, patience, determination, and support of the American people."

He suggested protest marchers and antiwar activity gave "the enemy hope that he can win politically that which he cannot accomplish militarily."

His remarks incited further protests from the usual cast of characters.

I wasn't old enough to vote, but I was old enough to go to war. What I had experienced of war in less than a month in-country had made me yearn for peace. I ached to go home and see my Mom and Dad, sister and brother, and be with Linda. Go out to Mickey D's for a hamburger, attend a movie, take a walk without fear of a mortar shell landing on my head, run with my old high school buds, engage in all those normal activities of young people who, unlike me now, thought they would live forever.

But at the same time I was a by-God Marine on a tough but noble calling. It was a dirty job, taking these hills, but somebody had to do it. Marines did not run away from hardship and danger with our tails tucked between our legs. *Semper Fi*, damnit! *Semper Fi!*

CHAPTER TWENTY-EIGHT

The Fall of 881S

"How many days since we left the graveyard?" Tony asked, referring to the Buddhist cemetery where we bivouacked after going ashore at Red Beach. It was the place, as Tony liked to say, where Dracula dwelled.

I gave it some thought. "Say, uh, about three years, minus a day or so?" At least it felt that long.

We seemed to live in a nightmare that went on and on with no distinction between yesterday and tomorrow, between Monday and Sunday.

"But it's still 1967, right?"

I shrugged. "I guess it is if we're moving out soon. We have our warning order."

Together we glanced upward at the Evil Twin, 881N. Tony shuddered. I felt the same chill run up my spine.

Back at the Pentagon, or IV Corps headquarters, or wherever such decisions were made, higher-higher must have been frustrated at how slowly our colored pins crept about on the Khe Sanh map. This was becoming more like the static trench warfare of World War I in France. Doughboys holding down their section of a trench, peering out over No Man's Land and wondering what horror came next. Not like World War II when colored pins made great leaps all over the globe. From North Africa to Italy, Britain to France, China to the Philippines, island to island in the Pacific—I could almost see ol' Texas hick LBJ getting up each morning in the White House, yawning, farting, scratching himself, twisting his beagle's ears, and taking a look at his Vietnam map and swearing when he saw the pins hadn't moved overnight.

Down at a grunt's pay grade, of course, we weren't privy to the president's "Big Picture." I ribbed Tony that, since he was my *assistant* gunner, I was his superior while he was the man at the very bottom of the pecking order. There was him, then me, then on up in the ascending chain of command through squad, platoon, company, battalion, regiment, division, troop command, Marine Corps Command, General Westmoreland, Joint Chiefs of Staff, Defense Department, Commander-in-Chief President Johnson—and then *God*.

I wondered if God had a map of the universe with colored pins on it.

Out here in the bush and the hills, things were a lot more immediate and personal than they were for the at-home brass moving pins on a map in the White House Situation Room for the president. Our tiny slice of the "Big Picture" played out in real life. Such was the battlefield concentrated as it was around the three hills—861, 881N, 881S—that whenever something happened over *there* on one hill or ridge, we over *here* became spectators. Not that we actually witnessed the details of individual maneuvering in the bush between Marines and enemy, although we occasionally glimpsed a group of unidentifiable stick figures darting to and fro. None of the blood and gore, just the fear and dread that we might be next. The illusion that we were sent over here like cavalry to the rescue to kick ass and go home had quickly faded.

We knew something big was up when our neighboring Twin, 881S, erupted like a volcano as Tony and I were taking our "Good morning, Vietnam!" piss. It seemed every howitzer at Khe Sanh, backed up by even bigger guns from Leatherneck Square, opened up at the same time to hurl steel across the sky. I almost jumped out of my skin. Damn! Why hadn't somebody warned us?

Tony, who wasn't through with business, wet all over himself in his haste to get back to our rat hole.

Exploding shells blotted out the morning patina of sky with colors even more vivid. Black smoke boiled into the sky. The bombardment continued for a full fifteen minutes before it lifted and a flight of jets reported overhead to carry out a second phase. The high-pitched screaming thunder of diving fighter-bombers culminated in a deep series of *Boom! Boom! Boom!* as 250- and 500-pound bombs went off. Napalm seared 881S with flames that appeared as a distant forest fire.

Crispy critters in the making.

I remembered as a kid being taken to a Fourth of July celebration that featured a flyover in formation by the US Air Force. The thunder of the jets and the glinting of their wings in the sunshine sent thrills through my bones, rattling them. I experienced that same sensation now, only magnified by this delivery of all the power in the universe. My bones weren't rattling; they seemed shattered into corn meal.

Only a few days before, Mike and Kilo Companies of 3/9 had been beaten off 881S while suffering significant casualties. Apparently, they and whichever other units were over there with them were going to take another shot at it, leaving 881N as an encore performance for the 2/3. Right now, Echo, Foxtrot, and Golf 2/3 weren't directly involved, but we nonetheless took sympathetic comfort with 3/9 in the bombardment. Each NVA destroyed by artillery and bombs meant one less enemy soldier for Marines to fight and kill going back up that damnable hill.

Not that the prep would kill all of them, even if the NVA were up there at Ground Zero, which I had begun to doubt. I kept hearing Sergeant Crawford's forewarning when the companies of BLT 2/3 landed on the airstrip of Khe Sanh that fateful whatever-day-it-was. Hill 861 absorbed this same beating while we Newbies watched, awe-stricken. Somebody remarked how there wouldn't be any gooks left. "That's what we thought at Iwo Jima," Big Ed had said.

A door seemed to slam when the flyboys packed their ditty bags and went home, followed by a deathly silence over the hills, ridges, and valleys. We field Marines of 2/3 waited expectantly on our toehold knobs below 881N while whatever elements of 3rd Battalion of the 9th led by Mike and Kilo jumped off in another attempt to wrest 881S from the enemy.

I felt guilty for even entertaining the thought—but, nonetheless, I had to admit some comfort in knowing that as long as the gooks were busy on 881S they would have no time or inclination to fuck with us. That meant a free day in the sun.

For some reason, I reflected back on the three gooks who surrendered to Tony and me when they emerged hands in the air from out of their destroyed bunker. They had dirt underneath their fingernails from clawing air holes through which to breathe. For all the NVA's fearsome reputation, these guys, incredibly filthy and reeking of body odor and decaying flesh, were frightened and homesick and, like us, would much rather have been home sipping brew and chasing women.

My guys over at 881S, my Marines, were preparing to go into battle against our prisoners' comrades. They would kill and be killed—*I* would kill and perhaps be killed when the time came—but somehow after seeing and recognizing the common humanity the prisoners and I shared I no longer felt the same fear and hatred toward them.

This one Vietnamese after he and his buddies surrendered squatted on the ground while Tony kept them covered with his M-16 and we waited for Captain Sheehan to come. He met my eyes with gratitude revealed in them.

"Thank you," he said in broken English. "Thank you . . . for not shoot. I remember . . . always."

I had nothing against these guys as individuals; they had nothing against me personally. All of them couldn't be savages who cut off heads and dicks. We were here to fight for the rights of the South Vietnamese to live free of communism. Uncle Ho sent his soldiers to force communism upon them. That was the black and white of it, but war wasn't always all black and white. As individuals, had we the choice, both sides would pull up and go home to our families.

"Maras, you can't change things," Tony advised. "You just live with it."

Nothing seemed to happen over at 881S for several hours after the Marine battle companies formed and started their approach through the jungle. With mounting tension, our eyes locked on the *other* hill; we below 881N waited for something to happen that might indicate how we in turn would fare when orders came for us to attack and take our objective.

"What are they *doing* over there?" Tony worried impatiently.

"Our time will come," I replied.

"You know how to lift a guy's mood, you know that, Maras?"

"Tell it to the chaplain."

"Can't. He went home. Too much sinning going on. Maras, if you hadn't been such a Boy Scout, we could have taken our Purple Hearts and been home too."

Distant explosions ended the conversation and jerked our attention back to 881S. Neither of us felt like talking after that. We simply waited quietly. It was a stupid conversation anyhow, fueled by anxiety and the need for human contact and companionship.

Mike Company's lead platoons reached the lower western edge of the hill and started up. The hill steepened and was covered with tall grass and thick brush. Fires crackled here and there from the recent prep. Large areas of the forest had been scorched black down to the ground.

The rest of the assault force maneuvered into position on Mike's flank. The sudden chatter of rifle and machine gun exchanges initiated the fight. Hostile mortar rounds fell on attacking Marines. Snipers in trees and gooks in camouflaged spider holes and bushes unleashed hell. NVA infantry attempted to break through in an effort to trap Americans in a killing box.

From our distant observation it was difficult to tell which side was winning and which losing. We saw little other than grenade and mortar smoke puffing up in the brush. Sounds of the battle provided only marginal information—the distinctive deep-throated banging of enemy AK-47s, the tinny Mattie Mattel rattle of M-16s, the ripped-cloth bursts of machine guns, both theirs and ours, opposing tracers in streams and waves, the low-decibel crashing of mortar rounds.

Huey UH-1E gunships joined the fight, streaking in like bumblebees to sting enemy positions with rocket and machine gun fire. Artillery from both sides hung fire as the two sides mingled in the forest and grasses to claw at each other's throats.

It went on and on like that—but then the fighting dwindled off. None of us could believe it. It appeared the NVA had made a wise choice and relinquished the field of battle. At least temporarily. No last-ditch stand at the Alamo for this crowd. It was like Sun Tzu in *The Art of War* recommended: Run today in order to fight tomorrow.

Word from our CP and commo shed soon circulated that, after only ninety minutes, 3/9 had reached the crest of 881S. Goal and touchdown! I felt vindicated in my cautious prediction that the NVA would not stand and fight at the top.

Days of bombardment had left the hill denuded. Virtually no tree stood intact. What remained was a shattered moonscape of craters, splintered timber scorched by napalm, torn earth, grass burned down to black stubble. Not a single live NVA soldier was found when Marines burst free of the lower forest onto the peak. Gooks seemed to have deserted their tunnels, trenches, and bunkers and mysteriously vanished. Like ghosts blending into the ether.

A familiar overpowering stench poisoned the air and made conquerors retch onto the ruined earth. The gook dead were not there. Left behind instead were the remains of Marines missing from previous encounters. They had apparently been dragged to the top of the hill and put on display as a message to the rest of us. One sergeant was left spread-eagled on a dirt bunker roof with his penis chopped off and stuffed in his mouth. Others were horribly mangled and then charred by explosives and napalm our prep fires had dumped on the hill. Pieces of them had to be scooped onto ponchos with E-tools to be ready for evacuation.

I was wrong about these people being human, *wrong!* They were savages, animals that deserved annihilating.

The 3/9 had seized their hill first ahead of us, but at a cost attested to by body bags that subsequently lined the strip of airfield below at the Khe Sanh Combat Base. Marines of 3/9 walked up 881S and took it. Now it was our turn against 881N. Did I dare assume the NVA would likewise abandon it at the end—or would they make their stand on 881N and demand the extraction of even more Marine blood?

CHAPTER TWENTY-NINE

Show Time

SERGEANT CRAWFORD WAS FROM PENNSYLVANIA. WHEN HE AND I MET during Vietnam up-training at Camp Schwab on Okinawa, I asked him if he had heard of Sally Star. Aunt Sally, my Mom's sister, was locally famous in Philadelphia for her TV show for kids.

"Oh, my God, yes!" he said. "My kids love her and want to be on her show."

I wrote my aunt and asked her to give Ed's wife a call. She invited Ed's children on her show and that sealed the friendship between Sergeant Crawford and me. Both of us would like to have seen the program. We decided to get together after Vietnam for a replay of it when we returned home. There was never any discussion of *if* we returned home.

I had made inquiries as to Big Ed's condition after his wounding in the draw. The only thing I learned for sure was that he was expected to live. What did that mean? I heard of guys "expected to live" who went home without their legs or an arm. Or with brain injuries that left them forever lost in Vietnam.

Since this morning when a new warning order jolted us awake—*Get Ready!*—I couldn't seem to shake from my mind thoughts of the mutilation of Lieutenant Sauer or of Jaggers. The lieutenant's body all carved up, his severed head on the ground at his feet, the face ghastly blackened with an expression of terror frozen on it. Imagine going to meet your Maker with your penis stuffed in your mouth! And Jaggers. Oh, God! I picked up his brain and cradled it in my hands like you might a puppy or a kitten.

I also thought of Gene Kilgore and his persistent premonition that he was going to be killed. His face when I last saw him this morning said today might be his last day. It was gray and drawn as though he peered at something scary deep inside his soul.

He had been all right yesterday when the gooks were too busy with the 3/9 on Hill 881S to fuck with us. Our holes were dry and we even got some sleep in shifts. Then came a last warning order. Yesterday, 881S fell. Today was the day of our Big Game when 2/3 broke for the goal and took our hill.

Kilgore was visiting my position when Gunny Janzen strode by passing the word. Prep fire against 881N had not yet started. It was easy to forget a war was going on as the sun prepared to break above the misty green peaks in that by-now familiar ritual of deceptive tranquility. The thick blankets of fog that lay in the valley between the Twin Sisters appeared soft and pastel-tinted, like a baby's blanket. Kilgore was his old self, smoking and grinning.

"Where you reckon they'll send us on R&R?" he wondered, anticipating our reward for capturing the gook prisoners.

"Maybe *this* is R&R," I said and pretended to read from a travel brochure. "'Enjoy an adventure-filled getaway in the alluring green wonderland in the north of beautiful South Vietnam. Where you awake each morning to life's harmony and the sound of artillery, to the hearty call of the red-plumed gook calling to you from the rain forest.'"

Kilgore chuckled, and Tony said, "Maras, you're full of shit, you know that?"

"Affirmative."

That was when Gunny came by with the word that we would be attacking 881N. Kilgore's cheeks and eyes suddenly seemed to sink into his skull, age lines dug furrows from the corners of his mouth. He became an old man right there before us.

Tony attempted to lighten him up with his Buddy Hackett routine. "Good morning, Vietnam, and all you little rug rats out there. It's a lovely day here in Shitsville."

It didn't work. Kilgore slumped off with his Starlite scope and his thermite grenade.

I sighed deeply, shook my head, and looked at Tony. His round face had turned serious. He nodded. We were Marines. If the hill was our duty, then we would do our duty.

Now was no time to think of Jaggers or Lieutenant Sauer. I had to prepare myself by thinking of better days. I imagined Linda and Mom at home doing little domestic things that normal people did. Anything to keep my mind occupied and off the terrors on the mountain ahead of us.

Back in high school, Linda and I and some of our teen friends sometimes partied on the sandy beaches at nearby Keystone Lake. Somebody would arrange for beer and we would guzzle suds, watch the red sun sink peacefully into the lake, split off into couples after dark to make out around the campfire, or take romantic walks along the shoreline in the moonlight.

I remember the last time we all got together at the lake. It was the night following graduation. I hadn't attended grad ceremonies because that day I went to enlist in the Marine Corps. Linda tried to talk me out of it. We walked together along the dark beach and I saw tears glistening in her eyes. She kissed me and withdrew.

"Bobby, you don't have to go."

"I *do* have to go," I insisted. "Linda, we got all summer to be together before I leave for boot camp."

"*Why* do you have to go, Bobby?"

I couldn't answer that question. Even now, or perhaps *especially* now, I still couldn't answer it. It was merely something I felt I had to do. War was intruding into our lives, even then, turning the beginning of our last summer together sour-sweet.

"War is so horrible," she said, her voice choked. "What if you're killed, Bobby? I don't know what I'd do if you never came back."

I remembered now her face lifted to me with the moon shining on her tears.

I *wasn't* going to die. I *was* coming back. I promised her. John Wayne always came back, right?

One day at Camp Schwab on Okinawa we were rope-bridging a creek when a squadron of Huey helicopters flew over. Sergeant Hard said they were Army Special Forces guys helping film a movie about the war in Vietnam. He said from what he had heard and seen of the production, it appeared very real to actual conditions. Except, and it was a very big exception, actors always came back because nobody ever got maimed or killed in the making of a film. The *real thing*, like in these hills, was brutal and bloody and if it didn't kill you, it killed someone you knew, and it killed something inside you.

Prep fire against 881N began with sudden alarming impact. The first barrages of 105s and 155s moaned and wailed across the sky over our heads like the revenant returning to claim lost souls. After that, the drum and howl of the Wicked Witch of the North blowing her top and spouting fire and brimstone dominated sight, hearing, and nerve endings.

Why, I demanded of myself, since no one else listened, did we keep bombing the tops when the gooks were probably waiting down below on the slopes? On second thought, if we *didn't* bomb the crests, then the NVA would be dug in up there waiting. Strategy and tactics were a bunch more complicated than they appeared on the surface. That was why generals and colonels and not privates ran the show.

Squad leaders and right guides, more commonly referred to as platoon sergeants, hustled between last-minute meetings with officers and keeping the rest of us informed. Lieutenant McFarlane's 1st Squad leader, PFC Taylor, looked stressed out.

"We move out in twenty minutes," he said. "Maras, you and Leyba are with me in Lieutenant Mac's Third Herd. Roger that?"

With the thunder of prep fire in the background, troops hurried to gear up for combat—buckling on web gear and helmets; honing edges on knives; filling grenade and ammo pouches; checking field dressings, just in case; writing last letters home; topping off canteens, and not from the dead gook crater either. Resupply had finally delivered.

Bolts ratcheted as men primed and dry-fired their rifles as a test. Teams swabbed out their 60mm mortar tubes. Anticipating casualties, Golf corpsmen stuffed their aid bags with pressure bandages, blood expander, bags of IV fluids, drugs and needles and tourniquets. Magilla came around to guys who smoked and collected cellophane wrappers from their cigarette packs to use in the emergency treatment of sucking chest wounds.

Beneath the surface of all this ran an undertone of apprehension as men fretted about. Would the M-16s jam just when we needed them most?

In addition to my Pig and Tony's M-16, he and I split the weight of a 3.5 rocket launcher and rounds between us. I carried the two parts of the launcher strapped to my back while Tony took the hard plastic backboard containing the rockets. I stuck my lunch of chicken noodle soup deep inside my pack where, hopefully, it would be safer than last time when a bullet found it.

"Maras," Tony observed as we team-worked getting things together, "you and I are starting to act like an old married couple."

"If that's a proposal, I'm already married. Besides, I wouldn't marry you anyhow. You is *so* ugly."

"You is *so* ugly too."

Best I understood it, the battle plan called for the refurbished and personnel-strengthened companies of Echo and Foxtrot to attack the hill from the south while Golf maneuvered to approach the northeastern slope. Hotel Company, not fully recovered from the fiasco in the draw that thinned out its ranks, stood in reserve on 861.

Golf Marines huddled in our holes—packed, strapped, and ready to go. Things got very quiet. No more banter, very little talking as we stared into the abyss and waited for cover fire to lift and orders to come down.

Gunny Janzen loped down the lines. "Saddle up, Marines! Drop your cocks and grab your socks. We're moving out."

CHAPTER THIRTY

Move! Move!

CAPTAIN JAMES SHEEHAN CONTINUED TO CONTROL THE BATTALION'S assault in the field while Colonel Pappy Delong commanded from his post at the Khe Sanh airfield. Not that Pappy would not have preferred to personally lead his men from the front, but a commander needed to remove himself from the minute-by-minute bedlam in order to maintain a view of the strategic "Big Picture." An officer under fire might make tactical decisions, but it required a certain detachment to make strategic ones. Captain Sheehan oversaw tactics primarily by radio commo with his junior leaders in Golf and with company commanders in Echo and Foxtrot, who remained subordinate to him during the operations against 881N.

At least that was the way I understood it as Golf organized into a skirmish line, just like in training, and we advanced on the hill through grasses that made the turtles thing again with our helmets. Brush and grass grew so thick and high in places that Marines lost sight of those on our flanks. I understood the "fog of war" concept, how it was confusing to keep track of what was going on when bombs started falling to fuck up the best laid plans of mice and men.

Sometimes I couldn't even see Tony ten feet over. My heart pounded in my ears, my mouth felt so dry I couldn't swallow. I felt compelled to look into that awful abyss from which no man returned. This too was part of the fog of war—and it wasn't pretty like the pink-tinted fog that snagged in the valley between the two hills. Nothing, *nothing*, was pretty about war.

Dead silence persisted as the terrain steepened. My labored breathing sounded like *The Little Engine That Could* panting up a mountain pass. Canteens of water sweated out through every pore. I stumbled over vines and stumps and rocks, barking my shins on fallen logs out of which rats and snakes and other little creatures scurried. I pulled myself up precipitous inclines with one hand while keeping the other near the trigger of the Pig slung from a strap over my shoulder, muzzle pointing forward, ready for action.

Tony labored along with me, appearing in and out of sight in the undergrowth. We tried to maintain visual contact with each other and with squad leader PFC Taylor in the event Lieutenant Mac required our services with the M-60. I heard Tony grunting, the clatter of his gear, the little under-the-breath curse when he tripped over some log and disturbed its occupants.

I suppressed a nervous laugh when he tumbled head first into a gully camouflaged with undergrowth. He came crawling back out with his helmet askew on his head, dragging his M-16 by its carrying strap, red dirt smeared on his chin and nose, glowering back over his shoulder with wide eyes for snakes. He hated snakes more than he had learned to hate gooks.

The anticipation of combat, the minutes leading up to the first shot or mortar going off, was always worse than the actual fighting. You lost all sense of self once the action started, became immersed in the machinery of it like you were a piston in a big engine operating by design. It was all instinct and training. No man was an island; we were a single organism, a machine fueled by blood and adrenaline.

Only afterwards were you human again, did you become aware of the cries of the wounded, the metallic stench of spilled blood, the sight of mangled bodies. Being human again wasn't always pleasant. Your bones began to rattle. Some guys vomited. Others wept with relief that it was over and they had made it through.

But we did our job, no matter. Our job was to kill people, break things, and blow shit up. We were Marines. We were good at it.

Up we climbed through the grass and trees, our nerves honed and aware of the snap of every twig, the whisper-rattle of wind through leaves, the mote-filled rays of yellow-bile sunlight sifting down through the forest canopy, the call of some distant bird, maybe a troop of monkeys getting the hell out of Dodge.

Where are they? Where the hell are the little bastards?

I could almost smell them. Feel hostile eyes watching. Their fingers on triggers posed to fire. Feel that first slug as it thudded into my chest and penetrated straight through into guts and lungs and heart. Hear my last wheeze of breath as I flopped onto the ground like a dying fish.

Damn! Next thing I knew Kilgore and I would be forming a Premonition of Death cult.

A kind of hump on the side of the hill ahead past a long narrow clearing sprinkled with sunlight caught my attention. I thought I saw movement.

Whump! Whump! The familiar sound of mortar rounds leaving their tubes.

The fight was on.

CHAPTER THIRTY-ONE

Timber-r-r-r!

MORTAR EXPLOSIONS WALKED BIG-FOOTED AND EAR-PIERCING THROUGH grass, trees, and undergrowth. Shrapnel, rocks, wood chips buzzed through the air, producing debris cuts and wounds on every Marine within range, some minor, others disabling. I automatically hit the ground when the first round went off. Snakes and rats, get out of the way! I could have dug to the center of the earth. No wonder monkeys were getting out of Dodge. This wasn't their fight and they wanted no part of it.

All along the skirmish line platoon leaders and sergeants bounced back to their feet after obeying their first instincts to go to cover.

"Move! Move! Keep going! Don't stop!" they yelled, their voices sounding as though they came from the depths of some cave because their ears were ringing from explosions.

Stop and you were dead. Close on the enemy, get at his throat, and the mortaring had to halt. Infantry always trained for this kind of scenario—and the drills worked. I sprang to my feet, calling out for Tony.

"Okay! Okay! Let's go!" he responded immediately.

Golf's skirmish line assaulted an invisible enemy through fire and smoke generated by exploding mortar shells. A single spontaneous, blood-thirsty roar erupted like a tsunami from the throats of Marines, louder and more chilling than the accompanying thunder of rifles and machine guns. A WWI bayonet charge out of the trenches, only without bayonets.

Yelling and screaming hysterically along with the rest of the company, surrendering to the passion and the fury of the mob, Tony and I together as always charging up the hill, burning rounds, shooting from the hip like John Wayne. No thinking now, just action. No attempt to pick out the source of hostile fire. Blasting away at anything that might conceal a gook. Thickets, clumps of grass. It didn't matter.

Enemy spider holes and machine gun bunkers were so well camouflaged that fire seemed to come right out of the ground. So I shot at the ground, at the occasional blaze-winking of a muzzle flash. Not seeing the enemy exactly. Anything that moved was fair game, even leaves trembling in the breezes.

Small-arms fire rippled like electrical surges back and forth along our skirmish line. Heavier here at one moment, rolling on the next to the other end of the line, then back again as the fast-moving firefight scrambled uphill into the enemy's teeth. It was what Marines called a target-rich environment.

The enemy had laid their defenses in layers, each echelon pulling back into the next to avoid being overrun. I began to glimpse shadows flitting through the trees as the nearest positions broke and withdrew before our onslaught. At least when we closed in on them, their mortars had to stop.

A *bush* moved in my peripheral vision. I swiveled the Pig's snout and cut down on it. I yelped with satisfaction, maybe even *glee*, when dying shrieks of pain erupted from it. I pumped another burst into the target for good measure. The screaming stopped.

Got the bastard!

As my section of skirmishers stampeded across a narrow clearing, a Marine to my left jerked up in mid-stride as though having collided with an invisible wall. He staggered back a step or two, blood pumping from his ruptured neck like red water from a garden hose. He went down hard out of sight in the grass.

I took one more look at him and kept going, my mind focused only on survival and what lay ahead, and on killing as many of the bastards as I could. Not giving a second thought about who the stricken Marine might be. He had to be one of my buddies in Taylor's 1st Squad, maybe even Taylor.

No time to consider it now. I yelped louder and louder, part rage, part fear, part . . . nihilism. If it were the end of the world, take as many with you as you could.

It proved impossible in this kind of terrain for the skirmish line to maintain form. It bent and shaped itself to the landscape, parts of it ranging ahead while other sections lagged. Tony and I came across a wounded Marine named Johnson who was bellowing like a beef next in line at a slaughter house. He had dragged himself behind a rock where blood sluiced from a severed artery in his leg with the sound of water gushing from a faucet. Tony and I dropped beside him.

"It's all right, brother, all right, all right. . . ." I muttered in a litany, willing it to be so as I jerked off his web belt and used it as a tourniquet to staunch the flow of blood.

The blood felt hot and sticky on my hands, the odor rich and nauseating. Tony rolled over on his back.

"Corpsman up!" he shouted.

Magilla seemed to appear out of nowhere to take over. God bless Navy corpsmen. They rushed into brimstone where even angels feared to tread.

"God protect the both of you," Magilla called out as Tony and I rejoined the herd.

Lance Corporal Ted West and his AG with their stubby 60mm mortar tube had passed us on the run while we were busy with Johnson. West, a member of my Weapons Platoon, was built close to the ground. His short legs pumped as the two Marines disappeared into the bush uphill.

Tony and I came upon them in an abandoned gook fighting hole where they were pumping out mortar rockets so fast the tube glowed red-hot. We tucked into the hole unannounced while West's AG, up on his knees, pissed on the tube to cool it down. No sense in wasting good canteen water. Urine sizzled on the hot metal and issued a rank cloud of ammonia.

"Man! You guys piss in your own living room?" Tony exclaimed. Buddy Hackett was how he coped with stress.

The grunt glanced at him and kept pissing. But in spurts. It was tough to keep a steady stream going when you were scared half to death.

Platoon leaders and sergeants kept at us. Tall, lanky Lieutenant Mac scurried past the mortar pit. "Marines! Keep moving! Run down the bastards!"

"Nice talking to you," Tony quipped as we leapt from West's hole and back into the melee.

"I really wanted to stay in that hole," Tony later confessed.

Dueling tracers of red and green snapped across the battlefield. The air was so full of steel it felt like you were breathing it. I dropped to one knee and turned the Pig loose on a grove of suspicious thorn trees, chewing them into kindling with a cone of red. Nothing ran out. There were no screams of pain. Shit! I thought sure gooks would be hiding in there.

Tony fed me another belt of 7.62 and we continued our crazy uphill sprint. A bullet plucked Tony's canteen off his web gear. Something whacked me on the back with such force that it drove me to my hands and knees. I felt the warmth of blood.

"I'm hit!"

Ever-faithful Tony skidded to the rescue, plopping down next to me. He quickly made his assessment. "Calm down, Maras. Look at me. You're not hit. It's your chicken noodle soup again."

"*What?*" That really pissed me off. "The sonsofbitches shot my chicken noodles? This is the second time the bastards did this. May they all rot in Hell."

Further up the incline we encountered actual human beings wearing pith helmets and tennis shoes. Tony and I dived for cover in a washout when a group of them opened fire on us from a short distance ahead and to one side. The firing stopped as soon as we were out of their sight.

They were still out there though, playing the old wait-for-the-squirrel trick. A squirrel when surprised dived into his hole. Wait a few minutes quietly, however, and, curious, he stuck his head out to take a look. That was when you bagged him.

We were hiding there trying to figure out how to handle the obstacle and warn other Marines in the area when a Mule armed with a 106mm recoilless rifle came charging up our washout where it extended in a downhill drainage. A "Mule" was like a flat-bedded go-cart with a cannon attached.

The operator driving the four-wheeler slid to a halt in the ditch, slinging mud, dirt, and leaves. He grinned with jaunty excitement as he flung himself onto the ground and crawled up to the berm-like lip of the washout where Tony and I sought cover. All he needed was a scarf around his neck to become the land-borne equivalent of the Red Baron, the famous WWII air ace. His little craft sat idling contentedly.

"Where are they?" he demanded.

I pointed in a direction. "About six of them, I think."

He pulled himself up to get a look. The NVA were well-disciplined soldiers who opened up only when they had clear targets. I pointed to a clump of bushes and trees, careful not to show myself and become the squirrel. Leaves shuddered as an enemy infantryman apparently peeped out at us peeping out at him.

"I see 'em," the Mule jockey announced triumphantly. He seemed to be calculating range and direction before he slipped back down to his carriage. "Keep down," he cautioned. "There's gonna be blood and shit in the air."

He made adjustments on his recoilless. He looked up toward Tony and me and gave thumbs up. The guy was one cool dude.

He gunned the buggy out of the low onto higher ground for a quick shot. He knew what he was doing and was good at it. The gooks weren't expecting *this*. He beat them to the draw. The cannon burped, its first shell followed almost immediately by a second. The powerful 106 rounds detonated spot on-target in the midst of the enemy, culminating their sorry lives in an iridescent vapor that slung chunks of flesh, cloth, leather, and weapons all over the landscape. A pith helmet leaped twenty feet into the air. A bloody tennis shoe ended up stuck on a high tree limb.

We waited another minute or two. When nothing moved in the trees, no sound, we assumed the standoff had ended successfully for our side.

"You call, we haul," the Mule driver remarked cheerfully as he raced on down the skirmish line like the Lone Ranger.

"He could have at least left us a silver bullet," Tony grumbled.

The advance continued. More NVA engaged Tony and me up the incline where they had gone to ground next to an isolated forest giant that stood twenty feet tall with a trunk about three feet in diameter.

Fortunately, Tony and I were moving fast, ducking and dodging, so that when the gooks opened up their aim was off. All they got were leaves and twigs that rained down on our helmets.

We fared more accurately with our return fire. My machine gun scored two of them who in their eagerness to bring us down had left the protection of the tree and jumped into the open. Tony's M-16 engulfed a third. So far his Mattie Mattel was working perfectly. I finished off the trio in case they weren't already dead. Tracers singed into their bodies and jerked them around like puppets controlled by a spastic hand. Hot tracers oozed tendrils of smoke from the holes they punched into flesh.

The confrontation turned into a standoff. The remaining two gooks proved smarter, or at least more cunning. They kept low behind the tree, popping up like gophers to rip off at us. Tony and I behind some rocks dueled back. Where was the Lone Ranger when you needed him?

I looked around for other Marines nearby that might offer a hand in eliminating the threat. Sounded like they were all busy with their own problems. Continuous gunfire raged from either side as well as forward and behind. Seemed to me like our skirmish line had disintegrated into a clusterfuck. FUBAR—Fucked Up Beyond All Recognition. Squads and groups and even individual Marines fought it out with counterparts all over our sector of the slope, while further away and around the hill more gunfire marked Echo's and Foxtrot's progress.

In this kind of environment, you dealt with any challenge yourself. I nudged Tony and pointed to a huge tree limb left broken and barely hanging eight or ten feet above our two opponents. Probably the result of a previous shelling of the area. The limb itself was about the size of a normal tree and likely weighed several hundred pounds. It was a long shot, but if I could dump it on these two guys, it would be like dropping a load of concrete blocks on a pair of rats. I explained to Tony what I intended.

"Go for it," he encouraged, eager to see what happened.

AK-47s rattled on full auto, the spray of bullets zapping the air above our heads. I waited until the gooks ducked back behind their tree where they were directly underneath the broken limb. I remained low to the ground out of their sight and let loose a long Pig burst at the strip of bark and wood that held the limb attached to the tree.

"*Timber-r-r-r!*" Tony cheered as the heavy limb crashed down on the two enemy infantry, eliciting from them amped-up banshee screams.

I sprayed the trapped gooks as we ran past, putting them out of their misery. I paused in astonishment. I had witnessed demonstrations in which 7.62 bullets from an M-60 machine gun ripped hog carcasses to shreds. I finally understood why our machine guns—even the heavy 50-cals—weren't tearing NVA soldiers apart when we unleashed on them. They wrapped their arms and legs with wire to hold flesh and bone together so they could continue to fight should they only be wounded and not killed. You had to respect these guys. They were hard core.

"Damn!" Tony exclaimed respectfully.

What a gory mess. I looked at my hands. They were trembling. It was not a good thing to stop and actually look at what you had accomplished in battle.

"Anyhow," Tony said as we turned away, "I'll bet we're the only Marines ever wasted gooks by dropping a tree on them."

CHAPTER THIRTY-TWO

Dig In, Marines

WHAT BEGAN AS A FULL-FLEDGED ASSAULT AGAINST A DETERMINED enemy gradually slacked off, breaking out again only in isolated pockets of resistance. It appeared the NVA could be withdrawing their delaying forces down here below and reintegrating them into their main force up on the hill.

From the sounds of it, Echo and Foxtrot were experiencing a similar lull in fighting. Only a spattering of small arms continued from their sector, diminishing into stray rifle shots, perhaps from jittery Marines popping at shadows or breeze-riffled leaves.

Still, no one thought the fight was finished.

Captain Sheehan utilized the breather to consult with Colonel Pappy at Khe Sanh and reconsolidate his companies for the final push. Our casualties appeared relatively light—relative in the sense that your chances of getting struck by lightning were remote, unless you were the one who took a bolt down your skivvies. At which point it became irrelevant how many casualties accompanied you in the body bags.

Captain Sheehan came to me and pointed to the top of the hill, which was concealed from view by what remained of forest after the beating it had taken from artillery, mortars, and air raids. He wanted to pop smoke on the summit as a guide to the objective.

"Maras," he asked, "you think you can put a Willie Pete on it?"

"Aye, aye, Skipper."

A WP (white phosphorus) burned brightly upon exploding and emitted a thick plume of smoke.

I broke out the 3.5 rocket launcher I had humped since morning, assembled the two sections, and loaded a round from Tony's pack board. I was about to fire it up when one of the platoon sergeants stopped me.

He was one of the kiss-ass sort. Troops mocked him behind his back for always trying to make points with the brass. Troops called him "Georgie Porgy." He was the type who, in high school, was the nerd in the front row who washed the teacher's blackboard and whose hand always grabbed for attention. "Me, me, teacher! Choose me!" Even in combat, he kept his hand in the air and his lips puckered.

He snatched the launcher from my hands with a smirk that seemed to say "don't send a private to do a sergeant's job."

Captain Sheehan shrugged.

Georgie made a production of prolonging the moment for whatever limited attention it attracted. He took careful aim and let fly. Tony rolled his eyes and pressed out a Buddy Hackett expression.

The rocket whooshed and trailed flame as it looped high above treetops and dived back down toward the point of 881N. The Captain's command element waited expectantly for the round to impact and send up its tell-tale plume of smoke. I couldn't resist calling it first.

"Dead miss."

The sergeant glowered.

"Give it back to Maras," Captain Sheehan instructed.

My round hit the target square. Smoke snaked into the air.

"That's how you do it, Sergeant," Tony taunted.

Judging from Georgie Porgy's scowl, I suspected he looked forward to Tony's and my being the next casualties.

Curiously enough, gooks on top made no effort to extinguish the Willie Pete, even though they had to know we were using it as a guide.

The hill grew steeper, more treacherous. Marines on line labored sweating and tense to make the final climb. All resistance seemed to have melted away. I couldn't help thinking this was just too damned easy.

How many Marines had died and NVA been slain in our savage dispute over the Wicked Twin Sisters? It made no sense that the North Vietnamese would give up so easily at the end. I still *felt* gooks, *smelled* them, *knew* they were up there waiting for us to trip their kill zone.

Foot by foot, yard by yard, the advance continued until Golf's skirmish line linked up with Echo's and Foxtrot's toward the peak. Tension continued to mount. Marines scrambled through tangled brush and over downed trees on our final few hundred meters either to the finish line—or to more chaos and destruction.

Why weren't the gooks mortaring us? Why no ambushes or snipers? I began to think, or *hope*, this might end as the taking of 881S had ended: with the enemy having abandoned it.

As a machine gun team, Tony and I were among the lead elements of Lieutenant Mac's Third Herd to venture cautiously out of the bush onto the hill's denuded crown. Platoon members hesitated and looked about, puzzled, not yet willing to accept that this might be over, that we had pulled ourselves to the top of the hill and it belonged to us at last without further resistance. There was no spiking the ball at the goal line, no little dance of triumph and *"Team! Team!"* No real sense of victory. It was all so anticlimactic. The gooks had simply pulled out. It was not a Mt. Suribachi moment.

Relative peace seemed a threatening stranger after so many days without it. Standing there suddenly in the open, crouched and my finger on the trigger, all I heard were the burr of insects and the calls of distant birds. As elsewhere, death and scorched human flesh hovered over the hilltop like a noxious cloud. Big green shit flies swarmed seeking lunch and biting the hell out of our exposed faces and hands.

Artillery and aerial assaults had obviously taken a terrible toll on the NVA. One-thousand-pound bombs had pummeled the crown into a dump site of splintered trees, destroyed defensive positions, craters, pulverized earth and rock, out of which threaded wisps of smoke and crackling tongues of flame. Shreds of clothing and bits and pieces of flesh were strewn about a wasteland that resembled a scene from some apocalyptic end-of-the-world flick.

Commanders quickly began organizing the companies into a defense. Tony and I were digging ourselves a gun position out of an NVA caved-in fighting hole when Tony uncovered a severed hand buried in the rubble. He picked it up and handed it to me for a look-see. Young men immersed in death and violence soon became conditioned to it. Tony reformed the stiffened hand into a one-finger salute and hailed Gene Kilgore, who labored nearby on his own position.

"Hey, Kilgore!" Tony thrust the hand aloft. "Gooks sent you a message."

Kilgore shook his head in pretended disgust. "You are some sick assholes, you know that?"

He had defied his nightmare premonitions once again and made it unscathed through another day with his Starlight scope.

As we decompressed, we began to take stock. While Tony, Kilgore, and most of us survived, we had suffered losses. Some were friends, some were not. All were brothers.

The most unusual losses involved Jim Hill's Bowie knife. The kid to whom Magilla handed the blade after Hill bought the farm had himself gone down. The knife passed to the next man, who subsequently fell. After that, Magilla or one of the others threw the knife into the bush, figuring it to be a bad omen.

Robert J. Todd out of Foxtrot Company was another freakish incident. Tony and I didn't see exactly what happened, but a sergeant eyewitness told us about it a few days after we conquered 881N.

Medevac choppers jinked in to evacuate our dead and wounded. Todd had taken a fatal bullet during the assault. His poncho-wrapped body was brought up and loaded aboard a hovering Huey. Although the NVA might have fled the hill, they were still in the area and full of venom. Apparently, they were moving back in to surround us. Shelling medevac birds was their way of letting us know the struggle wasn't over yet.

Mortar shells rained down fire and smoke on the Huey. Crewmembers piled in on top of the casualties, the pilot pulled collective, and the bird bounced into the air in a steep yaw with its blades clawing for altitude. It gained air as it soared in a steep bank out over the valley. Witnesses on the ground watched in disbelief when an object tumbled out the aircraft's open door.

"Somebody fell out!"

During the Huey's emergency getaway, crew had not had time to secure bodies on the helicopter's blood-slippery deck. Todd's body slid out the open door and plummeted to earth, crashing into thick canopy somewhere north of the Twin Witches. Every patrol from then on was instructed to be on the lookout for it. His body was never recovered.

After that and the renewed mortaring, frantic activity on 881N prepared for possible counterattacks. The NVA might have retreated, but they weren't beaten. They would want their hills back. Whether or not they could re-take them had to be seen. But most certainly they would try.

Captain Sheehan had earlier passed on to Tony, Kilgore, and me what the three prisoners Tony and I took from the ground revealed. Under interrogation, they said they were soldiers attached to the 325th NVA Division. They had traveled south on the Ho Chi Minh Trail in March in a vanguard of infantry massing against the Khe Sanh Combat Base. Uncle Ho was as determined as LBJ not to lose the fight. The POWs stated that many more communist troops were on their way—and, boy, were they pissed off.

Gunny Janzen looked worn out with his cheeks stuck to his teeth and his eyes like hollows in his skull.

"Well," he said after a deep breath, "we've taken the three hills. The question now is whether we can keep them. This fight's not over. Dig in, Marines, and stay alert if you want to live."

CHAPTER THIRTY-THREE

Knock That Shit Off!

I SHOOK MY CANTEEN, HEARING ONLY A WEAK SLOSH OF WATER. THERE was little chance of replenishing it until tomorrow when a resupply chopper *might* make it in. Nonetheless, I removed the crevette I used as a sweat rag around my neck, wet one corner, and with it reamed out my nostrils in an attempt to scrub out the sickening odor of *death*. I thought I might never rid myself of it.

Each guy had his own way of coping with war. In between events, some behaved like zombies, staring off into space to blank from their minds scenes of gore and brutality they may have witnessed, not wanting to recall dead and maimed friends and perhaps the extent to which their own humanity may have been tested and found wanting.

Others went dark, confronting violence and brutality with that barbarism I suspected may lurk in the hidden corners of the human soul waiting to be unleashed. One Marine notched off a dead gook's ear and stuck it in his pocket as a souvenir. One day he would be hanging around the pool hall showing off the dried and shriveled piece of flesh: "Yep, cut it off a dead gook myself." Another with a little Kodak camera had his buddy take a picture of him pissing on an enemy corpse.

Maybe they were just trying to prove they were tough, hiding their own fears and uncertainties. Maybe. I was no psychologist, just an amateur observer of human nature—and witnessing it at its worst. And, sometimes, to be fair, at its best.

The majority of us learned to compartmentalize for the sake of sanity. Doing what had to be done, which meant killing or mauling with bullets, clubs, knives, grenades, bare knuckles, teeth, or nails—whatever. As long as the gook was the one who ended up dead. Afterwards, we had to shut off that dark chamber and move to the light where we might still have a chance at "normality." It was in this recompression chamber that Tony's Buddy Hackett reemerged with "Good morning, Vietnam!" Or Wally Jacubowski demonstrated with his spastic chicken dance an enemy soldier getting chewed on by machine gun bullets.

Many of us, after all, were still teenagers barely out of high school and, in spite of Marine Corps training, largely unprepared for a *real world* that included war. Not so long ago we were attending house parties, camping out on the beach, teasing and pulling pranks on each other, going on dates. None of us wanted to lose that part of ourselves. We desperately attempted to hold onto it in spite of the grimness of the environment into which we had been thrust. In the process, we were discovering our capability for consuming both brotherhood and intense brutishness.

Tony carried a nostalgic expression on his face while he watched the sun edge down in the west. We were taking a short break from renovating our new "penthouse suite with a view."

"Guess what I'm thinking about," he piped up.

"Pussy?"

"Piss on her." He flipped me the middle-finger bird.

"I'm thinking about ice cream," he went on. "Me and my buds hanging out in air conditioning at the malt shop whistling at girls as they go by and having a banana split with cherries and pecans on top. What do you miss about home, Maras?"

I thought about it. "Linda," I said. "I miss Linda, Mom, my old friends. I miss the lake on lazy Sunday afternoons. You know, Tony, sometimes I miss being just a kid again."

We lapsed into that lonely silence of reminiscence.

"I wonder if it's true what they say," I mused finally. "That you can never go home again."

"This is getting too deep, Maras. Who do you think you are? Plato or something?"

I shrugged and dismissed the sudden uncomfortable image of Linda having a good time with some draft dodger. I mean, it happened to guys over here. Look at Tony's Peggy as an example.

Not Linda though. She was probably at home getting ready to go to bed at Mom's, completely clueless as to what was going on over here. So there I was on the other side of the globe, barely surviving, while people in America were sleeping in real beds, not being shot at, and getting up to go to work at their nine-to-five jobs, oblivious to people dying in a war in a part of the world nobody wanted.

Shit happens.

Captain Sheehan was good about keeping the troops informed, at least commensurate to what we had to know at our pay grade. Leaders like him, Lieutenant McFarlane, and most of the others were why Marines were considered the bad asses of the US military. Wind us up, point us in a direction, and somebody was going to get a butt kicking. He passed down the word through our junior leaders that Colonel Delong and the command element at Khe Sanh believed the enemy would not so easily relinquish the area and that we should be prepared to defend.

"He also says to tell every Marine he did a good job today. He's proud of us."

Pappy was proud of us! We all walked a little taller with our chests stuck out.

By sunset, 2/3 Battalion was well-mounted on the crest of 881N and set up for the night. Troops exhausted from the day's fighting sought sleep on a 50-50 alert basis. Tony volunteered to stand first watch at nightfall while I took my poncho and racked out on the ground nearby in a cool breeze. I closed my eyes and immediately sank into a deep fatigued sleep.

I should have known the gooks wouldn't leave us alone.

"*Incoming!*"

A hell of a way to be jolted awake. I lunged for the hole and dived headfirst in on top of Tony.

OP/LPs concealed down in the timberline to keep watch thought the mortar barrage signaled a pending ground attack. They raced up the hill shouting at the tops of their lungs so Marines in the perimeter wouldn't shoot them by mistake.

"*LPs! LPs! Don't shoot! Don't shoot! We're coming through!*"

Red-flashing mortar shells stomped the hilltop hard, contributing to the wreckage and overall denuding and ploughing up of the real estate. Sectors manned by Echo and Foxtrot on the south side of the crest took the brunt of the pounding. Gunnery sergeants counted ninety-two mortar rounds dropping from the sky in the span of several minutes.

Convinced we were under attack, Marines opened fire downhill into the darkness, adding to the noise and confusion. Shooting back served to relieve tension, even when targets were indistinguishable from the night. I burned through a belt of 7.62, streaming cones of red tracers downrange while Tony's M-16 malfunctioned. He crouched at the bottom of the hole and frantically worked with his K-bar knife to extract a fractured hull from the weapon's chamber.

I offered him my .45 pistol. "Take it. But first feed the Pig!"

While Tony pulled a fresh belt of ammo from its can, I peered downhill and noticed to my astonishment that we were receiving no return fire. No enemy muzzle flashes winking like angry fireflies in the dark. No bugles blaring or banshees screaming.

"Tony! Tony, there's nobody out there."

"Huh?"

I couldn't believe it myself.

We peeped out of our hole like a pair of perverts hid out in a ladies' room. It soon became apparent to everyone that we weren't facing a ground assault, although mortar rounds continued to thud the top of the hill, coming in so fast on top of Echo and Foxtrot that even the gutsy corpsmen dared not leave their hiding places to answer cries for help.

Officers and sergeants began shouting, "Hold your fire! Cease fire, damn it! There's nobody out there!"

Somebody was out there *somewhere*. God wasn't the one slinging lightning bolts at us for our sins.

Incoming gradually subsided and then ceased altogether, replaced by the even more nerve-shattering wailing and screaming of the wounded south of us on the hill. Foxtrot lost one KIA and a half-dozen wounded, several of whom weren't going to make it without immediate care back at Charlie Med. Corpsmen patched them up and moved them back to an evac area to wait for choppers to come in for a perilous night extraction.

Battered Marines emerged from our defensive posture and glared challenges deep into the dark—but nothing moved out there. Nonetheless, none of us found any rest for the remainder of the night. We kept expecting an attack. We hunkered wide-eyed and waited. Some of us prayed. Some of us simply stared.

Tony broke a long quiet spell after a Sea Knight dropped in, loaded up the wounded and the dead man, and took off again without a single shot having sought it out. Really weird. He watched the shadow of the big helicopter against the stars as it climbed out and poured on the coal back toward Khe Sanh.

"Maras?"

"Leyba."

"You know I love you like a brother, right?"

"You ain't gonna get all mushy?"

"We've saved each other's ass at least a dozen times since this shit started—but I want you to take this with all due respect: I'm hoping that if one of these rounds hits this hole it gets you and not me."

That triggered a relief valve. We sniggered and snorted at the bottom of our black hole like a pair of lunatics escaped from an insane asylum. Which seemed appropriate enough. After all, these hills were in fact a kind of loony bin populated by the mad and deranged.

A familiar voice boomed out of the darkness. "Knock that shit off!"

CHAPTER THIRTY–FOUR

Purple Haze

Tony rubbed his eyes. We climbed from our cramped den for our morning ablutions and a "Good morning, Vietnam!" salute. Other than the mortar attack that killed one of Foxtrot's men, our first night in possession of 881N passed without our having been otherwise hit. Another long and terrible night and we survived. At least most of us had.

Mankind, I pondered, had been terrified of the night since people first huddled in caves surrounded by bears, saber-toothed tigers, and other fearsome creatures. Since then, man himself had assumed the mantle of the most dangerous being on earth. You had more reason to be afraid of man lurking in the darkness than of beasts or demons.

Accepted scripture dictated that the NVA rarely launched full-scale ground attacks in the light of day. They, like thieves and assassins, preferred to work in the shadows. When necessary, they defended, ambushed, patrolled, snuck around, employed mortars and artillery in daylight, but for their major efforts they preferred a dark, cloudy night when, Zen-like, they became one with the universe.

Enemy soldiers started to come out in the quiet that followed the setting of the Vietnam sun. We heard them rustling about in the jungle outside our perimeter. Cloud cover over the stars and the absence of a moon assisted them in sneaking to within a couple of hundred meters of our lines, close enough that we could have had conversation with them. Jittery OP/LPs opened fire at sounds until Captain Sheehan ordered them back inside battalion defenses. Leaving them out there amidst blatant enemy activity amounted to signing their death warrants.

From the dark came the high-pitched tones of their voices, along with strange noises that sounded like a cross between the cackling of geese and the quacking of ducks. They seemed to be chatting and laughing nonchalantly, as though sharing a secret they intended to spring on us in the very near future as a dirty trick. Gunny Janzen said it was all part of a plan to psyche us out. If it was, it was working.

Marines taunted back in a vicious exchange of insults.

"You filthy scum!"

"You die, Marines!"

"Come on in, motherfuckers. Have we got something for you!"

"Marines, dinky-dow mamas!"

"Fire up their asses!"

"Damnit!" sergeants chimed in. "Knock that shit off."

"They started it, sergeant."

We held fire and took the verbal assault, waiting for orders or for an actual attack. We had become hardened and disciplined troops in the days after Red Beach. Since that first day when as a cherry I scrawled my inspiration on the cardboard C-ration box top at the airfield, I had come to realize I possessed no special insight, *none*, into what it meant to fight for life. The words must have been a whim, a fresh flight of fancy. Or perhaps, once in a while, some of us caught an omniscient glimpse into an alternate reality or truth.

There had been days and nights since we entered these hills that I expected never to see another morning. It wasn't only Kilgore and me either. The Marine collective mood had seemed to sour as our casualties mounted. Outfits left behind to guard Khe Sanh, the 1/26th or whatever, must have been continually stunned as bodies of Marines accumulated each day at the airfield, laid out neatly in body bags waiting for their last flight home.

You had to hand it to the enemy for having guts and for being as tenacious as ticks, leeches, or mosquitoes. But what, I wondered, did Uncle Ho hope to achieve now by hanging around in these hills? It should be clear to him by this time that he couldn't drive Americans out of I-Corps, the DMZ region, or Khe Sanh. He had missed his chance to create another Dien Bien Phu. If anything, we had reversed Dien Bien Phu on him.

Puff the Magic Dragon appeared overhead to drop flares and light up the terrain around the hill in eerie, flickering, greenish light. Fiery breath from the Dragon's mini-guns blistered the cockroaches and sent them scattering.

All right! Fuck you bastards!

The psyops boys in their invisible Huey arrived next to drop *Chieu Hoi* leaflets. Their loudspeakers blared from out of the night sky. Jimi Hendrix.

Oooo . . .

Help me . . .

Ahh, yea-yeah, purple haze.

Oh, no, oh

Oh, help me.

Tell me, tell me, purple haze.

I can't go on like this. . . .

Daylight came after the terrible nights. I watched a beautiful sun turn from pale pink to orange—beautiful because I was alive to see it. Funny, I thought, how the sun just kept rising and setting around the globe, unaffected by what we little ant-like creatures did to each other below. In a world away from these hills people were going about their normal affairs—having sit-down breakfast or lunch or dinner at a table, making love in bed, playing pick-up basketball at the park, indulging in quarrels, having family gatherings, working through a crisis, making plans for vacation or a weekend fishing trip, getting married, dying in bed of old age, giving birth, going to school, attending PTA meetings. . . .

How they took it all for granted while out here, in these bloody hills, men died and were being maimed, events that allowed you to take *nothing* for granted. Especially not life and the privilege of viewing another sunrise.

I took pride in preparing breakfast under less than ideal conditions. I arranged a small circle of stones on the ground near enough to our hole that I could tend it. In its center I ignited a heat tab and placed my canteen cup on the stones above the tiny blue flame. Tony contributed some of his last water to mine and I boiled water for coffee. We pooled our rations: I had one C-rat broadly defined as ham and eggs and one of fruit cocktail; Tony had a can of white cake and a John Wayne chocolate bar.

Tony lent his endorsement to my efforts. "Not bad. My compliments to the chef."

"Chef says you can wash dishes."

"You're getting fucking weird, you know that, Maras?"

"I thought you promised God to stop swearing."

"It takes time."

Little exchanges of domesticity, much of it obscene and bordering on the absurd, helped in escaping the stress of combat, made us feel almost "normal" under decidedly un-normal circumstances. It was this ability to find and hang onto an anchor that was part of a warrior breed's gestalt.

The reality of war often cut discussions short, whether philosophical or not. The distinct *Kerplunk! Kerplunk!* of enemy mortar rounds leaving tubes compelled us to duck and cover.

Incoming!

"Not *again!*" Tony raged.

About two dozen mortar rounds walked across the hill, then stopped, leaving smoke hazing the air and swirling around our necks. I listened for any cries of distress that might indicate wounded Marines, hearing nothing except the quiet that followed and the hollow-like vibrations of bruised eardrums. The dead never cried out, but I decided if any of us had been killed in one of the other companies, I didn't want to hear about it. Just shut it out for the moment. If Golf Company was okay, I was okay. The death of any Marine was personal, but it was especially personal if the dead guy was one of our own.

I thought of Kilgore and his premonitions. I called out to him in the aftermath. He and Rainey and a couple of other guys manned a machine gun post nearby.

"What do you want, Maras?"

"Just checking to see if you're all right."

"Why shouldn't I be?"

"You didn't notice? They were shelling us."

His dreams had him dying in an ambush, not from mortar fire.

Another voice broke in from down the perimeter. "Kilgore, still got your Starlite?"

Ribbing him about his duty to destroy the scope were we overrun had become a company pastime.

"Fuck you very much, pig breath," he retorted.

Kilgore never so much as *sounded* like he was smiling as long as he was on duty and in uniform. I had snapshotted the only known photo of him actually wearing a grin, although he claimed it wasn't so. He said he had gas.

We barely had time to catch our breath before a lookout on the northwestern sector of the hill sounded an urgent warning: "The gooks are charging up the hill!"

What? Didn't these cocksuckers know it was broad daylight? Did they not read their own tactical manuals?

CHAPTER THIRTY-FIVE

Kilgore's Starlite

COMMIE BUGLES INITIATED THE RARE DAYLIGHT MASS ATTACK. HIGH, strident notes that chilled spines, loosened bowels, and made some men doubt their courage. One night on Okinawa while Golf's new replacement trainees were gathered in the barracks scuttlebutting, somebody got Sergeant Crawford talking about Korea and how it had been when the Chicoms massed and charged with bugles tooting. We Newbies gathered around enthralled and curious. We didn't know enough at the time to be afraid. But what I saw on the vet's face, how his eyes narrowed and turned grim, how his jaw set, and sweat formed on his upper lip. . . .

"If there is a Hell," he said, "that's how it will be—demons and devils, the scourge of the underworld charging bellowing and tooting carrying red hot pitchforks with flames shooting from them. Boys, that's Hell on earth."

Echo Company on its hill knob had repelled a mass NVA attack that night previously while Golf across the lowlands that separated our two companies watched and listened with our mouths dry and hands shaking. Now—in broad daylight, no less—the rest of us were experiencing the bugle. I wasn't sure if it might not be better in the night *not* seeing the human infantry waves bursting from tree lines all around 881N and scrambling up the denuded slopes at us, firing their Kalashnikovs and light machine guns in throbbing claps of thunder, smoke, and fire that awoke the tormented gods of war. The Devil, that crazy sonofabitch, must have been clapping his hands in glee, whipping his barbed tail back and forth, and egging his advocates to scream and roar in his tribute. These guys seemed dead set on annihilating every last Marine on the hill—and there was enough of them to do it too. We were outnumbered at least four to one.

Colonel Pappy was right. These guys wanted their hill back. An image of Lieutenant Sauer's mutilated corpse flashed across the front of my mind.

King of the Mountain. Played with deadly overtones. I felt and heard the pressure and snap of lead and steel in a lethal hailstorm that buffeted the hill, geysering dirt, ricochets shrieking into the morning sky. Enemy soldiers howling like banshees loomed larger and larger as they closed in on us, firing from the hip and chugging grenades.

There was no time for fear, for rational thought even. A Marine reacted according to training. I laid on the trigger of my M-60. *Piggy, don't fail me now!* Sweeping my fire back and forth across the rushing masses in their pith helmets and tennis shoes. I *wanted* my bullets to explode the little bastards into mist and separate body components and leave nothing except unrecognizable chunks of human flesh. I couldn't help noting, even during the heat of chaos, that those I and others hit remained largely intact because of wire wrapped around their extremities. Blood, however, couldn't be wrapped. It misted and turned the air pink as bodies stacked up. Jaggers and Sauer and all the other Marines hammered by these devils deserved avenging.

What kind of control must communism have over the minds of its subjects that they would charge mindlessly to their own destruction?

It was horrendous, gruesome, frightening, and exhilarating all at the same time. I read once how it was good that war should be so terrible lest man come to enjoy it.

Enemy soldiers dropped at close range, some the victims of our fusillades of defensive fire, others to seek cover from which to lob grenades at us. Little Chicom hand bombs with wooden handles sailed through the air. Most landed short and exploded harmlessly in blinding sun-flashes of white fire. Throwing uphill was not an easy matter.

The evening before, sergeants and platoon leaders, anticipating a possible attack, had distributed cases of M-26 frag grenades to the line. Grenades were superior defensive weapons at close range, better than machine guns at clogging up a mass infantry attack before its components grappled with you in your hole. Marines got busy all around the perimeter hurling frags back at the gooks. Chain bursts of explosions sounding like the fiercest of thunderstorms cast a barrier of fire and steel against the enemy's assault.

Our downhill tosses were a lot easier and more accurate than the NVA's chunking uphill. That day's exchange with the enemy would go down in Golf Company legend as the "Big Grenade Battle." Every Marine on the hill, including company commanders, hurled grenades. In all the excitement, Marines yelled, whooped, and shouted insults at the Vietnamese.

Gooks were almost close enough to smell their breath. Tony and I emptied a whole case of grenades. Barely had one landed than I put another in the air, Tony right beside me in the bright sunlight doing the same.

"Piss on 'em! Piss on 'em!" Tony chanted, until I wondered if he might not be doing battle with his own army of Peggy clones.

"Fuck 'em! Fuck 'em!" Corporal Ted West over to our left flank bellowed each time he tossed a grenade.

I suspected my throwing arm would get as sore as my wounded elbow as we kept at it for what seemed like hours, piling up bloody clumps of enemy soldiers in final repose. Those merely wounded or in the agony of their death throes squirmed like beds of screaming earth worms. Marines put them out of their misery with bursts of fire. The Hill Fights had become so brutal that no quarter was asked or expected. The only way to win in this kind of fight was to become as nasty as the enemy—which posed the risk of your waking up one morning to find yourself even nastier than the enemy.

The fierce human tsunami finally broke. As it disintegrated, a company jokester high on adrenaline couldn't resist screwing with Gene Kilgore and his Starlite. It was an amazing thing that in the middle of gore and turmoil a Marine retained the sheer chutzpah to pull a boyish stunt on another.

"We're being flanked!" the jokester shouted. "They're overrunning us!"

Like the good Marine he was, Kilgore immediately stripped the scope form his rifle, flung it to the ground, and dropped his thermite on it. Nothing remained of it afterwards except a melted hunk of unidentifiable metal. Nobody ever learned who the culprit jokester was, but Golf Company enjoyed a collective chuckle at Kilgore's embarrassed expense.

Gunny Janzen chewed Kilgore a new one at falling for the prank. He shook his head, turned his back, and walked away before Kilgore could see his barely-suppressed amusement.

Peace settled on the hill. The sun rose higher in the sky as though it had witnessed nothing extraordinary in its long dominion over the affairs of men. Miraculously, no Marine had been killed. Only a few suffered relatively minor wounds. That was in stark contrast to the corpses of dead NVA that littered the killing ground. The tropical climate began to rot them almost immediately. Scavengers attracted to the slaughter sailed in circles above while swarms of big green shit flies magically appeared, buzzing with anticipation.

"Clean this mess up and bury the stiffs in a trench before they stink up the whole neighborhood," Gunny instructed.

Whereupon I commented to Tony, "This neighborhood already stinks."

CHAPTER THIRTY-SIX

The Few, the Proud . . .

SITTING ATOP 881N WAITING FOR GOD ONLY KNEW WHAT, JUST WAIT-ing, I had time to think, to chew on the past and try to digest events that at the time seemed inconsequential, with no future value to the rest of my life. Suddenly, I became inflicted with a bad case of homesickness and realized what real impact some stages of life exerted on subsequent stages. You made your choices and you enjoyed their benefits or suffered their consequences. For me, enlisting in the Marine Corps was one of those life-changing—and perhaps life-ending—choices.

I remembered when my cousin Jack Earl Woods came home wearing his Marine dress blues and how that inspired me to enlist. How naïve and Okie-innocent I must have been when, enamored by the uniform and the prospect of heroic adventure, I strolled into the USMC recruiting office in Tulsa and declared my intent to become a By-God *U.S. Marine.*

"Congratulations, boy," the recruiting sergeant said. "You've chosen the toughest and the best. So if you think you got what it takes, you've come to the right place. But if you got a yellow streak or you're a mama's boy, don't waste my time. Best you know it now and *swish* over to the Navy or Air Force."

"I got what it takes," I avowed with all the bluster and confidence of an eighteen-year-old in the fly-over middle of the country who had not yet graduated from high school.

General Chesty Puller, the most-decorated Marine in US history, had what it took. Why not me?

My brother George was four years older than me. "Bobby, are you out of your ever-loving mind?" he scolded when he learned I was enlisting.

Little sister Tammy was eight and still wide-eyed and innocent. "I don't want you to go 'way," she protested. "Will you come home again?"

"You know I will."

Mom tried to be reasonable. "Do you know what you're getting into, honey? There's a war on. They'll send you if you're in the Marines. You could join the Air Force."

Dad? Dad was Dad. He took everything in stride.

And Linda? A fun girl always up for a beach party, a hike in the woods, a horseback ride, or a fishing trip. Loyal, too. She was no Peggy. I would never get a Dear John from her.

Linda cried. But it didn't matter. My mind was made up.

Marine Corps training was designed to take raw material like me and, through a process involving torture, indoctrination, and tradition, mold it into an efficient machine whose primary function was to break things, blow up shit, and kill people. Tough drill instructors burned *Semper Fidelis* into our receptive young skulls. *Always Faithful.* In honor, courage, and commitment. You never shirked your duty, and you never left a buddy behind.

Marines were America's elite expeditionary force, the nation's point of the spear when military force had to be applied. No better symbol existed for the Marines than the Eagle, Globe, and Anchor for the purpose we served. We wore the emblem proudly. The Eagle with its wings spread represented the nation we honorably defended. The Globe signified our worldwide presence. The Anchor pointed back to our naval heritage and the Marine Corps' ability to access any coastline anywhere in the world.

How proud, how *honored*, I felt to come home to Tulsa on boot camp leave in my dress blues to marry Linda and show off in front of my neighborhood chums and former classmates.

"Did you hear? Bob Maras joined the Marines. You ought to see him in his uniform."

The history of the Marine Corps stretched back a long ways. Perhaps the earliest predecessors of marines were the Vikings. Other than that, the evolution of seagoing infantry began with the European Naval Wars of the seventeenth and eighteenth centuries. In 1731, the British government raised ten Royal Marine regiments for naval campaigns against the Spanish colonies in the West Indies and on the north coast of South America. The American colonies contributed one regiment for the campaign, with which George Washington's half-brother Captain Lawrence Washington served.

Marines from the American colonies also pulled duty on British ship detachments in the French and Indian War of 1756–1763. A dozen years later, the Battles of Lexington and Concord severed ties with King George and sparked the American Revolutionary War.

The Second Continental Congress issued a letter dated 10 November 1775 recommending the commissioning of Marines to conduct ship-to-ship fighting, provide fleet shipboard security, enforce naval discipline, and assist beachhead landings against enemy nations. That letter resulted in the birth of the Continental Marines and set the date celebrated by the Marine Corps as its birthday.

A piece of tradition that sounds just raunchy enough to be true holds that newly commissioned Captains Samuel Nicholas and Robert Mullan recruited the first Marines by holding muster at Tun Tavern in Philadelphia and luring prospective candidates into service with mugs of beer and promises of adventure on the high seas.

Captain Nicholas led the first amphibious beach landing in American history when he and 220 Marines stormed ashore on the British-held island of New Providence in the Bahamas and conquered Nassau.

The US Marine Corps was here to stay as the fledgling nation's first truly elite military force. During the First Barbary War (1800–1805) against the Barbary Pirates of North Africa, eight US Marines landed at the head of thirty Arab and European mercenaries in an attempt to capture Tripoli and free the crew of the pirate-seized USS *Philadelphia*. Tripoli became immortalized in the Marine Corps Hymn.

The deposed pasha was so impressed by the American Marines that he presented his Mameluke sword to their commander, First Lieutenant Presley O'Bannon, beginning a tradition of swords worn formally by US Marine officers.

Marines have fought in every American war since then. During the Mexican-American War (1847–1848), Marines conducted their first major expeditionary venture with the famous assault on Chapultepec Palace to capture Mexico City. The event added "From the Halls of Montezuma" to the Marine Corps Hymn.

The US Civil War (1861–1865) found Marines fighting in a minor role on both the Union and Confederate sides. In one notable event in 1859, a prelude to the war itself, Lieutenant Israel Greene led a hastily gathered eighty-six-man detachment in storming abolitionist John Brown's fortifications at a Union armory he and his men took over at Harper's Ferry. The Marines captured Brown and killed some of his followers.

From 1898 to 1914, Marines continued to demonstrate their readiness for deployment by being utilized throughout the Caribbean and Latin America in various capacities. They assaulted beachheads in the Philippines, Cuba, and Puerto Rico during the 1898 Spanish-American War.

Marines were therefore battle-tested when World War I erupted in 1916 and ready to serve a central role. The action that assured their reputation into modern history took place in June 1918 at the Battle of Belleau Wood.

Ordered to withdraw from taking on the Germans, Captain Lloyd Williams rallied his outnumbered troops with, "Retreat? Hell, we just got here."

Gunnery Sergeant Dan Daly, ultimately a recipient of two Medals of Honor, led the way into battle, bellowing, "Come on, you sons of bitches! Do you want to live forever?"

German troops fled, relinquishing the area to the fierce US Marines, whom they nicknamed "Devil Dogs." In honor of the American Marines, the French government re-named Belleau Wood *Bois de la Brigade de Marine*. Wood of the Marine Brigade.

In the meantime, Vladimir Lenin ushered in his socialist revolution in Russia that led to the eventual rise of the Union of Soviet Socialist Republics (USSR). During this "workers revolution," Marines landed at Vladivostok to protect American citizens caught up in the violence.

In between World War I and World War II, the USMC developed a specific mission to distinguish it from the army—that of a fast-reacting light infantry that could be shipped rapidly to far off locations via the Navy to land on enemy-held beaches. Success depended on waves of high-speed assault craft landing under the cover of naval gunfire and air power.

In 1941, as World War II began, American and British ship architects developed and constructed hundreds of LSTs (landing ship, tank) capable of steaming across open waters hauling infantry, tanks, and supplies to combat-offload directly onto hostile beaches. Joe Rosenthal's famous *Raising the Flag* photo of five Marines and one Navy corpsman hoisting the Stars and Stripes over Iwo Jima symbolized "island hopping" Marine campaigns against Japanese in the Pacific.

Although Marines fought primarily in the Pacific theater against the Japanese, they were used on a more limited scale in other regions of the war. A Marine brigade occupied Iceland during the early stages. Other Marines served as advisors and trainers during British and American amphibious operations in Africa and Europe. Some were sharpshooters to detonate floating mines and clear the way for the landings at Normandy on D-Day. At least fifty Marines became intelligence agents and saboteurs for the OSS, the Office of Strategic Services, a predecessor of the CIA, Army Special Forces, and Navy SEALs.

After the armistice, Secretary of Defense Louis A. Johnson believed there would be no future major wars and argued that the United States no longer required a Marine Corps, that America's monopoly of the atomic bomb was adequate defense.

He went even further and confronted Admiral Richard L. Connolly. "Admiral," he said, "there is no reason for having a Navy and a Marine Corps. General Bradley told me amphibious operations are a thing of the past. We'll never have any more amphibious operations. That does away with the Marine Corps. And the Air Force can do anything the Navy can do, so that does away with the Navy."

He was not just wrong, he was dead wrong.

In 1950, North Korean communist troops rampaged across the border into South Korea. The 1st Provisional Marine Brigade held the line at the Battle of Pusan. General Douglas MacArthur ordered a Marine amphibious landing at Inchon that collapsed NK lines and drove the North Koreans back north to the Yalu River.

Hordes of Red Chinese entered the fight on the side of North Korea. They surprised, surrounded, and overwhelmed the over-extended and outnumbered Americans. The U.S. 8th Army retreated in disarray. The 1st Marine Division inflicted heavy losses on the enemy during its own withdrawal to the coast in what became known as the Battle of Chosin Reservoir. It was during this fight that Big Ed Crawford was wounded for the first time.

Marines continued their battle of attrition against the NKs along the 38th parallel until the 1953 armistice. On the night of 26 July 1953, Buck Sergeant Crawford and his platoon were holding a hilltop overlooking the 38th parallel. Expecting a ground attack during the night that he knew the Marines could not hold off, Crawford assembled the members of his platoon.

"Write a letter home like it may be your last letter," he instructed.

He gathered the letters, secured them in an ammo can, and gave the can to one of the tank commanders. "What you have in this ammo box is more important than anything," he emphasized. "You have to get it out."

Crawford's outfit waited anxiously for an attack that never came. Shortly after midnight and the beginning of 27 July, word came through that an armistice had been signed. The war was over.

Between 1953 and 1965, Marines were dispatched to a number of regional crises: the 3/3 Marines evacuated Americans from Alexandria, Egypt, during the 1956 Suez Canal crisis; in 1958, Operation Blue Bat sent them to brewing trouble in Lebanon; five thousand Marines landed in Thailand in 1962 to support that nation's struggle against communists; and in March 1965, the Walking Dead landed at Da Nang.

Way I figured it, US Marines had been fighting around the world for nearly two hundred years. That was hard to contemplate. And now here I was in that long continuum of Marine history dug in on a hilltop in northern South Vietnam waiting for the commies to strike again.

"Wonder whatever happened to the troop who bashed his head against the shower tile?" Tony mused.

I shrugged. "Probably brain damage. He's sitting in some corner drooling and sucking his thumb."

"I suppose it might be better than being dead."

Okinawa when we were still young and foolhardy seemed like a lifetime ago, although only a few weeks had passed since we left the island. For some of us, like Hill and Jaggers and Doc Heath and the others, it *had* been a lifetime ago. Life had changed dramatically in a very short time for those of us who survived this far. Life indeed had a special flavor when you fought for it, when life hung by a thread subject to fate, chance, and whim, when tomorrow, or even the next hour, might be your last. I felt about a hundred years old, and tired, disgusted, and homesick.

I even harbored nostalgia for Camp Schwab. We had fun there, like at a Boy Scout jamboree. Even the name—Camp *Schwab*—conjured up thoughts of mystery and adventure.

Schwab was the name of a US Marine flamethrower who received the Medal of Honor during World War II. He had been a Tulsa boy. Wouldn't it be something if *I* went back to Tulsa with an MOH? Closest I was likely to ever actually come though was as a witness to Sergeant Crawford's feats. Word had it that he was up for the award for bravery during the NVA attack against Hotel Company in the draw.

Tony and I had been among about two thousand fresh trainees flown into Kadena, Okinawa, and loaded onto cattle cars for the short ride to camp where we were to be conditioned and prepared for combat in Vietnam. Most of us had been in training now for some six months and were eager to get it all over with and ship out to the *real war*. We were *United States Marines*. Hell, yes! The baddest motherfuckers on the planet. Go over, kick ass, end the war, come back home heroes.

Newbies were on the low end of receiving information, the last ones to know what was going on. That kept us focused on training without distractions. The USMC goal was to get us through it and put us aboard ships for the 'Nam. They were exciting times, those few weeks ago before the reality of war set in. Every swinging dick in the By-God Crotch was

0300-designated infantry. From the lowest slick sleeve right up to the commandant. That meant everybody was, first, a *warrior*, not a manager. We were proud of that. The Crotch always led the way.

Every single day we had jungle patrols, camouflage and concealment, hand and arm signals, call for artillery, react to ambushes, setting up ambushes, offensive and defensive operations, rope training, first aid, exiting helicopters.... Instructors wrung us out from dawn to dusk in jungle and hills like those in Vietnam. Even a "combat village" had been erected to add verisimilitude to training. Local Okinawans, who were Asians of similar stock to Vietnamese, populated the village so we would know what to look for and how to react during "search and destroy" missions once we were in-country.

One day, to teach us a lesson, the village turned against us. It was full of "Viet Cong," as the home-grown commies were called in South Vietnam. They ambushed our patrol and wiped us all out. Sergeant Baker, our principle instructor, was really pissed off at our carelessness. He ran amok jabbing each of us with his stick and chanting with each jab, "You're dead!"

"You're dead!"

"You're dead!"

"Damnit, you're *all* dead!"

Not many kind words escaped the stone lips of Sergeant Baker, more commonly referred to as "Sergeant Hard." Like Big Ed, he was a tough Korean War vet. Been there, done that.

"You pussy-faced cockroaches," he roared. "What, you wanna get your asses shot off, girls? This ain't no prep school. If you pukes wanna live, you do *what* I tell you, *when* I tell you. Now get down, get down and give me pushups."

"How many, Sergeant Hard?"

"Do 'em until *I* get tired."

Tony and I got volunteered to help him string a rope training bridge across a little creek. Damn! What rotten luck. Tony said he was as jittery about it as a dog shitting razor blades. I couldn't top that description, but I knew what he meant.

To our astonishment, once there were just the three of us, we discovered Sergeant Hard was *human* after all, with a sense of humor. He had two sides to his personality—the professional *Sergeant Hard* and the secret *Everyman* who surfaced for special occasions when he let down a bit.

We were laughing and joking and Tony was channeling his Buddy Hackett when our troops showed up to train on the bridge. It was like *Everyman* slipped into Superman's phone booth and came out *Sergeant Hard.*

"You bunch of pussies! You mama's boys are gonna come home in body bags."

Camp Schwab wasn't a boot camp. We had free days now and then to soak up some rays on the beach or sip suds at the bars in Honoko where the bar maids weren't too particular at carding us and the Shore Patrol left us alone, seeing as how we were bound for Vietnam, as long as we didn't break things, start fights, and fuck with the locals.

One Sunday, Tony and I dived for octopi off the coast to sell to natives for beer money. We got badly sunburned, a violation of the Uniform Code of Military Justice. A Marine's body was property of the United States; you did not abuse US property.

That was one of the first times Magilla Gorilla, the Navy corpsman, saved our asses. He had to pour water on our t-shirts to get them off without taking hide and all.

"I'll fix you up," he said. "Don't say anything to anybody about it."

Through all the fun, however, ran a threat. While the survivors of the ambush that all but decimated 2/3 participated in the up-training to integrate Cherries into the battalion, it was like they went through the motions without actually being there. They had seen their buddies mangled and dead, and now they would be returning to Vietnam with fresh meat. You looked into their faces, into their hardened eyes, and you realized all the training we endured had a real-life, practical application that could well mean life or death.

Now, in the Hill Fights, I had already experienced too much of death. Marines, some of them friends, so full of life before, suddenly empty and gray. I kept thinking: *That could be me. That could be Tony.*

Tony and I were best buds, closer than brothers, together since the first day of boot camp. We looked out for each other. What happened if Tony bought the farm? If so, why him and not me? I thought if he got it, maybe I should get it too. Maybe get it in his place. That was fair.

What about our other friends lost in these hills? How fair was that? Jaggers, Robert J. Todd, Hill with his bad luck Bowie knife, Boda, Carter, Schmitz, Corpsman Heath . . . all dead.

All dead, and many others as well.

Tony and me. We had to make it back to The World, to the Land of the Big PX, more so for our families than for ourselves. Sometimes, I imagined Linda and Mom, my Dad and my brother and sister all weeping together around a flag-draped coffin.

Crouched in my hole I smelled the thick nauseating air filled with the stench of decaying human flesh. I tasted sweat on my upper lip. Felt it dribbling from my arm pits. My elbow ached from the shrapnel wound. I heard a spatter of rifle fire down in the valley between 881N and 881S. I looked up and saw my friend the green parrot sail overhead. Higher up, white frigate birds glided south. Tony passed gas. Loudly. I sniggered.

I wondered if in another two hundred years from now, future Marines might not be dug in among these same hills fighting for their lives. Mankind seemed to keep repeating the same mistakes century after century.

CHAPTER THIRTY-SEVEN

Sleep Like the Dead

PAPPY DELONG DISABUSED US OF THE NOTION—CALL IT THE *HOPE*—
that the fight was over once we conquered the hills. We held them, but
the NVA were a long way from gone. Our next task, we were informed,
was to disinfect the valleys and draws of the perverted little bastards and
chase them back into Laos and North Vietnam where they belonged.
Pappy wanted to keep them off-balance to prevent their regrouping
against *our* hills.

He briefed the battalion's company commanders on his strategy. They
were required to send out daily patrols by platoon to maintain a constant
presence. S-3 Ops would provide each company its patrol responsibilities,
daily routes, and checkpoint grid coordinates.

"We want to let the NVA know we're out here and we're going to kill
them whenever and wherever we find them," he said.

My thoughts were that whoever represented Uncle Ho and General
Giap in the NVA 325th gave the same instructions to his officers in
sneakers. What it boiled down to was that the two sides killed each other
whenever and wherever we met. Sounded to me like a recipe for disaster,
a plan for knocking each other back to the Stone Age. At that rate, these
hill fights would never be over until the last two men met like David and
Goliath for the championship.

Each morning at first light, patrol duty platoons jocked up and prepared to set out. Golf Company's AO lay to the west and northwest off
881N. We humped out to whatever checkpoints were assigned us over

steep, rugged terrain and back again, returning to the perimeter at dusk dragging our asses. Much of the time we had to go out again the next morning, which left precious little time for chow, cleaning gear, and other housekeeping before nightfall when we went to ground against possible enemy attacks.

Add to this innervating schedule the misery of OP/LP and perimeter watches, the sun simmering against us in the jungle by day, and long, restless nights without a breeze. The troops were beat down to nubbins and praying for relief.

So let me get this straight: Our orders were to kill them, their orders were to kill us. So why all the blocking and feinting, like washed-up prize fighters reluctant to mix it up and get a bloody nose? Whenever we spotted the enemy on patrol, it was generally from a distance—gooks flitting through trees or disappearing over the next ridgeline. We discovered plenty of sign they were still out here. Trails, discarded or lost equipment, blood stains, camp fires, latrine slit trenches. . . . But the enemy was obviously avoiding contact. Which was okay by us regular grunts. I liked the NVA's new approach to the war: Live and let live.

Captain Sheehan and Lieutenant Mac thought Uncle Ho was biding his time and building up troops and resources in preparation for another major offensive. If so, sooner or later, we were bound to find ourselves butting heads in another desperate fight for control of the hills and in defense of the Khe Sanh Combat Base.

When not on patrol, we labored to build up defenses, just in case our officers were correct in assuming the present quiet was merely a lull before the storm struck again. Choppers ferried in C-4 explosives, wire, antipersonnel Claymore mines, and anything else we might utilize to construct a barrier between ourselves and the barbarians at the gate. Labor parties knocked down thickets and towering stands of elephant grass below the crest to enlarge our fields of fire. We laid out concertina wire and tanglefoot spiked with C-4 and grenades.

It seemed improbable that the commie NVA would even attempt to break through all this, especially in the dark. Even if by chance they made it through these first defenses, what awaited them were Claymore mines either command detonated or connected to trip wires. A Claymore was a nasty piece of work constructed of C-4 molded in a shape that sprayed fans of ball bearings to chop down anything within its radius.

I chose to believe we were impervious to attack, but nothing was a sure thing when it came to committed commies fanatical enough to sacrifice themselves for "the cause."

Nights, the enemy sent out teams to mortar us. Half-heartedly though, as if simply letting us know they were watching. Our arty at the airfield responded with heavy H&I to let the NVA know *we* were watching back. Random explosions targeting valleys, draws, and ridges where NVA might try to congregate, where they had in fact congregated before, kept our nerves on edge. But not nearly so much as when NVA mortar rounds dropped in uninvited among us, although not doing much damage except to our psyche and nerves. We went through most days pissed off and aching for a big set battle or something, *anything*, to put an end to this shit.

Yesterday, Tony and I had gone out on patrol with Lieutenant Mac's 3rd Platoon to search for a gook mortar site that kept harassing us at night. When we arrived at the suspected location, on the back side of a wooded ridge not far from the knob where Echo had fought that terrible dark battle, nothing remained except a couple of expended shell casings, an indention in the earth from the mortar base plate, and, nearby, a steaming fresh pile of feces.

We scoured around, but the Viets were still avoiding and evading. We had to pick up the pace to get back inside our perimeter before nightfall. You didn't want to be out here in the dark unprotected and vulnerable when Count Drac and the boys came out to play.

Safe inside our perimeter—or at least as safe as we might expect under present conditions—Tony yawned mightily the next morning and stretched out cramps and muscle kinks from yesterday's patrol hump. His leg still bothered him sometimes. The sun gradually rayed out to touch finger tips to the tops of the three hilltops that encompassed our entire world. We had become like rodents living in holes, who darted out to snatch crumbs while avoiding traps and predators.

Tony let out gas, loud and long, but the pervasive smell was of bodies and napalm.

Sometimes I was afraid the odor had ingrained itself into the pores of my nostrils so that I would smell it for the rest of my life. I had slept hard last night after our return, curled up in my poncho on the ground outside the hole during my 50 of our 50-50 alert. *Slept like the dead.* That was an old term people back home used without even thinking about it.

I hated that phrase now, vowed never to use it again, not even to *think* it. The dead weren't sleeping; they were *dead.* Speaking of which, I had no firm idea about how many Marines we might have lost so far in these hills. Word circulated that US Marines had killed 3,491 NVA in I-Corps up to last month while losing *only* 541 of our own. I supposed that was meant to be a morale booster to demonstrate how the body count showed we were winning.

So how many had we lost since the Hill Fights started?

Nobody was talking about it. Maybe the brass didn't want to scare the hell out of us. I spoke to a medevac chopper crew chief while I was helping load a mortar casualty aboard. He told me that during evacs at the worst part of the struggles for 881N and 881S he had used buckets of water back at the airfield to wash blood from the deck of his helicopter.

"That's exactly the kind of information I need," I responded wryly.

"You get used to it," he said matter-of-factly. But I noticed the strain and uneasiness in his eyes.

Killing and dying were part of war. You had to accept it or you went crazy. But you never got *used* to it.

"So," I mentioned to Tony, "we kill about three thousand gooks while at the same time they kill five hundred Marines. That's what, a ratio of about six-to-one? How long does it take us to wipe out all of 'em?"

"We won't," Tony pointed out. "There's a lot more of them than of us."

Heavy dew had settled on my poncho overnight after the patrol. I channeled the moisture into a low pocket and sucked it dry. Food and water remained a rationed commodity even though resupply choppers were coming in fairly regularly now, in spite of their still being targeted by antiaircraft emplacements along their routes. I looked back on the big monsoon rain and the bomb crater filled with water and dead gooks with a certain sentimentality. It was, after all, *real* water.

Gunny promised a resupply today. If an army traveled on its stomach, this army hadn't the stomach to go much farther. Except, we weren't army. We were *Marines*. Marines kept going while the army pussied out and took the day off.

"What's for chow this morning?" Tony asked. "We got enough water for coffee?"

I shook my canteen.

"That's it?"

I pointed downhill. "Unless you want to go back to the river or suck some water out of bamboo."

"I got something you can suck on."

We managed to score up breakfast and coffee with PFC Taylor's contribution and a little bartering with a C-rat pack of Lucky Strikes. Ham and lima beans.

"We're on the roster for another patrol," Taylor said, getting up and rubbing his belly. "See you in about fifteen mikes."

Tony had used his M-16 during the night for a "sound shot." When he broke out his cleaning kit, I wondered how many of our guys had died because of Mattie Mattell and some bigwig motherfuckers and politicians back in the Home of the Big PX getting rich off our blood by manufacturing cheap rifles they had to know were faulty.

Last night in the middle of my turn at sleeping, I startled awake to the strange quacking sound of NVA laughter downhill at the edge of the forest. Tony was tired and had had about all this happy horse shit he could stand.

"The bastards! The dirty little bastards!" he hissed. "Them motherfuckers are *laughing* at us, Maras."

"Piss on them."

The sound of gook laughter was what triggered his "sound shot" reaction. The muzzle of his M-16 flashed fire as he unleashed a burst into the distant dark outline of trees. The laughter stopped.

"Piss on them," he said. "And piss on her."

Always Peggy.

"Knock that shit off!" a sergeant shouted.

Due to the frequent usage of the phrase, I wondered why it hadn't been incorporated into *The Marine Corps Training Manual.*

CHAPTER THIRTY-EIGHT

Mushy Dianne

IT APPEARED THE MISSION OF THE B-52 BOMBERS THAT CHASED THE skies from Khe Sanh and the hills north to Ho Chi Minh Land and west to Laos was to pound North Vietnamese troops into the ground and annihilate even the memory of them. If not for their Arc Light bombings, so called because of the awesome display of power when their ordnance exploded on target, the NVA may well have been able to amass enough troops to drive through all the way to Da Nang. Everyone took note when a formation of the big swept-wing birds flew high above heading north or west, their silver wings glinting back light from the universe.

It was like the sun itself exploded when they let loose, a tremendous burst of blinding light that pulsated against the horizon. At first, all was deathly quiet while the light expanded. Sound and shock waves followed, rumbling and echoing through the hills so that you felt it in the soles of your feet and in the soles of your soul. Trees shuddered. Birds, rock apes, and krait snakes fled.

Witnessing it, even from afar, must have been a bit like at White Sands that day in 1945 when the first atomic bomb exploded and Dr. Robert Oppenheimer uttered his famous phrase: "Now I am become death, the destroyer of worlds." B-52s terrified the Vietnamese and caused them tremendous suffering. *I* was terrified, just watching it. But fuck 'em.

Kill 'em all, like some guys scrawled on their helmet covers, *and let God sort 'em out.*

CIA spooks, State Department "fact finders," congressional investigators, and Pentagon military brass trailed by reporters were constantly choppering in to take a quick look around, ask some questions, then shag ass back out before nightfall. No one wanted to be caught in these hills after dark. The rotating presence of so many dignitaries demonstrated the investment President LBJ and Washington placed in Khe Sanh.

Tony cynically diagnosed politics as the problem. "This would all end," he predicted, "if the fucking politicians would stop yapping, pick up their toys and go home. They strut around like banty roosters crowing and scratching in the dirt—but we're the fighting gamecocks who die, not them."

B-52s were starting to prowl shortly after sunrise when a Sea Knight slipped in with what I assumed to be another load of prominents, among them Pappy Delong and a lean, fit-looking man wearing a green foreign field uniform and a black patch over his left eye. The two stood together talking at the crest of the hill where it fell off into the green expanse of Vietnam that lay below and toward the north and west.

"Who's the Black Bart pirate?" I wondered as Gunny Janzen walked by carrying two tin canteen cups of coffee for Pappy and his guest.

"Moshe Dayan," he said.

"Mushy Dianne?"

"*Moshe Dayan.* Don't they teach you nothing in school?"

I was only fucking with the Gunny. Everybody knew the famous Israeli general, former Chief of Staff of the Israeli Defense Forces, hero of such campaigns as the Palestinian Arab Revolt, the 1948 Arab-Israeli War, the Suez Crisis. He lost his eye in 1941 when, during the early stages of World War II before the United States entered it, he was assigned to a small reconnaissance task force attached to the Australian 7th Division in preparation for the invasion of Syria and Lebanon. Wearing traditional Arab dress, the unit frequently infiltrated Vichy French Lebanon on covert surveillance missions.

On 7 June 1941, the night before the invasion of Syria, Dayan's outfit captured a Vichy police station. He was on the roof of the building using binoculars to scan Vichy positions on the other side of the Litani River when a sniper bullet struck his binoculars, driving metal and glass fragments into his left eye, blinding it. The black eye patch became his trademark.

"He's here to study the triad of ground, air, and naval warfare so he can use it in Israel's fight against the Arab Muslims," Gunny explained.

I thought about it. "Gunny, how many wars you reckon are going on in the world right at this moment?"

He shrugged. "I don't know. Maybe a dozen or so. The only one you got to worry about is *this* one."

"Gunny, you ever think about why God made us like this—always killing each other?"

"That's out of your pay grade, Maras. Your job is to shoot that machine gun when you're told to shoot it. Now cut the bullshit."

Gunny walked on, leaving me pondering on how *everything* seemed to be above my pay grade.

Speculatively, I watched from my distance while General Dayan and Colonel Delong sipped from their cups of bitter field coffee. Pappy gestured and pointed, explaining something. Both fell silent when an Arc Light opened a white gash on the western horizon. Moshe Dayan, I thought, would have made one hell of a US Marine.

Pappy intercepted Lieutenant Charles Chritton, who was preparing to lead a platoon-sized Foxtrot patrol into the bush. The battalion commander and the Israeli officer spoke with the lieutenant a few minutes, apparently concerning patrol procedures, before the platoon silently filed off the hill and the Marines one by one melted into morning fog that clung to the terrain's lower recesses.

Better Foxtrot than Golf again. Yesterday, Lieutenant Mac's 3rd Platoon with Tony and me once more attached to PFC Taylor's squad had suffered a long, uneventful walk in the sweltering sunshine. My legs were still sore, and Tony limped back into the perimeter on his bad leg.

An hour or so after the Foxtrot patrol departed the wire, a chopper delivered resupply and picked up Pappy, General Dayan, their aides, and a Marine escort to deliver back to Khe Sanh. I expected maybe some mail from Mom and Linda. Tony hunched down into his thick shoulders and scowled. I knew what he was thinking.

"Piss on her."

No mail came. Maybe tomorrow.

About noon as Foxtrot patrolled the lowlands, the stench of rotting flesh attracted Sergeant Chritton to a grassy clearing in a creek valley between the Evil Twin Sisters. Blood-soaked bandages, bloody web gear, scraps of clothing, bashed helmets, and other discarded or damaged items littered the clearing. The site appeared to be an abandoned NVA field hospital. Clashes with Marines and B-52 Arc Lights, along with arty barrages and air power, were obviously doing a bunch of damage to the NVA. How much longer could they possibly hang on?

Lieutenant Chritton radioed his find to Foxtrot's commander, who ordered him to proceed toward the day's final checkpoint. More bloody discards marked a track through the jungle leading toward Laos. The patrol followed it cautiously, climbing steadily out of the valley up one of the region's many ridges.

Every man felt an unseen malevolent presence. Hills seemed to have eyes. The disciplined Marines kept down noise as they walked, careful to avoid equipment rattles, their weapons ready, fingers next to triggers, expecting contact. The enemy would pick the time and place.

The patrol pushed another five klicks to the day's checkpoint without encountering opposition before it circled wide to return to 881N. A relieved platoon of Foxtrot Marines topped the hill ahead of the dark and passed through into the perimeter and the welcoming hearth of our mountain home.

CHAPTER THIRTY-NINE

The Ridge Finger

CAPTAIN MERLE SORENSEN, A THIRTY-ONE-YEAR-OLD KANSAN AND the commander of Foxtrot Company, was a man of few words—but when he spoke, people listened. He looked beat down from the day-after-day pace when Foxtrot went up on the patrol board for the third day in a row.

Foxtrot was not his first command. Two years ago, he had led Marine Alpha 1/6 ashore in the Dominican Republic to help put down a communist-inspired rebellion. Then, as now, he led from the front, a habit his Marines deeply respected. He refused to stay behind. From his viewpoint, a CO belonged with his troops.

After laying out the route and checkpoints, Sorensen, a small CP group, and two platoons of about seventy Marines departed the 2/3 Battalion wire at daybreak underneath a clear sky already heating up, and set out in tactical combat formation for the day's objective, the abandoned Nung village of Lang Xoa. Laid out on the map, the distance was less than three miles as the green parrot flies, but factoring in the terrain probably made it twice that far.

Order of march put Lieutenant Pat Carroll's Third Platoon on point, trailed by Lieutenant Jack Schworm's First Platoon, with Sorensen and his CP pulling drag. Due to the lay of the land, Foxtrot had to move slower than expected. Battalion Ops kept radioing Captain Sorensen to pick up the pace.

While Foxtrot cut across toward Lang Xoa, Lieutenant John Adinolfi led two Echo Company platoons on the day's second patrol, which roughly paralleled Foxtrot's to the southwest. Echo's checkpoint objective for the day was one of the lower hills, Hill 803 that lay south of the Nung village.

Shortly after noon, Foxtrot came upon a trail that led off the steep southwestern slope of Hill 778 in the direction of Lang Xoa. Prodded by Battalion Ops, Sorensen chose to save time by following the track, even though it was against his better judgment. He cautioned Lieutenant Carroll to keep point alert for enemy activity. The purpose of his patrol was to determine the numbers of NVA that remained present and viable in the AO and what their intent might be. That didn't mean you had to get among them and count heads.

Descending 778, Lieutenant Carroll's platoon entered a wide, flat ravine where his point squad led by a lance corporal shot up an "enemy near" sign that halted progress. The patrol went to its knee, weapons bristling and ready, while Carroll made his way to the front. The lance corporal indicated a fresh sneaker footprint imbedded in the soft soil of the ravine. He also pointed out a fresh pile of bodily wastes.

A short distance ahead, a second, smaller ravine intersected the first at a right angle. To one side rose a ridge finger that ran down from a larger ridge off 778. Carroll's survival instinct kicked in like a pounding hammer in his chest—a sudden premonition of impending disaster. He realized his platoon may have walked into an ambush kill zone. The high ground of the ridge ahead provided the enemy a perfect opportunity to catch the entire patrol in the open. If his feeling was right, the NVA were only waiting to trigger until the entire patrol ventured into the ravine.

Too late to turn back.

"Up there!" he suddenly shouted, acting on his instinct and pointing to the ridge finger, his training automatically seeking high ground. If he were wrong, he could live with his decision. But if he were right. . . .

"Get up the finger!" the lieutenant bellowed. "Don't let them get on the other ridge above us!"

Marines, recognizing the urgency in the platoon leader's voice, raced headlong across the wide ravine to scramble out and up. As they neared the finger's backbone, NVA soldiers hiding behind rocks and trees opened fire in a blistering barrage that filled the air with shrieking steel. Glancing back, Carroll spotted a large group of NVA charging out of the intersecting ravine to the right in an obvious maneuver to cut off and divide the Marine platoon.

He fired his .45 pistol as fast as he could squeeze the trigger. At least one of the gooks bit the dust; the others disappeared around a bend out of sight, still heading for Captain Sorensen and First Platoon bringing up drag.

The patrol's best chance lay in taking over the ridge finger and then the higher ridge beyond. Driven by desperation, Carroll urged his men forward.

"*Go! Go!*"

He grabbed his radio operator. "Contact Echo Six [Sorensen]. Tell him he's got gooks heading his way."

Sorensen would have to handle that part of the fight himself.

Marines fought valiantly, shouting back at the NVA and blazing away with everything they had in a mad race up the steep slope infested by enemy soldiers hurling grenades and firing their AKs. Wounded and dying men dropped on both sides. Corpsmen dashed through the confusion tending casualties and wrestling them to cover.

One corpsman came upon a Marine sprawled behind a rock and cursing with feeling as he worked frantically to clear his malfunctioning weapon. He was one of every four in the battalion that had actually been issued a cleaning rod. He rolled over on his back, cradling his M-16 against his chest while he hammered the rod down the muzzle.

"*Fuck, fuck, fuck, fuck . . .!*" he chanted.

The corpsman dropped next to him. "Here," he said, handing his pistol to the Marine. "Take it. I got too many wounded Marines to worry about."

The fight raged so intensely that Lieutenant Carroll failed to realize his .45 was empty. A gook armed with a bayonetted rifle lunged from a copse of trees. Carroll's pistol clicked.

From the corner of his eye he spotted a discarded M-16. He hit the ground and rolled, snatching up the rifle. *It better work, it better work . . .*

chorused through his mind. The gook was almost upon him, his weapon poised to ram its bayonet into the Marine's chest.

The M-16 worked. The enemy soldier fell not six feet away.

In the meantime, off to the lieutenant's left flank, howling Vietnamese overran a Marine fire team, swarming over the Americans like a pack of wolves, shooting wounded and able alike point-blank.

Up and down the ridge Marines were running out of ammo and desperately yelling for more. Lieutenant Carroll had got separated from his radioman. He came upon him now where a bullet had dumped him frightened and lapsing in and out of consciousness on the ground, his utilities blood-soaked. The radio he carried on his back still functioned. The lieutenant slung his commandeered rifle and the RTO's commo on his back and dragged the wounded man through a hailstorm of enemy fire toward the safety of a nearby tree.

A bullet slapped Carroll's thigh, knocking his leg out from underneath him and collapsing him on top of his RTO. Another slug plucked off his left thumb.

Things got worse, much worse. The two Marines were left fully exposed. The RTO lay unmoving, either dead or passed out from shock. Carroll refused to leave him. Though seriously wounded himself, he continued to try to drag his RTO to the tree.

He screamed out in pain as yet a third enemy round found its mark. This one shattered his lower leg and left his boot flopping with his foot still in it, all but detached from his leg. Now bleeding badly and unable to help himself, much less his radioman, he dragged his bullet-riddled body along by his elbows, struggling to gain the advantage of height while fusillades of enemy fire scorched the air around him.

He broke free of the kill zone by rolling into a shallow depression already occupied by several other walking wounded. Outside the sinkhole, Marines fought hand-to-hand with NVA infantry. Lieutenant Carroll and the others too badly injured to participate huddled together and prepared to fight to the end.

As the insane carnage continued, Captain Sorensen farther back fought through the enemy detached to stop him and drove the rest of the patrol straight up the side of the finger to join in the battle. A 30-caliber slug slammed into his right hip, dropping him to the ground where he found himself semi-paralyzed and unable to move. His RTO dragged him to safety in a clump of trees.

Foxtrot's attempt to secure the ridge finger and its adjoining high ground bogged down against stiff NVA resistance. All along the up side of the finger, individual groups of Marines sought cover and continued private and isolated little static wars of their own against enemy strongholds. It quickly became clear to the Marines that they were outnumbered. The tables had turned. Marines went on the defense as NVA swarmed and surged like big green shit flies over a carcass, stabbing and shooting wounded Americans.

Not far away, Echo's two-platoon patrol was approaching Hill 803, its checkpoint objective, when heavy shooting broke out on Foxtrot's route. To the Marines of Echo Company, it sounded like Foxtrot may have stumbled upon the entire NVA 325th Regiment.

Lieutenant Adinolfi picked up the distressed patrol's radio transmissions to Battalion: "*Pygmalion Six, this is Foxtrot Six. . . . We've got seven kangaroos and ten wolves. . . .*"

Seven dead, ten wounded. So far.

Adinolfi's platoons scurried up Hill 803, which looked down across a wooded draw to 788 and the ridgeline where the embattled Marines of Foxtrot fought for their lives. Adinolfi and Platoon Leader Lieutenant James Cannon gazed down in horror upon a scene of smoke and dueling tracers, heard screams of pain and fierce rage, glimpsed men of opposing sides fighting at each other's throats.

Cannon pointed out a giant tree on the ridge finger that appeared to mark the boundary between NVA forces and Captain Sorensen's Marines. Everything to the left of the tree was either NVA or dead Marines, while live Marines and dead gooks populated the right side of the tree. The distance across the draw was nearly a thousand meters, out of effective range for M-16s. Certainly grenades were out of the question. It would be suicide for Echo to try to cross the draw to relieve Foxtrot and make itself vulnerable in the low ground.

Lieutenant Adinolfi and Echo's Weapons Platoon sergeant hurriedly set up a pair of M-60 machine guns and opened up on terrain to the left of the big tree, raking NVA positions from the tree to the ridge crown with heavy 7.62 bullets, cutting a swath through the surprised NVA that promptly drove them back. After a few minutes of being hammered, the Vietnamese withdrew like ghosts into the jungle on the far side of the ridge.

Silence fell, eerie in contrast to the bedlam that preceded, punctuated only by the wailing and screaming of the wounded.

Battle over, Echo traversed to the ridge finger to help able-bodied Marines in the grisly task of policing up the dead and wounded. Some of the men who had been shot in the head execution-style at close range were unrecognizable.

While this was transpiring, a Marine detail sent to find a clearing in the trees that could be used as a medevac LZ discovered an enemy field cemetery that contained 203 fresh graves, mute testimony to the impact Marines and US artillery and airpower were exerting on the battle environment.

By 1700, helicopters had evacuated Foxtrot's dead and wounded to the Combat Base at Khe Sanh. Other birds lifted out the survivors to 881N, where those of us manning the perimeter watched the Sea Knights approach. We had listened since about noon with growing anxiety as sounds of the distant battle rambled and bounced among the surrounding hills.

A handful of dazed and bloody Foxtrot Marines exited the pair of choppers when they set down. Their utilities were ripped and tattered, red dirt ground into them, helmets and gear missing, eyes dull and sunken into their heads. They were quiet and withdrawn, as though not yet convinced they had actually made it back.

"Where's the rest of the patrol?" someone asked.

"This is it," came the terse response.

Twenty-four of their number died out there that day, and nineteen others were wounded, including Foxtrot's CO, Captain Sorensen, and one of his platoon leaders, Lieutenant Carroll, both of whom were in serious condition.

Tony and I watched stunned as the returning warriors milled about, not celebrating their salvation, simply staring at the ground, at the sky, at each other. Very quiet, withdrawn, like empty husks. We watched the helicopters take off again and whirlybird toward Khe Sanh. Watched them diminish in the sky until they disappeared. Said nothing to each other while we leaned on our elbows on the lip of our hole and watched the sun slowly sink into Laos.

Chapter Forty

Body Count

Viet fighters seemed to lose momentum after their big brawl with Foxtrot near Lang Xoa. B-52s expanded their bombing patterns up toward—and perhaps over—the Laotian border and north along the DMZ. They flew high above, specks against the tropical sky, dropping their loads farther away. The sound was like distant thunder rather than the approaching crash of an electrical storm.

Conditions on 881N—and probably 881S as well—got downright luxurious once resupply choppers were no longer subject to mortar attacks every time they skipped in for a visit. We ate better, although the menu consisted of the same old tin-can C-rats (only more of them); drank fresh water (but out of the same old canteens); and began to receive mail and care packages (without the doggie treats included). The stench of death faded gradually. If Tony whiffed something on an errant wind, he accused me of passing gas. I did the same to him. We took our morning piss together—"Good morning, Vietnam!"—without having to duck sniper shots or mortar shells. We dared to think the Hill Fights might be over and that we had won, although OP/LPs still had to be manned, perimeter watches maintained, weapons and gear cleaned, daily patrols run.

I spotted the green parrot flying over the hill. Probably a sibling or cousin, rogue daddy or slut mama, but no matter. I always thought of him as the same one, an old buddy with freedom under his wings and no worries. In a stream of idle whimsy, I saw him as a bird on a recon to report the state of the jungle to his fellow critters—tigers and elephants and deer and monkeys—few of whom I had observed so far. Couldn't say I blamed the elephants for packing their trunks and leading the other animals in evac'ing the AO. Had I my druthers, I would druther have packed my own ditty bag and departed with them.

Tony reminded me that we had had our druthers after being struck by mortar fragments.

"But *no-o-o-o*," he dramatized. "Maras had to be the hero. I don't feel like a hero. I feel like a fool standing in shit up to my neck, holding my nose, and pretending I'm in a Hilton Hotel swimming pool."

"You didn't have to stay. You could have left without me."

"And leave you out here alone with these poor gooks! How fair would that have been to *them?* Perish the thought."

He sighed, making a production of it. "It wouldn't have been right," he said.

Along with a rifle and name-stenciled skivvies, the USMC issued every recruit a sense of duty, responsibility, and, yes, guilt. One for all, all for one. The sort of mindset that prompted a Marine to forsake self interest in favor of doing what was expected in regard to buddies and the By-God Crotch. Living that maxim caused Marines to die for it and contribute a heavy body count.

The term *body count* had become common usage in Vietnam as a standard for gauging the progress of the war. After contact, higher-higher demanded an After Action on how many of *them* we killed. That was one of a leader's responsibilities. *Let's see, this guy is blown in two parts. Does that count as one body or two bodies?*

The news media took these gory stats and broadcast them around the world for entertainment and edification: *Today, in a major action near Da Nang in the Republic of Vietnam, the U.S. destroyed 308 Viet Cong soldiers while losing only 26 American lives.* Followed by an ad for *Things go better with Coca-Cola,* or *I'd walk a mile for a Camel.*

The NVA didn't have to keep their own body counts. Newspapers and TV in the West supplied them with a running tally of American losses, along with live coverage of the latest peacenik marches, draft-card burnings, antiwar demonstrations, and assorted hippie be-ins and stink-ins. Uncle Ho didn't have to have his Dien Bien Phu at Khe Sanh in order to win the war. I could almost see the old fucker wringing his hands in delight in anticipation of the United States winning every battle over here while losing the war back home.

I resented the term *body count* when applied to us. Doc Heath and the others were not *body counts*; they had been live human beings with names and ambitions and people at home who loved them. To refer to them collectively as *body counts* diminished their ever having been, reduced them to statistics and forgotten names hardly anyone would remember in a few years.

I wondered how long Linda would remember me if I never made it back.

How about *Khe Sanh*? Who would remember it and the Hill Fights after those of us who fought here were gone? I kept imagining LBJ in the Oval Office in his boxer shorts jumping up and down with joy and sending Uncle Ho nasty greeting cards over a victory *he* won a half-world away, a vindication of leadership policies that a generation from now everyone would have forgotten.

It wasn't as though Khe Sanh was D-Day or Anzio or Hiroshima or Pearl Harbor. Or even Pork Chop Hill, the Frozen Chosin, or Inchon . . . Belleau Wood and the trenches of World War I France . . . Teddy Roosevelt and San Juan Hill . . . The Battle of Bunker Hill . . . Gettysburg or Shiloh in the Civil War.

Khe Sanh?

"Papa, what's a Khe Sanh?" my little grandchild might ask one day, if I lived that long.

A tour of duty in Vietnam was one year. I had about eleven months to go. At the rate of the body count in the Hill Fights, the odds were stacked against me.

Christ, I was growing melancholy at the advanced age of nineteen.

Tony and I cornered Gunny Janzen. "When do we get our five-day R&R for capturing the POWs?" we asked.

"Way I heard it, they came up and *begged* you to capture them." He was poking at us. His sense of humor was returning now that things had slowed down. "Don't worry about it, boys. If the Marine Corps wants you to have R&R, you'll get it issued."

"We thought *you* were the Marine Corps." Poking him back.

"My daddy wore OD skivvies with a globe and anchor tattooed on his chest. My mama was a Tijuana whore. Does that sound like I'm the Marine Corps?"

I admitted it did. Gunny chuckled. "You'll get your R&R," he promised. "When we get to Hanoi."

The enemy was still out there—still being monsters in the dark—but they seemed to be fewer and with less bite. You could powder the hell out of Fido for fleas, but some always remained hiding in the hair. I supposed Uncle Ho left a few unlucky bastards behind to harass us and gather intel for when he might decide to try another Dien Bien Phu operation.

Rumors persisted that there were NVA base training camps hidden out in the jungles where the gooks bided their time and built up forces. We didn't want to make contact. Neither, apparently, did the gooks. What we heard was that they had written off the hills for now and were considering circumventing them in order to attack the Khe Sanh airfield directly and in overwhelming force.

Our daily patrols became little more than long marches in the sun. Rather pleasant strolls, actually. Once, we surprised an elephant basking in the sunshine by a watering hole, a highlight talked about within the perimeters of the two 881s. We had heard gooks used elephants as beasts of burden, like Genghis Khan and his Mongol hordes, but no one that I knew of had actually witnessed it.

Our patrols were reduced from platoon-sized elements to squads, there being no real need for larger forces. A squad could sneak and peek more on the quiet, without as much chance of being discovered.

Lieutenant McFarlane assigned PFC Taylor to lead his 1st Squad on patrol west in the direction of Laos to cop a look for possible enemy infiltration routes. Taylor chose Tony and me for heavy weapons, along with Ramirez as his point man. A patrol didn't have to worry about blundering into an ambush with Ramirez out front as its eyes, ears, and nose. He could *smell* gooks a mile upwind or a half-mile downwind.

First Squad reached our objective checkpoint and turned back. We had encountered nothing remotely suspicious—no tennis shoe prints, latrine cat holes, no sounds except those made by critters. Places in the forest were scorched and dug up from H&I artillery and air delivery, but it was easy to see why an entire NVA regiment could turn into ghosts and vanish into such rough terrain.

Not expecting contact, Taylor gave Ramirez a break and put him to the rear of the column on Tailend Charlie. Tony and I with the Pig remained near the front. The patrol took up an animal trail as it pushed through thick undergrowth that hazed the sun into twilight. Above our heads, a noisy troop of monkeys with black beards peppered us with handfuls of their own excrement to dramatize their displeasure at our trespassing.

"The gooks ambush us, monkeys ambush us," Tony muttered. "What comes next?"

"Invasion of the Cat People?"

We threaded in and out of jungle, crossed a dry creek bed and an open ravine where the sun beat down hard, then along a ridgeline.

Suddenly, Ramirez flashed up an alert from the rear. *Enemy near!* He had done it again. The entire patrol went to ground, eyes flashing anxiously in all directions, weapons ready. Ramirez crawled up the line to point out a small group of NVA well concealed below the ridge in a creek bed.

Carefully parting a few leaves allowed me to peep through and find them. Two or three men sprawled out on flat rocks sleeping with their weapons lying on the ground alongside. Another pair huddled together chatting. A third man yawned and scratched himself. His buddy laughed quietly. They all seemed unaware of our presence, having obviously failed to place out a sentry during their rest break. Looked like gooks were getting lax in also thinking the fight had ended.

Were these careless little bastards going to be surprised! Smoking and joking like that in the sun as if they were all alone out here in the wilderness. Allowing us to walk right up on them.

Our patrol was already on line. Taylor pointed with a pistol hand and let down his thumb like a hammer. We understood. When he gave the signal, the line exploded with rifle and machine gun fire. Lead and steel chewed through the somnolent Vietnamese. Those lying on the rocks died in their sleep. A couple of others, wounded in the initial shooting, jumped up to flee. They didn't get far.

Shouting and cursing, the patrol took revenge for all the atrocities and pain the NVA had inflicted upon us. On-line, we charged right over the gooks, shooting at anything that moved. The Pig and I were right in the lead, John Wayne-ing it, letting the Pig loose. *Da-Da-Da-Da*. . . . Splattering human parts and fluids all over the creek bed, turning the trickle of water in the stream red.

The surprised gooks ended up a bloody mess of tennis shoes, blood, and entrails by the time we ceased fire and they woke up in the arms of the Great Buddha. It was one easy body count. Because none of our guys suffered so much as a scratch, the victory produced an entirely different reaction than in the encounter when Foxtrot lost so many of its Marines. We held off celebrating, however, until the patrol returned safely to 881N. Then we let it all out.

"Did you see Carter's face when that dude's head exploded?"

"Man, that was some awesome shit! I reckon them gooks never knew what hit 'em."

"A dead gook is a good gook."

"That one kid we caught sleeping. Did you see him? He wasn't even twelve years old."

"It ain't no big thing. Give a kid an AK and as far as I'm thinking he could be forty years old."

"Hey, Carlisle! You missed the chance to collect some ear trophies."

"You're a sick motherfucker, know that, Jonesy?"

"Maybe we're all sick."

And maybe we were. A side effect of war.

CHAPTER FORTY-ONE

The Silver Dragon

WE HEARD THE NVA DRAFTED WOMEN INTO THEIR ARMY. NOT LIKE Catherine, the French journalist who came out to shoot *pictures*. They actually sent their females into combat. I hadn't personally run across any that I knew of, hadn't seen any among the gooks we killed. I doubted it was true. I thought about Linda and my mom. Come on! Why would any sane people send girls and women out here? It was Moshe Dayan the Israeli general with the black eye patch, whom I had gotten a look at that morning on the hill, who said something like, "Any nation that would send its daughters, mothers, and wives into combat is a nation not worth preserving." At least I thought he was the one who said it. Even if he didn't, he *should* have.

So, if the gooks really *were* running women out to fight, it proved how uncivilized communism really was.

But, then, on a patrol with Taylor's 1st Squad into the bush, I finally saw one of the fabled woman warriors with my own eyes. It was just like the other time when our faithful Indian scout spotted gooks taking a nap by the creek and we wasted them before they knew what was going on.

Ramirez on point did it again. This time there were four young men and a woman wearing NVA uniforms lollygagging in a patch of bamboo. The woman wore her pith helmet, the men had thrown theirs aside to cluster around the female and vie for attention. Their weapons lay on the grass.

While we watched, still surprised at seeing a woman out here, she giggled and playfully slapped one of the men on the shoulder. The men laughed and moved closer, like elementary school boys on the playground around a pretty classmate with a package of cookies. Clearly, they had their feeble minds on pussy and not on business. Another reason why you shouldn't send women into combat. Hard dicks and a pretty face were about to get the flock butchered.

PFC Taylor pointed to several 1st Squad men, designating them to trigger the ambush on his signal. I nodded when he looked at me. The Pig always got first call in such situations.

My finger tightened on the trigger. Tony sprawled belly-down next to me with his M-16. From the corner of my eye, I saw Taylor gesture with his pistol-hand. I squeezed and felt the quick jolting recoil of the machine gun stock against my shoulder as I whipped tracers into the four surprised targets. The tinny rattling of Mattie Mattels provided accompanying drama as everyone else opened up. Savage yells burst out above the cacophony.

It wasn't a battle; it was a massacre over in seconds. Not a pretty aftermath. Blood and gore splattered for yards about. Brains and bone and hair dripping from bamboo. Unlike other enemy soldiers we had encountered in actual campaign engagements, these had not wrapped their limbs in wire to keep from being blown apart. Bullets from my machine gun ripped open the woman's chest and tore out her lungs and heart. She died instantly, lying face up with her arms flung wide and her mouth and eyes open in astonishment. Only one of the four men survived. He lay curled up in a fetal position, emitting painful half-conscious groans, his eyes squeezed tightly shut as if to block out the world. If he didn't see it, it didn't really happen.

This time the aftermath was different, what with the woman involved. At least it was for me as I looked down on the dead woman and realized bullets from the Pig had slain her. The interaction we had witnessed among the gooks before the shooting started was as ancient and as human as mankind—guys preening and showing off for a female. The Vietnamese weren't specters and monsters after all; they were as human as we were. With all man's common natural desires, foibles, ambitions, weaknesses, and strengths. Kids became young men and women, grew middle-aged, then became old and died. The natural cycle of life.

Except these never had the chance to grow old through the cycle.

Best not to dwell on killing and death. But in *not* thinking about it, in experiencing it daily and dismissing it from our minds, did that not turn us hard and calloused? The violence and cruelty of war—was it not transforming us into monsters, both *us* and *them?* Monsters fighting monsters.

In order for war to work, you had to turn off your humanity. And pray to God you could reacquire it afterwards.

Tony, Taylor, and I searched the bodies for documents of intel value. The woman was an officer, according to her uniform markings. A *tee-wee*, a lieutenant. She carried a medical bag, indicating she was probably a doctor or nurse. So what the hell was she doing out here with these guys, other than getting herself killed?

She had carried a light carbine and a field pouch containing papers now strewn about by the force of our attack. As I collected them, I overheard Tony exclaim, "Damn! Would you look at that ring!"

The woman wore on her wedding finger a beautiful silver dragon ring with glowing ruby eyes. Her wrist was shattered and her hand all but severed from her arm, remaining attached only by a shred of sinew. I commandeered a communist hammer and sickle helmet band from one of her comrades as a trophy while Tony worked at removing the dragon ring from the woman's swollen finger. I slung my M-60 and the dead Dragon Lady's field packet of papers over my shoulders.

"Hurry, Tony. We gotta go."

"This damned ring won't come off."

I heard Taylor saying, "Somebody take care of the wounded gook."

The guy continued his pitiful wailing. I thought Taylor meant for us to administer medical aid. I was bent over one of the corpses relieving it of a map I'd overlooked initially when a single rifle shot startled me. I refused to look. I didn't want to know which Marine put the gook out of his misery. Nothing, I was discovering, could be as heartless as a teenage Marine cast into a wartime environment.

I wondered, though, afterwards, if the guy died with his eyes still closed.

Taylor prepared the patrol to move out. It was never tactically prudent to remain long at an ambush site.

"Maras, give me your knife," Tony called out.

I tossed my banana knife at Tony's knees where he knelt over the nurse's corpse. I presumed he intended to hack off her finger to get the ring.

"Get it and let's get out of here," I urged.

Taylor was getting impatient. "What's the holdup, Maras?"

"Go on. We'll catch up. Only be a sec."

The green caterpillar the patrol resembled got its legs underneath and headed out. I started to fall in, calling back over my shoulder, "Tony, what's keeping you?"

"I'm right behind you."

I stopped to wait for him at the edge of the bamboo and away from the carnage. It was already starting to smell. Tailend Charlie disappeared ahead of me in the jungle. I heard Tony panting as he charged up the trail with his M-16 slung and something clutched in one hand. He collapsed at my feet to catch his breath, his face red and his breathing rapid and hoarse like that of a thief flushed from a house he had just robbed.

"Come on, Tony! On your feet!"

"A minute. I got . . . have a minute," he gasped.

Up ahead, I heard the rattle of Taylor's halting the squad to wait for us. I reached down a hand to Tony. Then jumped back in sudden revulsion when I noticed he had *three* hands.

"Fuck, Tony. What do you think you're doing?"

He had cut the Dragon Lady's hand the rest of the way off. "I didn't want to mess up the ring," he explained.

"You crazy sonofabitch! Don't let anybody else see that. Get rid of it."

Having regained his wind, he concentrated on carefully sawing off the finger to remove and pocket the silver dragon. He returned my knife, stood up, and flung the hand and loose finger into the brush. I watched the delicate hand tumble in seemingly slow motion through the air before it crashed to earth like a wounded bird.

CHAPTER FORTY-TWO

Skinny Dipping

PATROLS VENTURED FARTHER AND FARTHER OUT FROM OUR HILL redoubts to seek confirmation that the enemy had indeed vacated the area and that the Marines had won the game.

"Don't let down your guard," Gunny Janzen cautioned. "That's when you get a haymaker from way out of left field."

None of our other recons found fresh signs of NVA presence, not even footprints in the soft soil along streams the gooks would have to cross. Birds and monkeys moved back in. One patrol even spotted a tiger. Animals seemed to know that the human fighting was over.

On an exceptionally hot afternoon's patrol when even insect activity receded to a soft, sleepy hum, 1st Squad's Faithful Indian Companion Ramirez called a sudden halt. We had skirted low around 881S and dropped unexpectedly into a little hidden valley shaded from the sun by growths of giant trees. The temperature seemed much cooler as gentle golden rays of cathedral sunlight penetrated the forest canopy. Monkeys and parrots chittered up in the lofts.

A sudden halt normally meant "bring the gun up." Tony and I dutifully pushed forward with the Pig and PFC Taylor while the rest of the squad assumed a tactical knee by the trail. I noted a peculiar scent in the air as we arrived forward and took to ground to cut down our profile. The fragrance in the air was surprisingly pleasant unlike the by-now-familiar stench of death that clung to these hills. I thought of the mingled innocent scents of girls together at one of the slumber parties my little sister used to throw.

Ramirez pointed to his nose and shrugged quizzically. Yeah, I smelled it. The four of us—Ramirez, Tony, the Pig, and me—edged on up through thick foliage toward the sound of running water while PFC Taylor and other Marines covered.

Drawing near the sound, we cautiously parted patches of ferns and peered into a spectacle like an idyllic scene encapsulated inside one of those little toy crystal globes sold as vacation souvenirs. I caught my breath in wonder at all the glory of the tropics displayed in one marvelous hidden setting.

A sparkling waterfall cascaded into a deep pool so clear that pebbles on the bottom glistened like gold nuggets. A terrarium of ferns and lianas and every manner of wide-leafed plant festooned the scene. Butterflies in an equal variety of hues and sizes performed ballets among the orchids.

Ramirez summoned the patrol to come forward. Curious Marines crept up and, as our advance group had done before, beheld the scene in bated-breath wonder. A monkey peeped silently from the recesses of a jungle behemoth. My green parrot—I chose to believe it was *my* parrot—led a flight of his buddies through the upper terraces of the forest, circled darting through the branches and landed with them all in a row on a branch overhanging the pool.

"Please don't shit in the water," Tony pleaded.

Clearly, this miniature paradise had remained untouched by the war, hidden away as it was in this remote corner, visited only by local residents of fur and feather. My parrot cocked his head and looked at us as though to say, "So? What are you waiting for?"

Smiles broke out one by one as young Marine faces turned into reserved but joyous laughter. I looked at Taylor from beneath a questioning eyebrow. Was he thinking the same thing I was? It had been weeks since any of us had had a bath. We smelled like a pen full of pigs, no offense to *the* Pig.

Most of us were teenagers, the rest not much beyond twenty. Hurriedly, as though by common consent, we began to strip. The entire patrol would have dived in together except for the memory of how we had twice surprised gooks out here and killed them while they were either napping or sucking up to a female soldier. PFC Taylor dispatched half the patrol as sentries to keep watch while the other half went swimming. Then we switched off.

For that one brief time in the war we reverted to being kids again. Like skinny dipping with my cousins in an Oklahoma creek, running and laughing with all the abandon that kids are capable of. That had not been so long ago either—but after these hills I feared I would never be a kid again. I might not even become fully human again.

We had done all the killing we could stand. I held my breath and sank in the water toward the gold pebble-nuggets on the bottom, shutting out the rest of the world. It was almost like being baptized. The clear, clean water washed off the grime of war. I felt young with revived hope that one day I might become the human I once had been.

CHAPTER FORTY-THREE

Picnic

COLONEL PAPPY DELONG'S BLT 2/3 WALKED OUT OF THE HILLS ON A morning when the green parrot was flying, the sun shone, soft fog lay close in the lowlands, and nobody was shooting at us. The date was 12 May 1967—a day, I supposed, when the colored pin markers with their maps declared the Hill Fights officially over and won. Dien Bien Phu II had been avoided. So sorry about that, Uncle Ho.

Unlike the Walking Dead of the 9th Marines, who fled Hill 861 carrying their dead in bloody ponchos, the 3rd withdrew in triumph, having soundly defeated a much larger force. With a little help, of course, from our friends. Yet, most of us felt no triumph. I felt nothing.

Less than three weeks ago, what seemed an eternity now, we had arrived at Khe Sanh fresh and green, barely out of USMC training, and, before that, for many of us, not long graduated from high school. I had been nineteen years old; I was now one hundred years old, ancient and wiser and more cynical than a young man ought to be. I would never view the world the same way again.

It was like I was empty inside, beaten emotionally and psychologically, exhausted, craving nothing so much as a real bunk to rack out in, hot chow, and time to decompress.

"Good morning, Vietnam!" contained all the enthusiasm of a worn-out old boot when Tony and I stood right out in the open in front of God and everybody and, hopefully, took our last piss on 881N. There would be time later to confront personal demons that we had relegated to our foot lockers aboard ship in the rear while we struggled day by day, hour by hour, sometimes moment by moment just to stay alive in these blood-soaked hills.

"Piss on her," Tony said, long-faced and with a tinge of bitterness. Peggy again.

"Piss on the world," I echoed.

War-weary, battered and filthy, eyes hollow in the thousand-yard stare, cheeks thorny and hollow, 2/3 Marines slogged back downhill using the same trails as before when we climbed up to Hill 361 and encountered Bravo 1/9 bearing their lifeless burdens in ponchos coming down. As per orders, we had refrained from speaking to them. They appeared then like we must have looked now; they probably wouldn't have talked to us anyhow.

I was astonished at how near we had been to the Combat Base all this time. The airfield and the big birds that could have lifted us out of here had seemed a million miles away while we were *up there*. They were actually only a day's march from any one of the Three Wicked Sisters. Colonel Delong and his command element met us in the forest to walk with us rest of the way where Sea Knights and crews waited to lift the battalion directly to our little three-ship armada from which we had launched so enthusiastically against Red Beach. No longer were we the eager cavalry boasting of saving the day, kicking gook ass, and winning the war by Christmas.

Not all of us who had walked up 861 walked back down. You could have put the surviving original members of some squads and platoons into a phone booth. Body counts, of course, were used to tally up the final stats: 168 Marines and Navy KIA, 443 wounded, two missing, including Robert J. Todd, whose body plummeted to earth from the helicopter's open door.

The enemy lost 940 confirmed KIA, which meant we slaughtered them on a ratio of about seven to one. I assumed that disparity signified a huge victory, body count–wise. Somewhere in the rear, at the Pentagon or the White House Situation Room, REMFs—Rear Echelon motherfuckers with their colored pins—were pushing back wearily from their maps and desks and sighing. It had been a tough fight and they were worn out.

But they and President LBJ had so far lived up to their vow that Khe Sanh would not become another Dien Bien Phu.

Later in the year, President Johnson would send Vice President Happy Hubie Humphrey to Da Nang to present a Presidential Unit Citation to Commanding General Bruno A. Hochmuth of the 3rd Marine Division. A copy of the citation went into the personnel file of every 3rd Marine who fought in the hills or in other Vietnam campaigns since March 1965 and the landing at Da Nang.

For extraordinary heroism and outstanding performance of duty in action against North Vietnamese Army and insurgent communist "Viet Cong" forces in the Republic of Vietnam from 8 March 1965 to 15 September 1967. Throughout this period the 3rd Marine Division, Reinforced, successfully executed a three-fold mission of occupying and defending key terrain around the Da Nang, Chu Lai, Hue, Phu Bai, and Dong Ha airbases, seeking out and destroying the enemy while also carrying on an intensive pacification program in areas already under its control. . . . The 3rd Marine Division, Reinforced, successfully executed 80 major combat operations in addition to more than 125,000 offensive actions, ranging from squad patrols and ambushes to company size search and destroy missions conducted in both the coastal rice lands and in the jungled, mountainous area . . . [that] denied [the enemy] access to his source of food supply, restricted his freedom of movement and removed his influence from the heavy populated, coast areas. . . . Through the period ending on 15 September 1967, the 3rd Marine Division, utilizing courageous ground and helicopter borne assaults, complemented by intense and accurate air, artillery and naval gunfire support, undeterred by heavy hostile automatic weapons and highly effective artillery and mortar fire, extremely difficult terrain, intense heat and incessant monsoon rains, inflicted serious casualties on the enemy forces. . . .

All right! Semper fucking fi!

The three ships upon which BLT 2/3 set sail from Okinawa—USS *Ogden*, USS *Monticello*, and the *Princeton*—stood offshore in the South

China Sea prepared to welcome us back aboard. From the air, I looked down upon a vast expanse of shimmering blue water that extended seemingly forever to the horizon, and beyond that to Okinawa and California, and, somewhere out there, to Tulsa and Linda and my Mom.

Sea Knights touched down gently one by one on the helicopter deck of LPH *Princeton* to disgorge the weary troops of 2/3. Tony and I, together with the Pig as always, dragged ourselves and our gear off our chopper with other battalion Marines. We stumbled bent over away from the rotor blast with our heads down.

First thing I saw when I looked up again was every sailor of the ship's company lining the deck wearing dress blues. They snapped to attention and saluted us. I felt my eyes watering. None of us expected *this*.

The entire battalion stank of mud and jungle and mildew and BO, and of death. Our utilities were blood-stained, ripped, and impregnated with the red dirt of Vietnam. Large metal containers, like trash bins, lined one side of the deck. A Navy lieutenant stood on an upside-down bucket and waved his arms.

"Attention, Marines! You all did a hell of a job out there. Now, we're going to clean you up. These bins are all marked. Strip down and put all your clothing in this bin, empty magazines in this one, grenades and other gear in this one. . . . Keep your weapons, helmets, and boots. You're all familiar with the ship. Showers and shaving equipment are below."

A shave, a hot shower! Every man stripped in place in record time. No one wore skivvies, so we all broke for the showers buck naked while Navy work parties held their noses and sorted through discarded equipment. Our utilities were rotted and unsalvageable; they were tossed overboard. Sailors petitioned us for war stories and battle souvenirs. Some offered as much as a month's pay for gook items like the communist helmet band I confiscated, and even more than that, a lot more, for an AK-47 or for Tony's Dragon Lady ring. Sailors gathered around him to ogle the treasure and question how he obtained it.

Tony managed a fatigued version of his Buddy Hackett: "I'd have to kill you if I told you."

I tried to avoid the hullabaloo and get to the showers.

"Pretty tough out there, huh?" a Navy petty officer commented.

The look I gave him, the hollow combat look, must have unnerved him. He stepped away.

I cast a tired look back toward the thin strip of land that was Vietnam on the near horizon. "I don't want to talk about it," I said.

Colonel Pappy threw a picnic for the battalion at China Beach, an area secured by American forces around Da Nang and used as a troop recreation area. White sand against warm blue waters stretched for several miles on a spit of land extending into the South China Sea. What was left of the battalion, now about the size of two companies since we had not yet received replacements for recent losses, loaded aboard AMTRACs and chugged ashore. Mess cooks preceded us to whip up steaks on a grill and prepare all the trimmings. I mean, French fries, beans not out of a C-rat can, real bread . . . cold *beer* that Ted West brought to the beach on a trailer behind a Jeep. Nobody asked how he got it.

Guys stuffed themselves, grabbing hot steaks right off the flames and plopping down in the sand to gnaw on them like starving dogs while guzzling cans of iced beer.

"Heaven! I've been killed and didn't know it and went to Heaven!"

"But the babes! Where are the women?"

"Women don't go to Heaven," Tony said, sotto-voce with his mouth full. Peggy again.

"If they ain't going," Kilgore declared, "then I ain't going either."

The beach sported an Air Force lifeguard in a little tower. He went ape shit when Marines began stripping and darting naked into the surf. He came running, tooting his little whistle. A hell of a way to spend a war, a tough job but somebody had to do it. He had the misfortune to latch onto Gunny Janzen.

"You Marines can't swim naked on this beach. Candy stripers and nurses from the hospital come down here."

"Go pound sand up your ass," Gunny advised.

A few minutes later the lifeguard returned with an Air Force butter bar lieutenant in a Jeep. This time Colonel Delong handled it.

"What's the problem?" he demanded.

"We have a complaint that your Marines are naked, sir."

Nodding, Pappy glanced down toward the beach. "Sure enough," he agreed. "They sure do look naked to me."

"Sir, we have women who come down here," the butter bar persisted.

"I'm sure my guys won't mind."

"Sir—!"

Pappy's voice hardened. "Look, lieutenant. We don't have swim suits. We just came from the Hill Fights—and if my boys want to go swimming, they're going swimming. You can take your candy stripers and nurses and . . ." He smiled. ". . . pen them up down the beach about a mile away where they won't offend my men."

Lifeguards blocked off the Marine portion of the beach and reserved another sector of it out of sight for women. Kilgore, Tony, and I lay au naturel on the warm sand with waves lapping at our feet and the sun and beer making us drowsy. Tony gnawed on a steak from one hand, burped loudly—"Excuse the fuck out of me, I intended to fart instead"—and shook his beer can to see if it was empty.

"Maras," he said, "you remember the feeling I had when they yanked us up out of Bo Diddley and landed us at Khe Sanh?"

"You say lots of things. I don't half-listen."

Kilgore tittered. He was about half-soused. "Amen," he agreed.

"You have to remember I was right though," Tony continued after another burp. "Something bad happens every time the Marine Corps feeds us this good."

CHAPTER FORTY-FOUR

Along the DMZ

AGAIN, TONY'S "FEELING" WAS RIGHT ON TARGET. "PARTYING" ABOARD ship and at China Beach lasted four days before warning orders came down from on high. BLT 2/3, now replenished in those four days by fresh troops from Okinawa and back to its full complement of thirteen hundred men, received orders to cavalry-up for Operation Hickory. On 21 May 1967, Sea Knight pilots airlifted the entire battalion to the northern edge of Leatherneck Square near the Ben Hai River, the first time US forces had officially moved into the DMZ.

The 1954 Geneva Agreement had established what was described as an inviolable five-mile-wide buffer zone along the 17th parallel between North and South Vietnam—which, of course, the North Vietnamese communists violated. To stop the incursions, Marines occupied a series of combat bases along Route 9—Khe Sanh, the Rockpile, Camp Carroll, Cam Lo, and Dong Ha. The NVA pulled sieges against the line beginning with Khe Sanh in the spring. It was through and around these forts that most of the fighting occurred in 1967.

As early as 1965, the Pentagon, led by Secretary of Defense Robert McNamara, had given serious consideration to occupying the DMZ with several US divisions to block infiltration. McNamara's proposal was to build the "McNamara Line," a fence of barbed wire seeded with ingenious little explosive devices and booby traps disguised as dog shit, bed bugs, gravel, and so forth, to discourage the NVA from crossing the border. Building that first experimental stretch of fence was one of the missions assigned Marines of Operation Hickory.

A secondary mission included clearing out all people living on or near the DMZ, some thirteen thousand of them, to facilitate unrestricted bombing of NVA positions. The previous July, the Joint Chiefs of Staff permitted bombardment of the DMZ and limited "search and destroy" missions up to the 17th parallel as long as no public disclosure of it was made. JCS authorized return fire across the DMZ in December 1966, followed in February 1967 with authority to conduct preemptive air strikes.

New US activity in the area attracted NVA like syrup attracted ants. BLT 2/3's mission was to "search and destroy" the enemy.

As the big Navy choppers skimmed in under a noon sun and put us out in the scrub at the north edge of Leatherneck Square and the southern boundary of the DMZ, I exited the bird running with Tony and the Pig. When I cleared the blades and caught my breath, I looked around in sudden dismay. North, the Ben Hai River threaded in gleaming silver through low jungle and scrub out of North Vietnam. But it was to the south and west that my eyes fastened. I stared. Out there somewhere, Hills 881N, 881S, and 861 loomed like a bad omen from the past. I had hoped never to see them again, never to have to even think about them and our days up there in the blood and filth.

Tony glared in the same direction. "Fuck! Fuck! Double fuck!" he exploded.

"You promised God to stop cursing," I reminded him drearily, feeling like cursing myself.

"When it comes to those damned hills, Maras, I'm sure God understands."

Pappy Delong's battalion dug in and set up a fixed position out of which to conduct operations against NVA within the DMZ. The enemy was near, watching, waiting for an opportunity. If Kilgore hadn't destroyed his Starlite, we could have watched them up on their side of the 17th marching around in strength and threat-posturing for our benefit. Some of our patrols ran right up to within seventy yards of them, less than the length of a football field, and made faces at them across the magic boundary line that separated us. Any closer, one step across the demarcation by either side, meant trouble.

Quite clearly, the NVA were massing troops to strike at our hill forts again. Our job was to kill as many of them as we could before they made it across the DMZ into South Vietnam. No easy task. The terrain was furred with thick scrub and jungle that allowed an enemy to sneak in right among us before we detected them. The same as in the Hill Fights. It was one haunted-looking place out there.

Same old familiar routine—digging holes, stretching defensive wire, setting out Claymores and alarm devices, putting out OP/LPs. Routine, however, soon began to unravel.

On 22 May, the day after the battalion inserted, Sergeant Crawford appeared out of nowhere, stalking down the line in that old cocky walk of a man comfortable in his skin and in his element. A grin crossed his broad face when he spotted Tony and me. We jumped out of the ground to give him bear hugs. We hadn't seen him since that day in the draw below 861 when the gooks shot him. He couldn't wait for full recuperation to get back to his boys in Hotel Company.

"Sorry I had to leave the way I did, boys. I kept hearing how things got real bad up there. While I was on the *Princeton*, I saw guys come in every day to the treatment ward."

Old home week didn't last long. US Naval aircraft began bombing Central Hanoi for the first time, their target the largest electrical plant in North Vietnam. An SA2 SAM missile shot down a US Phantom on its way back. From the ground, Tony and I along with the rest of the battalion saw the plane explode in a ball of flame and black smoke. A groan issued from the startled Marines—but then our hopes rose when we spotted two parachutes blossom when the pilots ejected.

We watched the parachutes settle to earth in low scrub brush. "Angel" helicopters picked up the pilots. On our hill, Colonel Delong's RTO tuned in on the chopper frequency and reported that the pilots were okay. The camp exploded in cheering.

On the night of 23 May, eleven hundred rounds of heavy artillery fired from north of the DMZ clobbered our positions. Tony and I whipped out our E-tools and, like a couple of terrified gophers, started digging our hole deeper. Afterwards, during the "all clear" when medevacs began whipping in, we learned that Sergeant Crawford had been wounded again and was on his way to the *Princeton*. No report on his condition.

This land would never let go until it had destroyed every last Marine. I climbed from our hole, which was still a long way from bottomless, and through the haze and smoke of the recent enemy bombardment shook my fists angrily in the direction of the Wicked Sisters.

CHAPTER FORTY-FIVE

Anything for R&R

VENTURING OUTSIDE THE WIRE WAS ALWAYS A RISKY AFFAIR. ON THE day after Sergeant Crawford got himself mortared and evacuated, Lieutenant McFarlane, who remained more or less in charge of Weapons Platoon, sent Tony and me outside the perimeter to plant a Claymore mine on a little rise covered with beetle nut bushes. The sun was shining and all the cockroaches should have scurried into hiding after a long night scuttering about in the kitchen and making Marines nervous. Seemed to me like Operation Hickory was about to become a replay of the Hill Fights—or a continuation of them.

Usually, machine gun teams were exempt from mundane tasks like setting out mines and pulling OP/LP. However, to coin an old Marine phrase: *Shit happens*. After the battalion's occupation of 881N and the losses Golf and the other companies suffered, plus being worn out from fighting and patrolling, every swinging dick on the hill was expected to pull dirty double duty. Tony and I had found ourselves out on OP/LP on one of the blackest nights in Black Night history. Just the two of us alone hunkered in a clump of bushes to listen for the enemy trying to sneak up on us. I had never spent a longer nor more nerve-wracking night.

I had turned the Pig over to Gunny's capable hands for safekeeping. That left the two of us armed with Tony's M-16, which had that bad habit of jamming when you needed it, my .45 pistol, and our pockets full of grenades. We lay covering each other's back while we peered warily out of the bushes, the grenades arranged between us with their pins straightened and ready for use. We weren't supposed to engage the enemy, just run back with a warning. Still, it never hurt to be prepared.

On 50-50, one of us could have slept, but neither of us did so. We lay wide-eyed all night, knowing, just *knowing*, gooks were trying to sneak up on us. I heard my heart beating, heard Tony's heartbeat. I listened to grass growing, heard lizards and insects crawling and hopping. Tony claimed later he heard a mouse fart.

Near daybreak, *something* out there in the pre-dawn moved across from our left to right. Stealthy footfalls. My heart pounded so loudly, like drumbeats, that I thought the enemy was bound to hear and charge. It was better that we seized the initiative than to become the enemy's initiative. On cue, the two of us chugged grenades and lit up our front with bursts of exploding flame. We figured afterwards that we may have annihilated a bamboo rat, two toads, a krait snake, and a colony of warrior ants.

Now away from those hills and up on the DMZ, hostile eyes must have been watching and waiting while my partner and I set the Claymore, camouflaged it, and hotfooted back to our hole and the Pig.

Next morning, Tony reminded me that today was our one-year anniversary in the Marines Corps. Curiously enough, we had both enlisted, though separately, on the same date on the deferred enlistment plan. It was about to become the most memorable anniversary of my lifetime.

As we took our ritual "Good morning, Vietnam!" piss, Tony looked at me and wryly suggested we break open the champagne and throw a party.

"Good idea," I agreed. "I'll get the champagne, you bring the dancing girls."

Instead, we went out to the beetle nut bushes to recover our Claymore. Patrols would be taking off soon; no one wanted an accident because of a mine left active. I carried a .45 in my hand as the two of us, keeping low and using available cover, approached the bushes.

The rifle shot from extremely close range, so near I suffered powder burns, slapped my left leg out from underneath me. I floundered to the ground, trying to hold everything together. *Where in hell did that come from?*

A second deafening report immediately followed the first. This bullet caught Tony. Ironically, it ripped at an angle across his chest muscles and grazed a deep furrow through his upper arm, in the process blasting off most of his tattoo, taking out the heart and all but the last two letters of *Peggy*. That was one way to finalize a romantic breakup.

He collapsed to the ground in a mist of his own blood. That was when I spotted our assailant. The sneaky little bastard was not four feet away. The camouflaged lid of a spider trap raised a little to allow the soldier inside to finish us off, revealing a netted pith helmet, a grim face, and dark eyes. The stubby barrel of his AK-47 pointed at where Tony lay writhing on the ground cursing up the proverbial blue streak in his pain and surprise.

Another moment and he would be dead from a second bullet. The gook couldn't miss at this range. But neither could I.

I beat the gook to the trigger, firing the .45, firing it again and again while the gook's head exploded in a blurb of blood and brain. The spider trap lid slammed shut on him, leaving one lifeless arm and his rifle protruding.

I scrambled over to Tony, dragging my wounded leg. It felt numb and about the size of an Oklahoma outhouse. Terror that I might lose my buddy after we had survived so much together made me forget my own injury. Blood stained the ground all around him, the leaves of bushes overhead, and his entire body, like he had run through a slaughterhouse.

"*Tony!* Don't you dare die on me, you hear?"

"Fuck off, Maras. Did you see that?" he cried indignantly. "That sonofabitch shot me."

"He won't shoot no other Marines. I blew his fucking head off."

I was so preoccupied with Tony's condition that I wasn't aware that we were still taking fire. Bullets whipped into the bushes around us.

I pulled Tony to cover behind a low outcropping of rock. He was still blackguarding and cursing every gook since the beginning of time. I parted bushes and spotted at least a half-dozen NVA protecting the mortar. They were up on their knees and craning their necks, trying to get a better look at where Tony and I had fallen. One of them pointed toward us.

Tony was hurting, and he was pissed. The gooks were out of range of my .45. Tony rolled over, pushed aside some intervening branches, and honed in on the enemy with his Mattie Mattel.

"Another fine kettle of fish you got me into, Maras," he muttered as he picked off at least three gooks one by one with his deadly accurate sight picture.

"Damn! I never knew you could shoot like that!"

"Why do you think they sent me with you, Maras?" he replied. "Hell, you can't take care of yourself without me around to wipe your butt for you."

AK fire slacked off. Tony dropped his head onto his arms and let out a muffled cry of pain.

"C'mon, man. We gotta get you out of here," I said.

"How bad they get you, Maras?"

"I'm not going to be dancing anytime soon."

Crawling on our bellies, helping each other as always, we dragged back to the perimeter. The first Marine we came upon, a newbie named Paul, looked pale and frightened. This was his first action.

"You guys hit?"

What did he think? We were covered in blood and crusted in red dirt.

"Go get a corpsman!"

A replacement corpsman, Doc Miranda, came racing across the field with his aid bag and skidded down next to us. The perimeter held its fire with remarkable discipline. Besides, the NVA mortars and their defenders remained under cover over the rise and away from direct fire.

Doc ripped open my jungle trousers. The bullet had entered my upper thigh, leaving the entire leg ugly with bruise and a tiny hole still leaking blood. I groaned in pain. Miranda pressure-wrapped the wound while others took care of Tony and carried him directly to the CP to await medevac.

My biggest concern at the moment was not my leg. "My Johnson?" I demanded.

"Don't worry," the Doc reassured me. "Your Johnson is still there. The bullet missed it. The ladies'll still like you. I'm going to give you some morphine."

He broke out a vial. A fresh new shake-and-bake lieutenant appeared before he had a chance to administer it.

"Do you know where they are?" he asked me. "Which direction?"
I pointed.

"Come on. Show me."

Couldn't the guy see I was hurt? Fuck it! Dragging my leg, I crawled with him back out to where I killed the gook in the spider trap. A lot of blood pooled on the ground, gradually soaking in where Tony and I were shot.

"The tube is there," I told the lieutenant. "Just on the other side of that little knoll."

I groaned and rubbed my leg. The dressing had come undone and left the wound exposed.

"What—?" the lieutenant began, before hesitating to notice my damaged leg.

"I got shot," I explained.

"Holy—! Okay! Okay!"

He radioed in coordinates on the bad guys, who were promptly smacked by our own mortar men. Then we crawled back to the perimeter as black and gray smoke marked the spot where the gooks had been.

The medevac landed. Tony and I were carried out on stretchers. Gunny Janzen saw us off.

"Some guys will do anything to get R&R," he said.

"You mean—?" I began.

He grinned. "Consider this in-country R&R for the POWs you captured."

"F-U-C-K-E-D A-G-A-I-N," Tony sang miserably to the tune of the *Mickey Mouse Club* theme song.

In that inescapable body count procedure that determined who won and who lost during this eight-day phase of Operation Hickory, Marines killed 789 enemy soldiers and disrupted the North Vietnamese command structure. Allied losses—Marines and Army of the Republic of Vietnam (ARVN)—were likewise heavy with 164 of us killed and over 1,000 wounded, including Tony and me.

The helicopter crew chief offered us cigarettes when corpsmen loaded our stretchers aboard. I didn't smoke, but I smoked it anyhow. As the blades whirred for takeoff, irrepressible Tony Leyba looked over at my stretcher from his.

"Happy anniversary, Maras," he cracked.

We were both laughing our asses off as the chopper lifted off. Before the doors closed, I took what I hoped would be my last close-up look of Vietnam and Hills 861, 881N, and 881S, the Trio of Wicked Witches where so many of my fellow Marines died or were maimed for life in what was to go down as one of the fiercest campaigns of the Vietnam War.

But it wasn't over yet. Not Khe Sanh. And not for Tony and me. We both recuperated from our wounds and returned to 3/2 to complete our tours of duty. Tony suffered another non-life-threatening wound; I was wounded twice more, the last time in October 1967 along the DMZ.

Chapter Forty-Six

The Siege

The week Tony and I departed the DMZ, me with a bullet in my leg and Tony with his "Peggy" shot off, President Lyndon Johnson publicly went on TV urging Hanoi to join him in "leading our people out of this bloody impasse" by accepting a compromise peace. Uncle Ho essentially snubbed the proposal and released General Giap to continue his campaigning out of Laos and along the DMZ in South Vietnam's northern provinces. He smelled victory. If not a military one, at least a political one.

Khe Sanh remained in the public mind back home, almost an obsession, and in the chants and demonstrations of dope-smoking draft dodgers.

"When I get home," I promised myself all over again as Tony as I recuperated aboard the USS *Princeton*, "the first cocksucker spits on me is going to spit on the next Marine or GI with no teeth in his head."

BLT 2/3 had pulled out of the Khe Sanh hills on 12 May 1967 to operate farther east along the DMZ. Less than five months later, in October 1967, intel reports indicated large-scale NVA infiltrations into South Vietnam from Laos and North Vietnam. Hidden sensors sown by the US Air Force went into electronic ape shit over the movement of more than a thousand trucks in the Khe Sanh area. That figure jumped to over six thousand trucks in December. In early January, intel reported division-level NVA units taking up positions in that strip of hilly jungle between the DMZ and Route 9, the only road connecting the Combat Base to the coast.

Undoubtedly, General Giap had Khe Sanh on his mind again. Dreams of another Dien Bien Phu died hard. By now, more than six thousand Marines of the 26th Division or under its operational control manned the Combat Base. They were well protected by batteries of 105mm and 155mm howitzers, plenty of heavy mortars, and by 175mm firebases at Camp Carroll and the Rockpile northeast of Khe Sanh in Leatherneck Square.

By mid-January 1968, NVA gunners up in the winter-foggy hills began to lob the isolated artillery shell at the Combat Base. Marine howitzers dished back H&I, with little effect. Targets were difficult to identify. Dense fog and low clouds made it almost impossible for airborne observers to locate targets and adjust Marine cannon fire. Sending out teams of Forward Observers on foot would be sending them to their deaths.

On the morning of 19 January, Base Commander Colonel David E. Lownds received disturbing reports from Captain Bill Dabney, commander of one of the companies holding the outlying hills. His India Company had bumped into a battalion of NVA while patrolling on Hill 881N and was presently engaged in a tough struggle.

Lownds was convinced the long-expected North Vietnamese offensive had begun. He ordered the base on full alert, cancelling the evening's main film, which was Elvis Presley starring in *Paradise, Hawaiian Style*.

India Company prevailed up in the hills where 2/3 had fought previously. But Colonel Lownds was right about an NVA offensive. The following morning, 20 January, artillery shells and 122mm rockets rained down on Khe Sanh. One round struck the base ammo depot. Over fifteen hundred tons of ordnance went up in a giant phosphorus flare, bowling over helicopters parked on the airstrip, demolishing tents and buildings, igniting aviation gas and oil supplies, and cooking off intense fires.

The NVA kept up the pressure every day for the rest of January. Some days over a thousand rounds of enemy artillery hit the base, reducing its living conditions to unbearable. The stench was appalling, what with huge piles of garbage smoldering and excrement burning in oil drums. In their underground bunkers, Marines endured the nauseating odor of sweat and urine while plagued by rats scuttering across their legs as they tried to sleep and pouncing from the rafters onto their chests.

Less than two weeks after the siege on Khe Sanh began, the American people received more bad war news. Before dawn on 30 January as Tet, the Vietnamese New Year, began, more than eighty-four thousand communist NVA and Viet Cong fighters appeared seemingly out of nowhere to attack cities and provinces all over the South. The scale of the surprise offensive was staggering, demonstrating after three years of US involvement in the war that South Vietnam was still vulnerable.

Within two days, the American Embassy in Saigon was hit, along with 36 of the nation's 44 provincial capitals, 5 of 6 autonomous cities, and 64 of 242 districts. Fighting between US forces and the communists raged throughout the month while Khe Sanh remained under siege. General Giap's and Uncle Ho's objective was not to overcome and take the nation by strong arm. Rather, they hoped to bring about the collapse of the South Vietnamese government by encouraging a popular uprising. Commies always thought the people were either on their side or could be *forced* to be on their side.

The NVA shelling of Khe Sanh continued for five relentless weeks. NVA infantry couldn't invade the base and in fact launched very few direct attacks to try. Marines at the same time remained trapped inside the wire. On one of the few occasions when a patrol ventured outside to locate an enemy mortar position hammering the base, only four of twenty-nine Marines returned. The bodies of the twenty-five remained outside the wire, decaying in the sun and rain.

The siege, as are all sieges, became one of attrition and wills. Who broke first lost.

While the NVA controlled the ground around Khe Sanh, Americans ruled the air. Designated Operation Niagara, the air war against the enemy resulted in a tremendous downpouring of death. Air Force, Navy, and Marine Corps fighter-bombers supported high-altitude Arc Light bombing missions by B-52s. Air traffic became so heavy that warplanes stacked up in "daisy chains," each waiting in the pattern for its turn over a target.

A new technique called "Bugle Note" brought streams of B-52s flying from Guam on a twelve-hour round trip in raids that contributed mightily to breaking up enemy concentrations before they could launch attacks against the Combat Base. The effectiveness of the bombing and the terror it sowed in NVA ranks became amply apparent when Marines captured an NVA soldier on Hill 881S.

A Marine jet screamed overhead minutes after the prisoner was taken. The man lost complete control of himself, psychologically destroyed by the constant pounding he and his comrades had endured from the air. He collapsed in a quiver at the bottom of a trench, whimpering like a beaten animal, his muscles in spasms, urinating and defecating all over himself.

In the meantime, by early March, the Tet Offensive had run its course and the last of the towns infested by NVA and VC cleared. In purely military terms, Tet was a resounding victory for General Westmoreland. He claimed that at least thirty-seven thousand communists were KIA. The final tally may have been as high as fifty thousand.

But while Westmoreland might declare Tet a military victory, Uncle Ho was claiming a political one. The American public even saw it as a win for the communists.

Public opinion was turning against the president. His numbers were tanking. By late March, only 26 percent of Americans approved of his handling of the war. Fearing Khe Sanh would become a military disaster, President Johnson spent sleepless nights haunted by "another damn Dien Bien Phu."

In the middle of nights, looking worn and old, LBJ endured his own siege in the White House's basement Situation Room where he read and re-read the latest cables and casualty reports from Khe Sanh and studied a terrain model of the Combat Base and surrounding landscape. He demanded daily reports in minute detail from the Joint Chiefs of Staff and General Westmoreland. Westmoreland himself was often summoned to the Situation Room at midnight or later. For two months he was forced to sleep in the Combat Operations Center.

"Can Khe Sanh hold?" LBJ repeatedly asked his generals.

Furthermore, he required the entire JCS to "sign in blood" a declaration that Khe Sanh would hold no matter what it took. The image of

Marines retreating down Route 9 with their tails between their legs was too horrible to contemplate.

At 9:00 p.m. on Sunday night, 31 March 1968, while the siege at Khe Sanh continued, President Johnson seemed to give up. Before a bank of TV cameras and radio microphones in the Oval Office, looking tired and discouraged, he began a speech that many considered an admission of failure in Vietnam.

"Tonight," he began, "I want to speak to you of peace in Vietnam and Southeast Asia. No other question so preoccupies our people. . . ."

He offered Hanoi an olive branch, proposing to slack off US bombing against the North if the communists would agree to engage in serious negotiations. Ho Chi Minh, smelling military success, more or less spat on the olive branch.

The president ended his speech with a shocker: "I shall not seek and will not accept the nomination of my party for another term as your president."

General Westmoreland piled on the Marines a bit of insult to injury when he placed the US Army in charge of siege ground and air activities and tapped the army's 1st Air Cavalry to lead Operation Pegasus, the effort to fight through to the air base and break the siege. The relief movement began at 8:00 a.m. on April Fools' Day. Colonel Pappy Delong's 2/3 Battalion advanced west along both sides of Route 9 while the AirCav conducted heliborne assaults to clear the surrounding hills.

Eight days later, the AirCav passed through the destroyed Khe Sanh village, finding little but rubble, craters the size of houses, and rotting corpses, and from there slogged on to meet up with Marines who had defended the Combat Base during seventy-seven days of siege. By this time, the Marines did not need relieving. Most of the enemy shelling had ceased. NVA in the hills were already pulling in their claws and preparing to withdraw.

On 15 April, General Westmoreland declared the relief of Khe Sanh complete. During the two weeks of Pegasus, the relief effort cost the lives of 92 Americans KIA, 667 WIA, and 5 MIA. Defenders at the Combat Base lost 205 Marines KIA.

On 11 June, General Westmoreland relinquished command of US forces in Vietnam, succeeded by General Creighton W. Abrams. Abrams immediately initiated Operation Charlie—the destruction and evacuation of the Khe Sanh Combat Base. The base was officially closed on 5 July. Marines withdrew east on Route 9.

Abandoning the Combat Base on top of Tet helped foster the perception of Khe Sanh as a defeat in the minds of the American public. Ho Chi Minh scored his propaganda win. Never mind that the American stronghold successfully defended itself against a much larger force while sustaining only a fraction of the losses imposed upon the NVA.

Neither was it as though the United States had turned tail and run, abandoning the base to General Giap and the communists. The Americans pulled back from Khe Sanh only a few miles on Route 9 before establishing a new forward base at Ca Lu, a location much easier to defend and supply. There, Marines and soldiers continued to carry out mobile infantry and recon against the NVA to close off infiltration routes.

No matter. Antiwar protests escalated in the United States. Although it prevailed against the enemy at Khe Sanh and during the Tet Offensive, and in almost every battle before and after, to the American people the war was lost. Ho Chi Minh was to comment afterwards how America's wavering encouraged him to continue the fight. After the final withdrawal of troops from South Vietnam in 1975 in the famous helicopter rout from the roof of the American Embassy in Saigon, Uncle Ho admitted that he was "ready to give up, but the Americans pulled out."

Front-page headlines brought the news of Khe Sanh's closure home. By that time I had been sent home to Tulsa to recuperate from my wounds. A friend dropped by Mom's house with a copy of the *Tulsa Tribune.*

"Bobby, you were at Khe Sanh, right? What do you think about this?"

It didn't make sense. Not only had the Combat Base been abandoned, I felt like we who fought there had also been abandoned. Why did we go through all that misery and dying in the Hill Fights to save Khe Sanh, only to give it up? I was more stunned than angry, like somebody had just punched me in the balls. Like our sacrifices were unnecessary and meant nothing.

Linda curled up on the sofa next to me. "Bobby? Bobby, it's all over. You're home again. That's what counts."

For those who fight for life, it has a special flavor the protected shall never know.

At the moment, the special flavor I savored was a bitter one.

AFTERWORD

"DID YOU KNOW SO MANY GUYS WHO DIED IN THE WAR?"

That question posed innocently by a bystander echoed in my mind and back across the decades as Sergeant Ed Crawford, Tony Leyba, and I stood silently and misty-eyed before The Wall, with its 58,191 names of servicemen and a few women who died in a war that ended twenty-seven years earlier. Our names could have been on that black wall with those we fought with and who died for what now seemed a hopeless cause. We won the war militarily and lost it politically. We bailed out with our tails tucked between our legs. Uncle Ho's communists swarmed in, took over, and slaughtered tens of thousands of innocent people in the name of "the workers." Tens of thousands more, the "boat people," fled to sea on rafts, inner tubes, boats—anything that would float. Chancing death rather than accept state slavery.

I sometimes felt guilty, as though I had somehow personally let the South Vietnamese down.

Names on The Wall were arranged according to the year the men died. The year 1967 was a big "body count" year. I touched with my fingertips the names of the Marines who died in the Hill Fights. Faces seemed to emerge from the black granite, the serious countenances of young grunts who took being Marine so earnestly that they died for it.

During the Hill Fights, Gene Kilgore lived with the premonition that he would die in Vietnam. He even described how he would die. That it would be by machine gun fire in a surprise ambush. I remembered now what he wanted inscribed on his tombstone: *PFC Gene Kilgore. A Marine Who Died For His Country.*

News reached Tony and me months later that he had indeed been killed. In an ambush. I searched for his name on The Wall, but the only Kilgore I found was a "Danny" Kilgore. I wondered if "Danny" could have been part of Kilgore's name. No matter now. This "Danny," if not Gene, had still been *there*. And, like the other names on The Wall, he had died there.

Tony stood at my side at The Wall, the same as when we were in Vietnam. We had lived together in the holes, ate together, slept together, pissed "Good morning, Vietnam!" together, were wounded together. My brother by another mama and daddy.

He had gained weight in the thirty-five years since the Hill Fights, which made him look even more like Buddy Hackett. I had gained weight too. We were in our mid-fifties now, not quite old men looking back on an old war, but close to it. I reached and squeezed his arm with my left hand.

With my right, I reached for Sergeant Crawford. He reached back and gripped my hand. Big Ed had been mentor to young Marines. *What would Big Ed do?* had guided our course.

Big Ed was now in his seventies. A little stooped, a bit slower, shuffling one leg due to wounds, his face lined and his hair thin and gray. But the Marine bearing remained in the way he held his head, the proud square of his shoulders. Once a By-God Marine, *always* a Marine.

Big Ed had been waiting for Tony and me when the USS *Princeton* with a sick bay full of wounded Marines pulled into Subic Bay, the Philippines, to transfer us to the Navy hospital. Ed had been wounded for his second time in Vietnam two days before Tony and I got hit. He was already up and about and planning on going back into the fight.

"Have you guys notified your parents that you were wounded but you're okay?" was the first thing he asked.

I hadn't. I wanted to make sure I was *really* okay before I called Linda. There was a possibility, a real probability, that I would go home half a man. I wasn't sure how Linda would accept it.

"We may have to take your left leg," the surgeon said when the medevac offloaded casualties aboard the *Princeton.*

I thought of how Vlasek died that day with his face shot off. How he wouldn't have wanted to live that way.

"Doc, please, sir?" I begged. "I can't go home with one leg. Let me die first. Doc, you don't understand."

The drawn expression on his face told me he *did* understand, that he had confronted situations like this many times before. Turned out his home town was Sand Springs, Oklahoma, a Tulsa suburb. We were practically neighbors.

"Son," he said wearily, "I'll do everything I can to save your leg."

He did. I wasn't going to lose it. Tony and I would return to the war.

"You'll both phone your parents and tell 'em," Big Ed decided. "I'm taking you to the Petty Officers' Stork Club on the Navy base for dinner and a drink where you can use the phone."

We were in the ship's sick bay. We weren't authorized to leave. We didn't have Liberty Cards. Even if we somehow got off the ship, we had no transportation.

"I'll take care of it," Sergeant Crawford promised.

He did. Somehow, he obtained Liberty Cards for Tony and me, as well as dress uniforms with lance corporal stripes. We hobbled down the gangplank to the liberty boat and went ashore, me on crutches, Tony wrapped about the chest in bandages, his "Peggy" arm in a cast and sling. Big Ed waited for us dockside with a Navy staff car.

"Ask no questions, I'll tell you no lies," he said.

Late that night, Big Ed arranged our return to the *Princeton* in style: he commandeered the admiral's barge.

Sergeant Ed Crawford, a Marine's Marine, had been a legend in the 3rd Marine Division. Now, these years later, he was an old man, and Tony and I were getting there. The three of us turned away from The Wall clutching our name etchings and climbed the few steps up toward the larger-than-life bronze statue of American warriors in combat. Sniffles from some of the onlookers accompanied our departure. Come on! We were not to be pitied; we were Marines and we had done our duty.

Heads high, shoulders square, in step, we marched out of the scene. Never let 'em see you cry.

Index

About the Authors

Following Vietnam, **Robert "Bobby" Maras** served in the Oklahoma Army National Guard. He was a police officer with the Tulsa Police Department for over twenty years and is now retired. This is his first book.

Charles W. Sasser served twenty-nine years in the military (active-duty and reserve): four in the US Navy as a journalist, the remainder in the US Army, including thirteen years in Army Special Forces (the Green Berets). Like Maras, he is a combat veteran. He was also a police officer in Miami, Florida, for four years, and in Tulsa, Oklahoma, for ten years, where he was a homicide detective. Maras and Sasser served together on the Tulsa Police TAC/SWAT team. He is the author of over sixty published books.